D0660782

Israel's Fateful Hour

YEHOSHAFAT HARKABI

Translated by Lenn Schramm

PERENNIAL LIBRARY

HARPER & ROW, PUBLISHERS, New York
Grand Rapids, Philadelphia, St. Louis, San Francisco
London, Singapore, Sydney, Tokyo, Toronto

To the victims of their leaders—
Jews and Arabs

This book is based on a Hebrew work, *Hachraot Goraliot.* Copyright © 1986 by Am Oved, Tel Aviv.

ISRAEL'S FATEFUL HOUR. Copyright © 1988 by Yehoshafat Harkabi. All rights reserved. Printed in the United States of America. No part of this book may be used or reproduced in any manner whatsoever without written permission except in the case of brief quotations embodied in critical articles and reviews. For information address Harper & Row, Publishers, Inc., 10 East 53rd Street, New York, N.Y. 10022.

First PERENNIAL LIBRARY edition published 1989.

Designed by Karen Savary

The Library of Congress has catalogued the hardcover edition as follows:

Harkabi, Yehoshafat, 1921–
    Israel's fateful hour.

    Rev. translation of: Hakhra'ot goraliyot.
    Bibliography: p.
    Includes index.
    1. Israel—Politics and government. 2. Jewish-Arab
relations—1973–   . 3. Israel-Arab conflicts.
4. Begin, Menachem, 1913–   . 5. Religious Zionism.
6. Religion and state—Israel. I. Title.
DS126.5.H357213   1988   956.94   88-45513
ISBN 0-06-016039-X
ISBN 0-06-091613-3 (pbk.)

91 92 93 CC/RRD 10 9 8 7 6 5 4 3 2

Contents

Acknowledgments   v

Preface   vii

1. The Arab-Israeli Conflict: The Arab Positions   1

2. The Arab-Israeli Conflict: The Israeli Position   42

3. The Two Streams of Zionism   70

4. The Likud in Power   84

5. Nationalistic Judaism   138

6. What Is There to Do?   194

Appendixes   227

References   249

Index   253

Acknowledgments

I WOULD LIKE TO THANK ANNE ENAYAT, WHO INVITED ME TO publish this book in English, and Connie Wilsack for their tireless editing of the British edition.

The American edition is a much expanded and updated version of the British edition. For this I am indebted to Ted Solotaroff, who not only edited the English translation but actively assisted me in revising the original text, written for the Israeli public, to be more useful and effective for its American readers.

Preface

I WROTE THIS BOOK BECAUSE I BELIEVE THAT ISRAEL STANDS at a crossroads. The course it chooses will not just affect the tenor of the nation's life but will determine whether it can continue to exist. My purpose was to deal not so much with current affairs as with the underlying factors that mold Israel's thinking and condition its behavior. Many of the disasters of recent years, such as the Lebanon War, Israel's economic crisis, the increasingly degenerate standards of Israeli civic and political life, and above all the attempt to annex the occupied territories of the West Bank and the Gaza Strip, which have led to the recent riots and repression, stem, I believe, from a failure to view the country's situation correctly. Not only have the policies of a particular group of leaders bequeathed to Israel a painful legacy, but also, behind the fiascos they have perpetrated, is a dangerous and misleading world view.

Since the Likud came to power in 1977 this world view, which derives from the Revisionist Zionism of Ze'ev Jabotinsky and Menachem Begin, has become increasingly ingrained in public attitudes and is rampant in the broad coalition created by the Likud movement and nationalistic religious circles. I believe that Israel's survival requires a fundamental challenge and widespread opposition to their position. If a national debate can be launched and large segments of the Israeli population can be persuaded to change their minds about the occupation of the West Bank and Gaza, then government policy in time will follow suit.

It sometimes happens that peoples and nations persist in a wrong political direction they have taken. When they wake up to their mistakes it is usually because history has slapped them in the face, in the form of a trauma such as military defeat or revolution or a major loss of domain. Israel's special predicament is that it cannot afford to learn from adversity; its national policy has to be in Israel to commit national suicide and, if that happens, I will be with them. But it is my duty, and the duty of others with similar views, to warn them against such a course.

The most fateful of the crucial issues I analyze in the book is the Arab-Israeli conflict, because the way it develops affects all aspects of Israel's life—political, social, and cultural—and even the status of Jews abroad and the standing of the Jewish religion. Four years ago, when I began to write the book, the urgency of changing Israeli policy arose from the opportunity offered to Israel after Jordan and the PLO, in February 1985, reached an agreement based on a principle unprecedented in the history of Arab positions in the Arab-Israeli dispute—namely "the land for peace" (see Appendix C). That "the land" meant withdrawal from the territories Israel has occupied since 1967 was not spelled out in this document. But that this was the Arab demand was stated specifically in the resolutions of the Fez summit held in September 1982 (see Appendix B), and endorsed by Syria and the Palestine Liberation Organization. I thought that Israel should seize the opportunity to withdraw and conclude a peace settlement, even if this meant painful concessions.

True, the Arab readiness to achieve peace was expressed in equivocal terms, creating suspicions of their intentions and reminding one of their old commitment to Israel's destruction. Nevertheless, since the Camp David Accords with Egypt, there has been a basic change in some Arab positions, in particular Jordanian and Palestinian, culminating in Arafat's acceptance of American conditions for recognition of the PLO in December 1988. This has come about because many Arabs have realized that a continuation of the conflict will be calamitous for them as well as for the Jews. They too have a vital interest in extricating themselves from its deadly clutches. I believe that the longer Israel waits, postponing negotiations and deferring a settlement, the more the situation will deteriorate and the worse off Israel will be in future negotiations when, instead of going to the negotiating table of its own volition, it may well be pushed there by events or by the superpowers.

Unfortunately Israel rejected the Jordanian-Palestinian proposal. At first King Hussein hoped to enlist the United States to exert pressure on Israel to negotiate. But for this purpose the PLO had to legitimize itself in the eyes of the American government by accepting Security Council Resolution 242 (see Appendix A), acknowledging the right of Israel to exist, and by renouncing terrorism. The PLO was ready to take a position close to this but still avoided expressing itself explicitly, finding refuge in verbal sophistry. In time relations between Hussein and the PLO leader Yasser Arafat deteriorated again, to the point that, in a speech delivered on February 19, 1986, the king suspended their agreement.

The rift between Jordan and the PLO has been a setback to the cause of peace, although attempts to mend it have continued and are periodically renewed. The radical organizations, such as Dr. George Habash's Popular Front (PFLP) and Naef Hawatmeh's Democratic Front (DFLP), which seceded from the PLO during the 17th Palestine National Council of November 1984, attended the 18th Council held in Algiers in April 1987. Significantly the PLO did not agree to pay for their return by changing its basic position on a political settlement of the conflict. Still, the presence of these organizations at the PNC signaled a radicalization of the PLO position.

Once the possibility of achieving a settlement, with the United States as an intermediary, receded, King Hussein considered it necessary to include the Soviet Union in the negotiating process in an international conference under the auspices of the United Nations. At the same time, fearing that in the absence of a settlement the situation might get out of control, he took steps to improve his relations with Syria and organized a summit meeting of Arab states in Amman in November 1987. This was for the purpose of reconciliation between Arab states in the face of the Iran-Iraq War and the Arab-Israeli conflict. On the Arab-Israeli conflict the Amman summit's resolutions, leaked to the Paris-based weekly *al-Yaum al-Sabi'*, stipulated: (1) That the Arab-Israeli conflict is the central issue for all Arabs (thus downgrading the Iran-Iraq War). (2) That no Arab principal should try to resolve the conflict on its own. (3) That the Syrian principle of "strategic parity" be adopted as a Pan-Arab principle, i.e., Arab states should achieve a military readiness that would allow them to escalate and use violent means against Israel or, in modern strategic parlance, acquire "escalation dominance." (4) That a settlement of the conflict should be reached within the framework of an international conference. (5) That the Fez resolution is reaffirmed and that the PLO should be included in all negotiations as the sole legitimate representative of the Palestinian people. The summit also decided to terminate the diplomatic boycott of Egypt, declared after the conclusion of its peace agreement with Israel.

A month later, in December 1987, riots broke out in Gaza and

the West Bank. These erupted spontaneously, without PLO insti-
gation or direction, and are often referred to as the "Intifada."
The Uprising expressed the Palestinians' humiliation and indigna-
tion over the Israeli domination and, although predictable, came
as a shock to the Israeli authorities and public.

In my book *The Bar Kokhba Syndrome* (published in Hebrew in
1982 and English in 1983), and in this book (first published in
Hebrew in 1986), I warn that Israeli control of the occupied territories will become less and less tolerable and that civil unrest will
bring about the "Belfastization" of the situation. Now wider circles
in Israel have begun to doubt the possibility of keeping the West
Bank and Gaza under Israeli control for much longer.

The events in the West Bank and Gaza have renewed interest in
the position I advocate, and in its analysis and argumentation.
More and more people in Israel have become alive to the demographic problem I highlighted. Meanwhile, the Likud has been
unable to devise a meaningful answer to the powerful challenge
this problem presents to its gospel of reclaiming "Samaria and
Judea"—namely that by holding on to the occupied territories, the
majority of the population of Greater Israel will soon be Arab and
that a Jewish state in such conditions is not viable.

Before the Uprising and now even more so, many Israelis, including the élite of the Likud, have come to the painful conclusion
that a full-blown annexation of the occupied territories is a forlorn
hope. Nevertheless they indulged in hopes that there were still
alternatives to complete withdrawal and the establishment of a
Palestinian state. One of these halfway solutions was shared sovereignty with Jordan through a condominium that would allow Israel's settlement activities on the West Bank to continue. Another
was an arrangement that allowed Palestinians residing in the occupied territories to exercise their political rights by voting for representatives in the Jordanian parliament, thus avoiding the demographic threat to the Jewishness of Israel.

The Likud coalition and particularly Herut, its principal party,
refuse to admit, at least publicly, that Israel will have to give up the
occupied areas. This refusal stems from an excruciating political
predicament: such an admission would be tantamount to the
Likud's declaring its ideological and political bankruptcy. So Yitzhak Shamir and its other leaders cling to the interpretation that the
autonomy to be granted to the Palestinians, as stipulated in the
Camp David Accords, is not necessarily a transient phase culminat-

ing in full Palestinian independence; it can be "frozen" in the form of continuing self-rule under Israeli supervision. Furthermore, autonomy is presented as a test to examine the Palestinians' ability to rule themselves—the presumption being that in the event of their failure Israel would be called upon to renew its domination. This part of the old, misleading interpretation given to the Camp David Accords by former Prime Minister Begin was not challenged by the United States as arbiter of those negotiations; the result was to delegitimize in Arab eyes any continuation of the negotiation process for the Palestine question set forth in the "Framework for peace" of the Accords. America's failure to dispute the official Israeli interpretation of the Accords has also inadvertently strengthened public belief in Israel's ability to keep the occupied territories forever, and has thus helped to recrystallize popular support for the Likud policies and leadership.

The hope for in-between solutions such as a condominium suffers from three main flaws. First, to be workable these solutions must be founded on good working relations with the Jordanians and Palestinians. Yet, by rejecting the "land for peace" principle and maintaining Israeli domination, current policy severely antagonizes the Arabs, increasing their hostility and obduracy. Second, there is no prospect of Jordan's coming to terms with Israel independently. Despite its latest break with the PLO, Jordan repeatedly stresses its inability to achieve a settlement without the PLO—more emphatically so than at any time in the past few years and most blatantly in its statement at the Arab Summit meeting in Algiers on June 8, 1988. Finally, this approach is based on the warped assumption that politics is a laboratory in which, if one experiment fails, another can be tried. But the policy of continued Israeli domination means that Israel will forfeit the possibility of reaching a settlement, for in the meantime Arab positions will harden in the face of Israeli rejection, and Israel's political position will deteriorate.

Israel must withdraw from the occupied territories with their growing Arab population. There are pro-Arab and -PLO circles that make similar demands; I make them because I am pro-Israeli. Given the provocations of 1967, Israel cannot be blamed for its occupation of the West Bank and Gaza, but it should be criticized for attempting to retain them; occupation was justified, annexation is not. The settlement of the conflict cannot be by symmetrical compromises, with both parties offering commensurate concessions, because the situation is asymmetrical: Israel dominates areas thickly inhabited by Palestinians. Nevertheless the onus of making concessions does not fall on Israel alone, and the Arab contribution must not be limited to an august condescension to make peace with a Jewish Israel. The peace is as much for the sake of Arabs as for Jews. The acid test of the Arabs' peaceful intentions will be their readiness to meet Israel's security needs at the negotiating table. Palestinians and Arabs are not such a weak party to the negotiations that they can only receive concessions. Both sides must bring themselves to consider the adversary not as an object to be manipulated and attacked but as a subject with whom to communicate and finally come to terms.

Israel will inevitably have to negotiate with the PLO. There is no hope of a local Arab leadership distancing itself from the PLO. Any attempt to drive a wedge between the PLO and the Palestinians in the West Bank and Gaza is doomed to failure. Even the Muslim fundamentalists who criticize the PLO for its moderation still declare that it represents them. By describing the PLO as a basically terrorist organization we criminalize it and thus, unwittingly, criminalize the whole Palestinian community, which hails the PLO as its representative and leader. Such a stance is both politically and morally wrong.

Imputing political traits as though they were permanent ones—expansionism to Zionism, terrorism to the PLO, or unrelenting aggression to the Soviet Union—has proved to be a false approach, and should be banished from political discourse. Human history repeatedly demonstrates the ability of peoples to transcend the negative characteristics that were once justifiably ascribed to them.

The Middle East is a region of volatile changes. However, the developments that have taken place since the publication of the book corroborate the cogency of my previous analyses. For example, on July 31, 1988, King Hussein announced his decision to sever administrative connections with the West Bank.

The delusions of a "Jordanian option," or of a Jordanian/Israeli condominium in the West Bank, or of West Bankers being represented in Jordan's parliament have been finally exposed.

Israeli, and even some American, spokesmen and commentators have tried to brush aside the importance of this event. Prime Minister Shamir has asserted that it "did not create anything significantly new." Nobody likes to admit that his prophecies have failed. Others describe Hussein's decision as a ploy. Many in Israel and the United States had to eat their words.

For years there have been rumors of a debate between King Hussein and Prince Hassan, his brother and heir apparent. Hassan, advocating a smaller Jordan, wanted to extract the kingdom from the complexities and travails of the West Bank and the PLO and concentrate on modernizing Jordan. The king, however, was unwilling to relegate Jordan to a lesser role in the Middle East. He also understood the danger of pressuring the Palestinians, who constitute at least half and perhaps the majority of Jordan's population, to decide whether they are Palestinians or Jordanians.

Hussein has now come to accept his brother's line. His previous equivocal position, which gave rise to suspicions that he continued to harbor ambitions to regain the West Bank, led nowhere. Neither the Israelis nor the Americans believed Hussein when he repeatedly emphasized that he could not negotiate without the PLO since such negotiations would have no legitimacy in the Arab world. If the Americans and Israelis wanted to retain Hussein as an active partner in the negotiations, they had to bring the PLO into the peace process. The road to Amman went through the PLO. Nevertheless, both Israelis and Americans treated Hussein as if he was malingering and defaulting on the role they had allotted to him.

Hussein is not completely detaching himself from the Arab-Israeli conflict. Geography does not allow it. In his speech he did not refer to the possible confederation between an independent Palestine and Jordan, probably so as not to give rise to the suspicion that he wants to come back through a confederation to control the West Bank. He knows how strong the Palestinian national emotions are. He will be the king of the Jordanians, not the Palestinians. But one can surmise that he still holds to the project of confederating the two states.

Meanwhile the Uprising has continued unabated. The Palestinians in the occupied territories demonstrate their unflagging readiness to sacrifice, both economically and physically. For the Palestinians, this tenacity is a source of pride, a proof of the authenticity of the Palestinian commitment, as if atoning for their previous subordination to Israel and resignation to its domination. The Israeli political leadership underrated the political significance of the Uprising, whereas the military leadership recognized its nationalist nature and warned their government that the Uprising could not be subdued by military means but would require a political solution. The subordination of the military to the government is deeply ingrained in Israel so that this development was particularly significant. Corroborating the view that there is no escape from eventually negotiating with the PLO, a military intelligence report was leaked to the public in early 1989 and published in the Israeli and international press. This finding, by an Israeli institution whose patriotism cannot be doubted, will perhaps be allowed to testify that a position such as my own is not an unpatriotic heresy.

As the main arena of the Palestinian national struggle, the Uprising has tilted the balance between the Palestinians "outside"—in the Arab world and foreign countries—and those "inside"—in the occupied territories—in favor of the latter. It is now recognized by all Palestinians that those living under occupation by Israel carry the main burden of confronting it. Paradoxically, it is the Palestinians in the occupied territories, whose animosity and acrimony should presumably have been reinforced by Israeli repression, who have exerted effective pressure on the PLO to moderate its positions. These pressures have even prevailed upon the radical wing of the PLO, inducing it to mute its opposition to the moderate line.

Thus the 19th Palestinian National Council (PNC) was convened in Algiers, November 12–14, 1988. The two documents that were promulgated, "The Final Statement of the 19th PNC" and "The Palestinian Declaration of Independence" (Appendix E), ushered in important changes in the PLO's positions. Both hailed the Intifada as the greatest event in the Palestinian national struggle and called for support and reinforcement of it. The Intifada supersedes in these documents the traditional "armed struggle," a phrase which conspicuously is not used in them. Absent too are deferential references to the Covenant, as well as the ominous expressions of "liberating" Palestine, which in the past implied a call for the demise of Israel. Instead of "liberation" the goal of achieving Palestinian "independence" is repeatedly stressed. Security Council Resolutions 242 and 338 are referred to in these documents, not, as previously, to reject them (as, for instance, in the 18th PNC), but in connection with the international conference (Resolution 338 calls for negotiations under "appropriate auspices") in which the PLO would participate on equal footing with the other parties.

The most important change was the reference in the "Palestinian Declaration of Independence," read ceremoniously by Yasser Arafat, to the United Nations General Assembly Partition

Resolution of November 22, 1947 (Resolution 181), as the source of legitimacy of the Palestinian state. The Declaration states that " . . . following upon UN General Assembly Resolution 181 (1947), which partitioned Palestine into two states, one Arab and one Jewish, yet it is this Resolution that still provides those conditions of international legitimacy that ensure the right of the Palestinian Arab people to sovereignty and national independence." It should be noted that the Israeli Declaration of Independence read by Ben-Gurion on May 14, 1948, was also based on the same Partition Resolution.

This Declaration, which was accepted in the PNC by a unanimous vote, directly contradicts a basic PLO doctrine enshrined twice in its Covenant. This stipulates that "Palestine . . . is an indivisible territorial unit" (Article 2) and that "the partition of Palestine and the establishment of the State of Israel are entirely illegal" (Article 19). Ironically, what was deemed "entirely illegal" now serves as the source of legality for the Palestinian state.

The right of Israel to exist is not acknowledged in the Declaration. But if the legitimacy of a Palestinian state is now based on the Partition Resolution, it tacitly acknowledges the legitimacy of the other party to the partition—the state of Israel. Thus Arafat could justify his subsequent explicit recognition of Israel as authorized by the Algiers PNC's resolutions, in defending himself against the criticism of his radical wing. Both the implied, and subsequently explicit, recognition of the state of Israel contradicts another basic tenet of the Covenant—that the Israeli Jews do not constitute a nation and thus do not deserve to have a state and cannot sustain one. This contention was meant to invalidate the raison d'être of Israel—the need of the Jews to have a state of their own. Stated in Article 20 of the Covenant, it reads: "Judaism being a divine religion is not an independent nationality. Nor do the Jews constitute a single nation with an identity of its own; they are the citizens of the states to which they belong." Such tacit negations of the Covenant may well constitute an important stage in the process of incrementally abrogating the Covenant.

The 19th PNC affirmed the principle of "Israeli withdrawal from all the Palestinian and Arab territories that it has occupied since 1967, including Arab Jerusalem." Thus the reference to Resolution 181 does not imply a demand for Israel to return to the narrow boundaries that were specified in the resolution of 1947.

Despite King Hussein's severance of administrative ties to the West Bank, the 19th PNC "confirmed previous resolutions concerning the privileged relationship between the two fraternal Jordanian and Palestinian peoples, and that the future relationship between the two states of Palestine and Jordan will be established on confederal bases." Thus it did not call for a Palestinian state existing independently, but for an independent state within the framework of a confederation with Jordan "on the basis of the voluntary choice of the two fraternal peoples."

Arafat's final statement in his Geneva press conference on December 14, 1988, reads: "Our desire for peace is a strategy not an interim tactic." This is meant to negate the accusation of a policy of "phased" conquest. Arafat continues: ". . . I also made a reference to our acceptance of Resolutions 242 and 338 as the basis for negotiations with Israel within the framework of an international conference . . . we mean our peoples' right to freedom and national independence according to Resolution 181 and the rights of all parties concerned in the Middle East conflict to exist in peace and security and, as I have mentioned, including the states of Palestine and Israel. . . . As for terrorism, I renounced it yesterday in no uncertain terms, and yet I repeat for the record that we totally and absolutely renounce all forms of terrorism, including individual, group, and state terrorism."

On the same day President Reagan authorized the State Department to initiate a "substantive dialogue" with the PLO. Secretary of State Shultz announced: "The Palestine Liberation Organization today issued a statement in which it accepted UN Security Council Resolutions 242 and 338, recognized Israel's right to exist in peace and security, and renounced terrorism. As a result, the United States is prepared for a substantive dialogue with PLO representatives."

A new era may thus have opened in the history of the Arab-Israeli conflict. By acceding to the American demands and accepting the two-state settlement, the PLO has created a reversal of positions in the conflict, which may well prove to be of great significance. Originally, it was the Zionist community, or Yishuv, and subsequently the state of Israel that upheld the two-state formula by agreeing to partition plans that culminated in the UN one. This conciliatory position enabled it to gain the support of international public opinion and of many governments. Without such support Israel could not have come into being, much less thrive. During this period, the Arab states and the Palestinians insisted on a one-state—an Arab one—solution: an Israeli state should not come into being, and when it did, they called for its demise. But now it is Israel that calls for a single state in which the Palestinians will have at best an "autonomy" under Israeli control. That this autonomy is not intended to be a transitory stage toward independence can be seen from the repeated declarations of Prime Minister Shamir that it is "folly and nonsense" to expect his government to give up any part of the West Bank and Gaza to the Palestinians. (See, for example, the *New York Times*, February 13, 1989.)

A settlement of the Arab-Israeli conflict can only ensue from a negotiated peace, not from a dictated one, whether by the Israelis or by the Arabs. A negotiated peace is, by nature, between parties of equal status, though it does not require equality in all respects. The Palestinians cannot accept the idea that the Israelis deserve to have an independent state while they should be content with an autonomy supervised by Israel. Their rejection of autonomy on Israeli terms is not motivated by false hopes inspired by Israeli moderates, as Israeli hard-liners contend. Such a contention maligns the Palestinians, who clearly do not need anyone else to do their political thinking for them.

The Palestinians believe that the U.S. demand that they agree to the principle of a two-state solution and recognize Israel's right to exist as a precondition for their participation in the negotiation process is discriminatory. A parallel recognition by Israel of the Palestinians' right to an independent state is deferred to the outcome of the negotiations. This asymmetry in demands contravenes the egalitarian nature of a fruitful negotiation. A mutual recognition of the two-state formula is a necessary prerequisite if there is to be real progress toward a settlement. The Palestinians have already begun insisting on this aspect.

Palestinian circles also complain that they have offered concessions without reciprocation from the Israeli side. The frustration could undermine the conciliatory mood in the PLO, driving it to act against its best interests and annulling its recent gains in the international arena. Public opinion expects progress toward a settlement, and a continuation of the present stalemate for which the PLO will bear even part of the responsibility—for instance by an offhand rejection of the idea of elections in the occupied territories, recently put forth by Prime Minister Shamir, without offering an alternative step or a more acceptable version of elections—will be charged against the Palestinians. Public opinion would then suspect that the PLO's recent changes of position were not genuine.

A continuing stalemate is what both Israeli and Palestinian extremists hope for, and they may collaborate in bringing it about. Both groups tend to believe that in a situation of competitive attrition their side will prevail and eventually there will be only a Jewish Israel or an Arab Palestine.

The Israeli moderates can maintain their ground for a long time. Whether the Palestinian moderates can do so without some positive gains from their recent concessions is, for me, an open question. This feature of the conflict creates a degree of urgency in the need for progress toward a settlement. The parties concerned—Palestinians, Israelis and Americans—should take this factor seriously and exert themselves to produce some movement forward, even if the conditions for negotiation are not fully clear or completely satisfactory. The conditions may clear up only during actual negotiations.

However, negotiations cannot be expected to begin without Israel's acceptance of an eventual two-state solution. A gradualist approach of first granting autonomy to the occupied territories may be acceptable to the Palestinians provided they are assured that this would not be the final stage. Because moving from autonomy to independence would require Israel's assent, Palestinians are apprehensive that Israel would balk, a stalemate would ensue, and the autonomy arrangement would be frozen indefinitely. No American promise to promote the final transition can dispel this suspicion.

"Moderate" Palestinians, in Shamir's vocabulary, are those who agree to "coexistence" with Israel, though this does not connote a desire for Palestinian independence, but rather a willingness to live under Israeli supervision. Such "moderates" do not exist and thus cannot be found. The announcement by governmental circles that now Israel will seriously search for them is a travesty.

Palestinians in the occupied territories will be unwilling to serve in place of the PLO in substantive negotiations. Let us remember that the Jewish side in the negotiations prior to 1948 was not represented by the leaders of the Yishuv but by the heads of the Zionist World Organization and the Jewish Agency. Limiting Palestinian representation to those from the occupied territories symbolizes, for all Palestinians, an unacceptable reduction of the issues. The fact that the Palestinians are dispersed over many countries makes the problem much broader than that of the territories, and its solution will require development policies outside of, as well as within, Palestine and will necessitate the participation and contribution of regional and other states, including the super-powers.

Demands should be made upon the PLO as well. Its claim to being the sole legitimate representative of the Palestinians incurs responsibility for their actions and the need to impose discipline on recalcitrant Palestinian groups. Noblesse oblige. No doubt it is not an easy task. At the very least the PLO must demonstrate that it is making a determined effort. Also worrisome are the contradictory messages that emanate from the PLO leadership. Of course, no movement can impose absolute homogeneity of viewpoints and consistency of expression on its members. However, the divergences in the policy statements emanating from the PLO are not about nuances, but involve substantive issues such as their objective in Palestine, the revision of their Covenant, and the scope of the Palestinians' "right of return." It would also be helpful if Palestinians in general become accustomed to distinguishing between "the Land of Palestine" and "the State of Palestine," as the Israelis differentiate between "the Land of Israel" and "the State of Israel." So long as the Palestinians do not make this distinction and as long as the term "Palestine" continues to refer to all the territories west of the Jordan River, a statement such as "we shall continue the struggle until Palestine is liberated" inevitably evokes their former aim to destroy Israel.

Some Palestinian factions will continue to harbor vicious intentions toward Israel, but their plots can be foiled only by a political settlement, while the lack of one nurtures them. Vicious intentions are not grounds for refusing to negotiate but for making a settlement that will withstand them. The negotiations and the agreements should also be very specific to prevent different interpretations which can become dangerous disputes. The agreements' wording should be concrete and clear, garnished neither with so-called "constructive ambiguities," nor catch-all slogan phrases like "self-determination," which can apply both to the choice of its government—which is acceptable—and to the ambition to decide unilaterally size and borders—which is bound to renew the conflict. International safeguards will be needed to rivet the agreements, reinforce each side's obligations, and nail down once and for all Palestinian demands.

It is extremely doubtful whether Arabs and Jews, left to themselves, can reach an accord. The call by some Israeli circles for direct negotiations only means stalling. There is a need for international midwifery if such negotiations are to start and to succeed. Can there be in our world important political transactions without the great powers' direct or indirect intervention?

As relations between the superpowers improve, both will be in a better position for a joint venture to bring about a settlement of the Arab-Israeli conflict. Under Gorbachev, the Soviet Union is changing its attitude toward regional conflicts in general: rather than viewing them as an opportunity to extend its sphere of influence, it now tends to regard them as either a burden or an impediment to improving relations with the West. This revision of general policy has extended to the Middle East. The Soviets are counseling moderation to their Arab allies and the PLO. They may prove to be particularly useful with the extremist groups in the PLO such as George Habash's Popular Front, Naef Hawatmeh's Democratic Front and the Palestinian Communist Party, which, since the 18th PNC of April 1987, has been part of the PLO Executive Committee.

Reportedly, the Soviet Union exerted pressure on these organizations before and during the 19th PNC in November 1988, urging them not to hamper Arafat's efforts to moderate the PLO's position, and thus made a considerable contribution to the PLO's changes of policies.

The Soviet Union continues to support the principle of Palestinian self-determination. But in their recent statements Soviet officials have played down the principle of Return which was prominent in Brezhnev's statement of policy in September 1982. The new regime appears to recognize that Israel cannot allow itself to be deluged by a flood of repatriated Palestinians. There are signs too of the Soviets' desire to improve relations with Israel, which may culminate in the renewal of full diplomatic relations. If the Soviet Union hopes to play an active role as a mediator, it cannot limit its contacts to the Arabs.

It is not true that the Arab-Israeli conflict has been simply a reflection of the Cold War. Such a view was maintained in the past by both Arabs and Israelis, for it enabled both sides to diminish their responsibility. The Cold War did not create the conflict but, rather, aggravated it. Now the thawing of the Cold War may allow the superpowers to consider and take measures to prevent the conflict from drawing them into its vortex. Both are concerned about the potential for violent escalation in the Middle East, which is greater than in any other regional conflict because of the accumulation there of sophisticated and immensely destructive weaponry such as missiles and chemical agents.

However, any movement toward resolution is doomed to fail unless its main features are formulated and accepted by both parties. Negotiations cannot begin, for example, on the terms that both Israeli security needs and the legitimate rights of the Palestinians must be satisfied. That is too vague to serve as a basis for even meaningful discussions. I for one do not see the possibility of viable negotiations unless there is first a mutual acceptance of a Palestinian state and of Israel's withdrawal. Only when these principles are agreed to can the method and details of a negotiated settlement be worked out. In other words, objectives must precede the process—such as that of an international peace conference. Thus in the arms control negotiations the general principles are agreed to by the parties prior to the commencement of the negotiations, which then deliberate on the details.

In Secretary of State Baker's speech of May 22, 1989, the United States took a more aggressively even-handed line in urging both parties to move toward a settlement. He advised Israel that "now is the time to lay aside, once and for all, the unrealistic vision of a greater Israel." Baker went on to provide a list of positive steps: "Foreswear annexation; stop settlement activity; allow school to reopen; reach out to the Palestinians as neighbors who deserve political rights." Turning to the Palestinians and speaking no less forthrightly, he said, "Now is the time to speak with one voice for peace. . . . Amend the Covenant. Translate the dialogue of violence in the Intifada into a dialogue of politics and diplomacy. . . . Reach out to the Israelis and convince them of your peaceful intention. . . . Finally, understand that no one is going to deliver Israel for you."

Perhaps the most significant implication of Baker's speech was that "the legitimate rights of the Palestinian people" in the Camp David Accords and in President Reagan's speech of September 1, 1982, are now referred to as *political* rights." Even though U.S. policy still does not support the creation of an independent Palestinian state, the phrase "political rights" implies the recognition that the Palestinians constitute a political entity, which may be a first step in the recognition of their right to statehood.

The settlement of the Arab-Israeli conflict can only be founded on this principle: One cannot persuade Palestinians that Jaffa, Haifa, and Nazareth are not part of "Palestine." One cannot persuade Diaspora Jews and Israelis that Judea and Samaria (the West Bank) are not part of Eretz Yisrael. The solution of the Arab-Israeli

conflict requires that both Israelis and Palestinians resign themselves to the arrangement that their respective states in which they
will be citizens will occupy only part of their homeland, to which
they will both bear sentimental allegiance.

Having a common homeland may well, in time, lead the Palestinians and the Israelis toward economic and perhaps political
collaboration. However, slogans like "Benelux" are premature. It
is hard to conceive that the parties can leap from hostility to partnership. Nevertheless, such slogans may have the merit of allaying
apprehensions that a settlement would entail complete disengage-
ment between Israel and its neighbors, and may even kindle some
hope that the peace achieved may become more than a cessation
of violence.

Accepting the final outcome of two small states will be difficult
for Jews and Arabs alike. The Diasporas of both the Palestinians
and the Israelis exacerbate this problem. Since the state of Israel
and a putative Palestinian state have been integral to the identity
of Jewish- and Palestinian-Americans, both are reluctant to resign
themselves to a smaller, as though mutilated, homeland. They
need to become conscious of this psychological blinder in their
viewpoint, which is frequently more hawkish than that of many
Israelis and Palestinians in the occupied territories or even in the
PLO establishment.

The states of Palestine and Israel will have space for only a
fraction of the world's Palestinians and Jews. Both will have Diasporas larger than their own populations. Both will need to develop
more realistic relationships with their respective Diasporas. However, the situation is not symmetrical. Most Jews living abroad do
not plan to immigrate to Israel, even if they like to leave such a
possibility open. Many Palestinians, especially those living in Arab
countries that have not granted them citizenship, still consider
their present residence a transient one. A paradoxical outcome of
the Intifada and the moderation of the PLO position has been to
make many of these exiles aware that the putative Palestinian state
will be a small one, with a limited capacity to absorb people like
themselves. Thus settlement of the conflict will entail a painful
process of converting the transient Palestinian Diasporas into permanent ones.

The main accusation leveled against me in Israel is that my
position is unduly pessimistic. My belief in the possibility of a
settlement that may in time blossom into real peace is optimistic.
The real pessimists are those who hold the view that we must

forever live by the sword. It is tempting, and therefore common, to present the Arab-Israeli conflict as a Gordian knot. Such a stand is defeatist. It denies the human ability to find solutions to seemingly intractable political problems, and implies that resignation is the better part of wisdom. This conflict cannot be settled, in the manner of some disputes, by a process of containment; too many bombs lurk in its folds. Time cannot, in this instance, heal.

I am not a solitary voice in Israel. The Hebrew original of this book has to date run to four editions. There are many in Israel from all sections of the political spectrum who recognize the perils I warn against in this book and acknowledge the need for a change in policy. However, they are powerless to bring it about unless a long-overdue public debate begins and the political climate changes. The Labor coalition (the "Alignment") should have been concerned about opening a debate on national goals as a means of changing the Likud politics it criticizes. However, the creation of a government of national unity has blocked such debate in the name of national consensus, and dissent has become unpatriotic.

The second government of national unity formed at the end of 1988 has been even more unfortunate for the prospect of peace. The Labor Alignment has become so "aligned" with the Likud that it has abdicated its former role of criticizing the Shamir position and offering an alternative one. What we need in Israel is not a united front behind a wrong policy, but searching self-criticism and a careful examination of our goals and means, so that we can differentiate between realistic vision and adventurist fantasy. We need clear, rational, and, above all, long-term, comprehensive political thinking. Politicians frequently focus their gaze on the pebbles they may stumble on, ignoring the precipice. Some are brilliant in their analysis of events of the past weeks, but myopic in their perspective on what can happen in the coming months or years.

Jews in the West, particularly in the United States, should participate in this debate. They should not be squeamish and discouraged by the fear that the arguments they air may help their enemies and those of Israel. The choice facing them, as well as Israel, is not between good and bad, but between bad and worse. Criticizing Israeli policies may be helping the enemies of Israel and of Jews in general, but refraining from criticism and allowing Israel to maintain its wrong policy is incomparably worse.

If the state of Israel comes to grief (God forbid), it will not be because of a lack of weaponry or money, but because of skewed political thinking and because Jews who understood the situation did not exert themselves to convince the Israelis to change that thinking.

What is at stake is the survival of Israel and the status of Judaism. Israel will soon face its fateful hour. The crisis that faces the nation will be all-consuming. It will be bitter because many will have to acknowledge that they have lived in a world of fantasy; they will have to shed conceptions and beliefs they have held dear and prepare us for a reorientation of our national thought. Let us hope that we shall meet the challenge, transforming it into a cleansing and revitalizing experience that will prepare us to abandon the "Zionism of acreage" for a "Zionism of quality."

A Personal Note

Over the last twenty-five years I have written a considerable number of books and articles about the Arab-Israeli conflict. At first I described the Arab positions as very harsh, leaving no leeway for Israeli political initiatives. At that time public opinion, both in Israel and in the world, was reluctant to believe that the Arabs really wanted to destroy Israel. This opinion was conditioned by history, in which conflicts between nations, however fierce and desperate, have not sought the total destruction of one of the parties. I, therefore, had to validate my position by drawing upon many sources that demonstrated the ideologies underpinning their objective. On the whole, I think my analysis that the hardness and harshness of the Arab line should be taken at face value was correct. But, despite the adamancy and extremism of the Arab position, I advised the Israeli public to understand the Arabs' grievances, putting ourselves in the shoes of the Palestinians, as it were, and I warned against the distorting effect of our own biases as well as of the blindness of involvement.

I am frequently asked how and why my position has changed. My answer is that mostly it came as a result of changes in the situations and positions of the Arab states and of the Palestinian people and their leaders, rather than of any changes in my outlook. I analyzed these changes in several articles collected in *Palestinians and Israel* (1974) and *Winds of Change* (1978). Many readers, both in Israel and the West, who were impressed by my early writings but not cognizant of my later ones, tended to "freeze" my position and often express astonishment that I should have revised it.

Once I concluded that there were positive changes in the Arab position, I wrote about them. My main intention from that time until now has been to search for a policy by which Israel can get the best possible settlement of the conflict in the Middle East. In time I concluded that the best way to such a settlement was to develop and follow a moderate policy. Thus, jokingly, I dubbed myself a "Machiavellian dove."

As early as mid-1970, only three years after Israel had occupied the West Bank, Gaza, and the Sinai, I wrote: "Israel would be wise to declare openly its readiness to withdraw as a part of a peace settlement" (Ma'ariv, May 10). In the same vein, I wrote a few years later:

> It is very possible that Sadat truly yearns to liberate
> Egypt from the bondage of the dispute and to arrive at a
> settlement with Israel. . . . Realistic considerations
> should make it clear to us that we cannot maintain the
> present borders and refuse to withdraw or refuse to
> abandon settlements. . . . Israel's proclaimed
> unwillingness to enter into negotiations with the PLO
> seems to be misguided. (Ma'ariv, April 13, 1974)

Both of these statements also appeared in my book *Palestinians and Israel* (pp. 176, 255, 256, 258), published in 1974.

Because I believed in this position I decided to resign from the position of Intelligence Adviser to the Prime Minister. In my letter of August 30, 1977, to Mr. Begin, which he allowed me to publish in my *Winds of Change,* I wrote: "For us to rule Judea and Samaria for an extended period of time is, I believe, impossible. Would that I be proved wrong."

There has been a philosophical change in my approach, which I should note. In the early years I regarded the Arab-Israeli conflict as a case study of a stark conflict that may serve as a vantage point for understanding international relations; in other words, proceeding from the particular to the general. Nowadays, I am more inclined to view the particular case against the background of the history of international relations, since I believe that the latter helps us to see more clearly the fundamental factors that underlie and shape the Arab-Israeli conflict as well as its possible solution.

Though the brunt of my criticism in this book is aimed at the political thinking and policy of the Herut party and the Likud coalition, I would like to emphasize that I have never been a member of the Labor party or of any other Israeli party. My book is not meant to serve as an apology or an attack on behalf of the Labor party. I concentrate on those patterns of political thinking which I believe have led Israeli policies astray. I see them to be directly connected to the content and tone of the Herut ideology and mentality. However, these mistaken ideas and this mindset have spread widely through the Israeli public, including into the Labor party itself.

1

The Arab-Israeli Conflict: The Arab Positions

THE RIOTS IN THE WEST BANK AND GAZA AND THEIR REPER-
cussions amply demonstrate that the Arab-Israeli conflict is the
dominant issue of Israeli life. It casts its shadow on almost all our
activities—our politics, social relations, economic development,
and military deployment. As such, it determines our present and
our future—as individuals and as a nation. If we want to influence
our destiny, it is important that our perception of this conflict be
based on fact rather than myth, however deeply rooted. This intro-
ductory chapter provides a summary of the way in which the conflict has evolved so far and presents a framework for the analysis
that follows. It focuses on the large picture, dealing with general
trends rather than specific details, and it attempts to draw some
conclusions.

What Is a Goal?

The analysis of a conflict should start by examining the goals of the
adversaries. These are the focal points of their positions, which in
turn create their collision. The concept of "goal" is equivocal,
however, ranging from "ideal" or "grand design," on the one
hand, to "policy" on the other—that is, from what one hopes will
happen or what one aspires to, without necessarily knowing how
it will be brought about, to a set of actions designed to achieve
what is considered possible and attainable. In a similar way, Arnold
Wolfers distinguished between "aspirations" and "policy goals."
For example, the grand design of the Soviets may be to destroy the
West, but this is not the policy actively followed by the U.S.S.R.
Similarly, the grand design of the United States may be to bring

about the collapse of the Soviet regime, or at least to end Soviet hegemony over Eastern Europe, but this is not American policy. The policy followed by the United States, even if unwillingly, recognizes that Soviet domination of Eastern Europe will continue.

The distinction between grand design and policy, between ideal goals and realistic goals, is fundamental to human life. It is not limited to states, but can also be found governing the behavior of individuals. It is found, for example, in the difference between what a particular society and culture consider worthy accomplishments and the practical goals that the individual works toward. These latter objectives are often much more modest, reflecting the limits imposed by personal ability. Thus, despite the desire of many to be learned, very few are willing to study seriously, and though one may want to be rich, one may not be willing to economize in order to save and invest. This is the distinction between what we wish to be or have and what we actually expect ourselves to achieve, between what we hope for abstractly and what we expect concretely. Thus the questions "what does an individual want?" or "what does a state want?" are ambiguous; are we speaking in the abstract about imagined aspirations, or about the more realistic goals that shape one's behavior? Since we are dealing with states, I shall develop the distinction as that between "grand design"—abstract hope—and "policy"—the practical intention that guides actions.

What is unique about the Arab position in the Arab-Israeli conflict is that for many years both grand design and policy focused on the destruction of Israel. This was seen not merely as an abstract aspiration but as a practical goal, in the realm of international politics. This gave the Arab position the harshness that I have described in my earlier writings on the conflict. It affected the way in which the Arabs built up their military forces, organized their societies, developed their economies, and modernized their countries. Liquidation of Israel was a tangible objective, which could be achieved through appropriate effort—by developing an ideology, analyzing the requirements for implementing it, and making practical preparations. Precisely because the goal of destroying a country is extremely rare in international conflicts, the Arabs spent a lot of energy justifying it to themselves and others, convincing themselves that it was attainable, and thereafter working out the details of a program that could achieve it. The integration of grand design and policy made the Arab position *absolute,* of the sort that demands realization of the goal *in toto* and leaves no opening for a political settlement—which is always a compromise.

But even the most ardent idealist must at some stage come to terms with reality. In this case, the Arabs' bitter experiences throughout the course of the conflict—the repeated disappointments, especially the results of the 1967 and 1973 wars—have led to a recognition of the need to divorce grand design from policy. This is what brought President Sadat to Jerusalem. It is possible that the negative world reaction to the repeated calls for the annihilation of Israel—"politicide" would be an uncomfortable precedent in the international arena—also played a role in bringing about this change. The Arabs understood that in order to realize this goal they would have to overcome not only Israel, whose might they could describe to themselves as transient, but also the global powers—a task that even the most ardent idealist had to recognize as daunting.

Sadat had always taken a harsh stand against Israel and the Jews. The decision to sign a peace agreement with Israel did not reflect a change in his belief that the world would be a better place if Israel were to disappear, not a sudden love affair with the Israeli people. It was simply a recognition that the Arabs, or more precisely the Egyptians, were unable to realize the grand design of liquidating Israel, then or in the foreseeable future. He came to his recognition through a protracted process. In 1970 Sadat offered Israel a separation-of-forces agreement and a sort of nonaggression pact, while deferring the possibility of a peace treaty to a later date, or even a future generation. It was only in 1977 when he saw the virtue of divorcing the grand design from policy that he was ready to negotiate a peace agreement.

When human beings divorce grand design from policy they relinquish their responsibility for realizing the grand design in favor of history. For example, the Soviets claim that capitalism in the West will come to an end, but this will occur because of the dialectic of its internal contradictions. Likewise, the Americans foresee the crumbling of the Soviet empire not as the result of any action on their part, but as the result of its incompatibility with economic growth and competition, or of pressure from the ethnic minorities in the U.S.S.R.

It may be that deep in his heart Sadat hoped that Israel would eventually disappear, that Allah's will would ultimately be done, and that through the working out of historical processes Israel would wither away and be assimilated into the Arab world. All the same, he concluded that the time had come to make peace with Israel. By separating ideal and policy, Sadat made the Egyptian stance more flexible. This influenced the world's image of Egypt, and Sadat himself received world-wide public support and acclaim for having the courage to make a revolutionary change.

It would appear that all that can be achieved in an international dispute is to bring one's adversaries to differentiate between their ideals, as expressed in their grand design, and their policies—to get them to moderate the policies without requiring them to give up their hopes for realizing the grand design. Throughout history peace agreements have imposed restrictions on deeds and policies, but not on dreams. People or states can be constrained to refrain from action, including plotting and planning—which are actions of a sort—but not to abandon all their hopes and aspirations.

The distinction between grand design and policy is expressed not only in the temporal framework, as a progression by stages, but also in the nature of such gradualism. Those Arab radicals who are committed to the grand design of liquidating Israel can adopt a step-by-step approach, breaking down their course of action into stages. One stage may even include a peace settlement. For them, however, this stage is meant to be temporary, a stratagem that will make it easier for them to attain the goal of liquidation that informs the grand design. This is the nature of the Arab theory of stages, an expression of tactical incrementalism, which was contrived to obviate the consequences of separating the grand design from policy. By contrast, for moderates who distinguish the grand design from policy, the stage represented by a peace agreement is not temporary. They do not scheme to bring it to an end or plan to go beyond this stage to a more extreme situation. It has no fixed expiration date. This is *strategic gradualism.* The goal represented by the grand design is not seen as practical or feasible, but is relegated to the domain of distant dreams.

These two types of gradualism were analyzed as far back as 1965 by Fayez Sayegh in a well-known article "A Handful of Mist," which is fundamental for understanding the Arab positions. Sayegh distinguished between open escalation, which enables the Arabs to continue their struggle against Israel until its final liquidation—a sort of "take . . . and then ask for more"—and closed escalation, which brings about the end of the conflict.

The gradual approach adopted by the Palestine Liberation Organization (PLO) at the twelfth session of the Palestine National

Council in June 1974, expressed in its willingness to settle for a Palestinian mini-state, was tactical. To highlight this it was accompanied by a demand for the "restitution of all [Palestinian] rights, and first among them the right of return and of self-determination on the entire soil of the homeland." At the same time, certain steps were forbidden: "The Liberation Organization will fight against any plan for a Palestinian entity whose price is recognition, peace, secure boundaries, the concession of national rights, and denying the right of return and right to self-determination of our people on the soil of our homeland." Implicit in these demands was the intention to accept a Palestinian mini-state in the West Bank and Gaza Strip, but without paying for this with any concession that might even symbolically obstruct the path toward the attainment of the grand design: the "liberation of all Palestine." On the contrary, the mini-state was explicitly intended to serve as a staging area for attaining the grand design.

Sadat's gradualism was of another sort. He agreed to peace and the principle of normalization (the Arabic word he used was *tatbic,* making relations natural), that is, to engender peaceful relations by creating facts that could forestall the possibility of turning back the clock.

True, the distinction between grand design and policy is not so solid as to defy reversal, but no peace comes with a lifetime guarantee. Wars always break out of peace. But this is the most that states are able to achieve in their relations—guarantees that peace will endure forever are utopian. Nations therefore do not disarm in peacetime; they maintain their military preparedness so as to be able to defend themselves, but without the anxiety that characterizes a state of conflict.

The cornerstone of modern strategic thinking is the concept of deterrence, which is designed, by threatening a resort to violent means, to induce one's adversary to desist from his grand design and follow a less-threatening policy. To this concept we must make an important addition: the longer the divorce of grand design from policy continues, the greater are the chances that the grand design will be discarded and that the peace will become a true peace. Peace agreements that endure do so not because the sides involved have made a commitment to abide by them forever—such promises have been given in abundance—but rather because a mutual interest has been created in not reverting to a state of war.

The separation of grand design and policy that Sadat began did not spread to encompass all the Arab countries; Arab circles elsewhere have mostly remained firmly attached to the old policy. Sadat's approach has nevertheless spread in some measure into other parts of the Arab world—to Jordan, to the Arabs of the West Bank, and even to certain factions within the PLO. Abu Musa's rebellion in Tripoli in 1983 was launched against Arafat's inclination to detach policy from the grand design. The separation of ideal and pragmatic goals is no more than a beginning, but it is an important beginning that merits our attention. From the Israeli perspective everything must be done to see that it solidifies.

There is another problem with Arab positions toward Israel that we must recognize. Moderate Arabs are willing to recognize Israel de facto on condition that this is not accompanied by recognition de jure. That is, they are willing to recognize that Israel is a fact, but not to agree that this fact should ever have come into being; in their view, Israel's birth was the result of an act of aggression, the theft of land that had been Arab and its forcible conversion into Jewish land.

Some Arabs exploit this distinction as a rationale to refuse to recognize "Israel's right to exist," as if doing so would also imply recognition of Israel's right to have come into existence. We must not be deterred by this tactic but we should understand the Arabs' problem. There is no need to make peace with the Arabs conditional on their de jure recognition of Zionism—that is, on their agreeing that justice was on the side of the Jews when they took over a land populated by Arabs and made it into a Jewish country, as if the Arabs had somehow been there illicitly. Israel need not ask the Arabs to become Zionists, only to show some understanding of why the Jews became Zionists. On the other hand, a demand that the Arabs recognize Israel's right to continue to exist is reasonable; the refusal to accept such a formula is indicative that the Arabs are holding fast to the goal of liquidation as a policy.

It is true that de facto recognition that is not also de jure recognition is incomplete, being the recognition of something that exists but ought not to. Israel should discuss this problem with the Arabs with complete candor. But from the Israeli perspective it suffices if the Arabs recognize Israel's right to exist now as a state, even if they do not accept that it should have been established. This problem will be resolved after peace has endured for a while. The old arguments over the rights of Zionism will then lose their relevance and eventually be forgotten.

The Palestinians and the Israelis have a similar problem when it comes to recognizing their adversaries' right to self-determination, since each side may fear that implicit in such recognition is an acknowledgment of the other side's right to define itself as the exclusive proprietor of the entire land. Simply calling the Palestinians "Palestinians" ostensibly indicates that they are the owners of Palestine, which is what is implied by the identity between the name of a people and of the country they inhabit. (Thus, France belongs to the French.) However, calling the country Eretz Yisrael denotes that it belongs to the Jews; this name is an acknowledgment of the historic right of the Jews to the entire land, in the past and present, with the implication that the centuries-long Arab residence in the land was legally and morally flawed.

The way out of this semantic tangle, which conceals fundamental political meanings, is a mutual understanding that the other side's right to self-determination is restricted: to part of the land, not all of it. Without this the conflict becomes absolute, a conflict that leaves no possibility of a settlement—which is always a compromise based on a relativist approach to the demands of the opposing sides.

The Debate Among the Arabs

An examination of the ongoing inter-Arab discussions about the conflict will help us understand the problem of separating grand design from policy, since the discussions tend to revolve around it. For simplicity's sake I shall polarize the positions as between moderates, who tend to separate the two, and extremists, who do not.

The extremists within the PLO and in Syria claim that separating the two is premature and a symptom of defeatism; the struggle against Israel must be pursued until that country is destroyed. Precisely because they do not see the divorce of policy and grand design as merely a stratagem or tactical stage, they reject it vigorously. They are afraid that such separation might become permanent and lead to the final acceptance of Israel as a state in the Middle East. On the other hand, the vehemence of their opposition to the moderates on this question is evidence that, for the moderates who suggest it, this separation is no mere tactical maneuver.

The extremists claim that from a historical perspective the Arabs are the stronger side, even if they now appear weak, and that Israel's present might is ephemeral. Israel's strength is less an objective fact than it is a reflection of Arab weakness. True, Israel was victorious in 1967 and expanded, but this expansion will have serious repercussions. Israel's conquests will lead dialectically to its collapse, and by the irony of history its strength will lead to its defeat. The annexation of the West Bank and Gaza Strip, with their Arab inhabitants, will change Israel's ethnic balance and create a situation of instability, tension, and civil strife within Israel, weakening it from the inside until it becomes an easy prey for the Arab states. In the language of the Arab left, just as capitalism is digging its own grave, so Israel will bring about its own doom, or at least will unwittingly help the Arabs to do so.

True, the continuation of Israeli rule in the occupied territories causes hardship to their Arab inhabitants, but this is the price that must be paid for the cause of Pan-Arabism. For the Syrians, the Arab-Israeli conflict is a pan-Arab issue and cannot be reduced to simply achieving a Palestinian state.

Moreover, and paradoxically, the Israeli domination of the territories is for the moment in the Arab interest, as it increases the unrest and riots there. This view was amply confirmed by the riots that began in December, 1987. The repercussion of such strife in Israel will discourage Jews abroad from immigrating to Israel, and encourage emigration. The link among the Jews, in this view, is merely that of religion. They do not constitute a national group, and do not share the consensus of interests needed to sustain statehood in the long term. Moreover, the world condemnation of the policy of annexation that Israel is pursuing will serve to further weaken Israel's position.

The Arabs, assert the extremists, do not have to destroy the Israeli state but merely the Israeli success story. Israeli society is so unnatural that it contains within itself the seeds of its own demise. It is therefore sufficient to fuel the process of disintegration that is intrinsic to it. Eventually the Arabs will only have to provide the final *coup de grâce.*

One of the strongest arguments used by the extremists against the moderates in the Arab camp is that moderation must fail because military successes have so dazzled the Israelis that they can no longer perceive reality. Hence they will reject all overtures by Arab moderates to resolve the conflict, until the moderates themselves become disillusioned. It will then be clear to all that in practice the radical path is the only one open to the Arabs.

The latent strength of the Arabs, claim the extremists, is their capacity to wait. Patience and endurance have always been stressed as traditional Arab characteristics. The Middle East has suffered repeated invasions—by Crusaders, Mongols, Turks, and European imperialists. In the end they were all expelled, and the region has remained Arab. The Zionist invasion will suffer the same fate.

Moreover, one of the Arabs' great advantages is their ability to bear the burden of war and absorb casualties. Israel may be victorious at first, but repeated wars will lead to exhaustion; heavy losses will undermine the ability to persist. Thus, each war is part of a continuing process of attrition, in which the imbalance in resources and numbers will eventually tilt the scales in the Arabs' favor.

Even extremist Arabs recommend avoiding open confrontation with Israel for the moment. But the Lebanon War has taught them that Israel can be severely hurt by terrorism, much more than has been achieved by the Palestinian organizations. In this view, even if such terrorism leads to Israeli reprisals against the Arab civilian population, it achieves its effects because such reprisals incite rebellion and more terrorism, shaking the Israelis' sense of security and marring their image in the eyes of the world. This position has probably been strengthened by the insurrection in the occupied territories.

Some radicals hold that the Arab-Israeli conflict has a positive role to play in Arab nationalism. In the absence of an Arab proletariat with a revolutionary class consciousness to be the vanguard of the social revolution, Arab leftists hope that the motions aroused by the conflict will produce revolutions in the more conservative Arab states. Such revolutions would have a homogenizing effect on the regimes within the Arab states, which may then facilitate Arab unification. Thus far it has been the differences in regimes that have thwarted all attempts at cooperation. A kingdom cannot merge with a republic. The nationalist circles that view Arab unity as the supreme national goal describe the Arab-Israeli conflict as the type of external threat required to provoke the Arab states to merge. Peace with Israel would be a social and political loss for Arab nationalism. This idea recurs in the publications of the Center for Arab Unity Studies in Beirut, and is stressed in the writings of Professor Nadim al-Bitar.

Syria's contribution to radical Arab thinking is conspicuous, and may well reflect the personal involvement of President Assad. The problem is that it is hard for leaders to content themselves with policies that offer only long-term results. They would naturally prefer results to become apparent during their period of office or rule and be credited to them. Thus, Assad seeks strategic parity with Israel, which would permit Syria alone, unaided by other Arab states, to attain some—however limited—military successes against Israel in the foreseeable future.

Syria's nightmare is that, given that Egypt has regained Sinai, and that there is a possibility of negotiations between Israel, Jordan, and the PLO which may end in Israeli withdrawal from all or most of the West Bank, Syria might find itself the only country with territory—the Golan—occupied in 1967 still in Israeli hands. Thus Syria opposes the possibility that Israel, with the support of the United States, may conduct separate negotiations with each of its neighbors individually. This was its quarrel with President Sadat. Syria argues that when Arab countries go it alone they impair their own bargaining power.

The Syrians further insist that any agreements that may be reached between Arab states and Israel should leave open the way to continued pressure on Israel. Syria is the main proponent of "salami tactics" that call for destroying Israel gradually, step by step. The only permissible separation between the grand design of Israel's elimination and the policy of concluding a settlement with it is tactical—an armistice of sorts, not a peace treaty.

The moderates do not dispute the long-term historical perspective of the radicals that sees the Arabs as ultimately victorious. This should be emphasized. Where they disagree is over the cost of this policy. Most of the inhabitants of the West Bank and the Gaza Strip have particularly strong reservations, since they are unable to accept the view that they should be sacrificed in order to attain the destruction of Israel. Thus they too have a stake in a political resolution of the conflict.

The other moderates tend to estimate that the direct price exacted by war with Israel is too high, while the indirect damage is even greater, since the conflict drains their national energies and thus delays their advancement. The more the Arabs delay, the more difficult it will be for them to catch up. Because of the broad economic revolution created by the rapid advances in electronic technology, nations that tarry in catching up are all the more destined to backwardness. The Arabs' position in the world order therefore depends on their liberating themselves from the conflict. It is better for them to suffer Israel as their neighbor and have the benefits of progress than to oppose Israel and suffer the handicaps of backwardness as a result.

Those moderates also cite the historical experience of the Palestinians, whose uncompromising position as far back as the British Mandate has been detrimental to them. The moderates' fears that continuation of the conflict would radicalize the Arab world and increase the influence of Islamic fundamentalism also increases their readiness for peace.

The moderates have another argument. The Syrian demand that any agreement should leave open a way to continued pressure on Israel is simply not practical. Even if the Arabs were to intend a purely tactical settlement, Israel could demand arrangements to buttress the peace that would make it difficult to reopen the conflict. In this Israel would be supported by the world community. The Syrian demand is thus self-defeating: an agreement that is perceived as a temporary measure will strengthen the Israeli refusal to withdraw from the conquests of 1967, and the Arabs will continue to pay the price. The moderates also caution the others not to rely too much on the demographic factor because Israel may adopt pressure tactics to make the Arabs emigrate or even use some international upheaval to expel them.

A comparison of the moderate and extremist positions regarding an Arab state on the West Bank and Gaza Strip will highlight the differences between them. The radicals claim that Arab acceptance of such a state as part of a peace agreement would serve only to perpetuate Israel's existence; the dream of an entirely Arab Middle East would vanish forever. In PLO jargon, an agreement means "liquidating the [Palestinian] problem" instead of "liquidating Israel." The moderates, on the other hand, claim that the establishment of an Arab state on the West Bank will not necessarily preclude further Arab pressure on Israel. But, even if an agreement is tantamount to the final acceptance of a Jewish state, it is worth it when compared to the damage caused by the alternative path.

Comparison of these two concepts highlights the different extent to which they have been worked into an ideological framework. The radical view has been more thoroughly developed, both as ideology and as policy. The moderates have found it much more difficult to express their views fully and confidently. There is a basic reason for this. The radicals' view stands on its own, independent of the position of the adversary or of third parties. The view of the moderates, however, is by definition affected by Israeli positions. Thus Israeli policies, actions, and failures are a factor in the debate between Arab moderates and radicals. Following the logic presented here, Israel should abandon the hard-line policies that have led to a de facto alliance with the Arab radicals in favor of policies that would strengthen the Arab moderates. Without such assistance the Arab moderates cannot persevere in their position.

Moreover, the radicals can survive indefinitely in the absence of an agreement, but for the moderates the continued absence of one is a negation of their position. As Israel's hold on the occupied territories is consolidated, so the moderates' claim that the territories can be regained becomes less persuasive. The recent Uprising may well have strengthened the hope of the moderates that Israel's hold may be short-lived. The moderate position is not autonomous; the extremist position is. The radicals can live with a political intensification of the Middle East conflict, the moderates cannot. For the moderates, then, the clock is ticking. They fear that delay of a settlement will allow Israel, through its settlements policy, to take over the West Bank and Gaza Strip, eliminating the possibility of a peace agreement and leaving no alternative to further wars.

In short, Arab moderation is born first and foremost from a recognition of the Arabs' inability to achieve the goal of destroying Israel. Another factor at work is the discomfort of maintaining a position that is in contradiction to the present world order and to the main norm upon which it rests, i.e., recognition of the integrity of present states. The Arab radicals do not deny that the Arabs are weak, they merely counsel against despair and against seeing the situation as final. Moreover, they believe that Israel's perceived "intransigence" will help accommodate world opinion to the Arab goal of liquidating the country. The moderates, for their part, assert that a long wait until fortune shines upon the Arabs will cause them great harm. However, they are trapped in the dilemma that Israel might exploit their highlighting of the Arab need for peace. Later we shall see that there is a parallel problem on the Israeli side.

The suffering engendered in the past and the nightmare of a violent future that will lead to great destruction are the reasons why Israel's Arab neighbors fear the absence of an agreement and have moderated their positions (except for Syria, primarily because of Israel's holding of the Golan). By contrast, the more distant Arab countries—Libya, Yemen, and Algeria—are sheltered by their remoteness from the front lines and can allow themselves to hold fast to the old radical positions.

The PLO has long understood this difference, and suspected

that the front-line states are liable to abandon the struggle and prefer their own interests. This suspicion has not been groundless, as the peace treaty with Egypt demonstrated. For the PLO the problem has been how to keep these Arab states from moving toward peace. On the other hand, because the PLO leadership has become more moderate, its attitude toward these countries has also been changing, and they have become its allies. Today the PLO leadership does not seek to prevent a settlement, but rather to guarantee that it will be a party to it. Iraq, which traditionally held a most extreme position, has also revised its position. The Iraqis' explanation for this is most instructive; they present it as required by the need to make their position conform with that of the PLO, which is the party directly involved in the conflict.

Arabs differentiate between pan-Arab nationalism *(Qaumiyya)* and the nationalism or patriotism of each of the Arab states or peoples *(Wataniyya)*. Palestinian nationalism developed not only as a reaction to Zionism but as a reaction to the Arab states' attempts to make the Palestinians subservient to their interests. Thus, until the establishment of the PLO in 1964, and more so until the changes that were promulgated by the PLO in 1968, the Palestinians hoped that their salvation would come through pan-Arab efforts and they emphasized *Qaumiyya* rather than *Wataniyya*. Only as they despaired of the former joint approach did they turn to the do-it-yourself approach of the latter.

The Palestinians and the PLO

The special status of the PLO stems from the fact that in the eyes of the Palestinians and many others it symbolizes the Palestinian struggle for recognition of their collective identity. Were a referendum to be conducted among the Palestinians in the occupied territories and the Palestinian Diaspora, most of them would say that the PLO represents them, or, to use the familiar formula, that it is "the sole legitimate representative of the Palestinian people." This does not mean that they are enamored of the PLO, or that they do not have bitter criticisms of the organization and its leaders, or that they identify with every clause of the PLO Covenant. On the other hand, the criticism of the PLO occasionally expressed by Palestinians or other Arabs should not be seen as calling into question that it represents the Palestinians.

In this context, we should distinguish between the PLO as an idea and the PLO as an institution. The idea is that the Palestinians are a people whose collective existence should be recognized and should find political expression in a state. The condition for realizing the idea is the existence of an institution to fight for this goal. The institution is thus an agency to implement the idea. It is reasonable to assume that the vast majority of the Palestinians, and perhaps even all of them, identify with the idea, and this is the source of their identification with the PLO as an institution. As long as no other institution represents the idea, the Palestinians have no alternative to identifying with the current framework, however strong their reservations may be about it.

The principal conclusion entailed by this argument is that since a political solution of the conflict will involve the territories, and since the territories are inhabited by Palestinians, any political settlement must include Palestinian representatives, that is, the PLO. In the past Jordan was willing to negotiate the future of the West Bank without the PLO. Those days are gone, and not only because of the pressure of Arab countries that defined the PLO as the "sole representative of the Palestinians" (secretly and with Jordanian reservations at the sixth Arab summit, held in Algiers in November, 1973, and publicly and by general agreement at the Rabat summit in October, 1974), but also because of a principled Jordanian position that advocated political cooperation with the PLO.

Today, any demand for a settlement without the PLO is equivalent to demanding no settlement. Israel must recognize that the role of the PLO in an agreement is determined by the PLO's status and not by its conduct. In other words, recognition of the PLO is not according it an affidavit of good behavior, but is dictated by the function that it fulfills. To insist that Palestinian representatives to negotiations not be identified with the PLO is merely an act of self-deception: even Palestinians who are ostensibly not identified with the PLO will take their instructions from that organization. If diplomatic exigencies require the Palestinian negotiators to pretend to distance themselves from the PLO, their subservience to the PLO will increase in proportion to their "declared" distance from it. Thus any negotiations with the Palestinians will be negotiations with the PLO, and it would be better if they were direct and open.

Unconditional Israeli rejection of the PLO and its participation in a political settlement is doomed to failure. On the other hand, it is of course possible to confront the PLO with explicit demands and conditions that it change some of its official positions. But the more vehement Israel's rejection of the PLO, the more painful will be Israeli retreat from that position.

The Palestinian Covenant, a summary of the PLO's ideology, is ugly, totally one-sided in its refusal to recognize that Jews and Israelis too deserve their own national identity. It asserts an absolute position that leaves no room for compromise. This unwillingness to compromise has, not surprisingly, had its effect on the internal norms and behavior of the PLO, which is riven by internecine quarrels and bloodshed. The elevation in 1968 of armed struggle as the PLO's main principle of action has exacted a high price from the organization and its constituent groups. Time after time fighters have been sent to their deaths with no sense of responsibility on the part of their commanders. Nevertheless, the Palestinians have persevered in their struggle and made many sacrifices. Those Israelis who trumpet the great bravery that the Irgun militia and Lehi underground displayed during their comparatively brief fight against the British Mandate should remember that in numerical terms their sacrifices were very small when compared to the lengthy caravan of Palestinian martyrs who have given their lives in their national struggle.

The predicament in which the Palestinians found themselves after 1948 gave them the impetus to acquire education that would permit them to advance themselves in the societies where they were living. Paradoxically, it was the example of the Jews that motivated them to do so. Palestinian families outside Palestine made great efforts to send their children to schools and universities, much like Jewish families outside Israel. Today there is a broad stratum of Palestinian university graduates and academics of renown. Israelis who base their opinion of the Palestinians as a whole on their impressions of the Palestinian workers they encounter in Israel make a serious mistake. There *is* a considerable Palestinian working class—a class that in Israel has become so shrunken that the economy has become dependent on Palestinian labor— but there is also a flourishing and expanding intelligentsia.

The Palestinians are notable also for their nationalist spirit. This too is partially a result of the lessons they have learned from the Israelis—collective spirit and a willingness for voluntary activity unknown among them in the past are today widespread. The individual sees himself as in the service of the national mission.

Because of their strong sense of identity, many Palestinians feel themselves strangers in the Arab countries. Consequently they tend to marry among themselves and to preserve their own identity and dialect. In Arab societies the Palestinians are seen as rivals for success, and there is much jealousy of their achievements and their social and economic status. Politically, Palestinians are considered a dangerous element, seditious or at least promoting instability. The other Arabs also hold the Palestinians responsible for the suffering that has resulted from the Arab-Israeli conflict. But it is important to remember that Arab dislike of Palestinians, and even open animosity, do not indicate any kindred feeling with Israel. The Arab states may not be enthusiastic about the creation of a Palestinian state, but they are even less enthusiastic about continued Israeli rule in the territories. Confronted with a choice between a Palestinian state and continued Israeli domination, they would be fervent supporters of a Palestinian state.

The Arab states further recognize that as long as there is no Palestinian state they too will have no rest. Their commitment to the Palestinians stems not only from national sentiments but also, and most importantly, from calculations of their own self-interest. They are apprehensive that the Palestinians, if they do not settle down, may destabilize their own countries. For the Arab countries the establishment of a Palestinian state is a means to rid themselves of the encumbrance of the Palestinians and their pressure. This consideration does not have the same weight for all the Arab countries; nevertheless, it represents an important achievement for the PLO.

Palestinian self-recognition as a national group may be rather recent, but it is a mistake to deduce from this that it is superficial and weak—as did the late Professor Benjamin Akzin in *Ha'aretz* (October 16, 1984), in speaking of "an artificial product of successful advertising semantics, called 'the Palestinian nation.' " The Palestinians see themselves as a people, not as a nation: the language of Arab nationalism distinguishes between a nation *(umma)*, which is pan-Arab, and a people *(sha'ab)*, which refers to the territorial groups into which this nation has been subdivided over the course of history, and one of which is the "Palestinian people." The Palestinians demand recognition of their collective existence like all the other Arab peoples.

For many years, the Arabs referred to Israel as the "so-called" or "alleged" Israel, as if verbal denial of its existence could be translated into nonexistence in the real world. The use of verbal tricks as a device to make an unwanted entity disappear has now entrenched itself in the Israeli attitude toward the Palestinians. Israeli denial of the existence of a Palestinian people will not bring about its miraculous disappearance. Similarly, in years gone by, it was the Arabs who avoided contact with Israelis and were distraught if they discovered they had shaken hands with an Israeli. Today the position has been reversed: contact with Palestinians who are members of the PLO now carries social stigma and legal penalties in Israel.

The avoidance of the term "Palestinian," as if its use constitutes recognition of the Palestinians as a political entity, leads to absurd situations. This can be seen in the public pronouncements of Menachem Begin and thereafter in the Hebrew translation of the Camp David agreements, where "the Palestinian people" is rendered as "the Arabs of Eretz Yisrael." However, the Camp David Accords also express the first stirrings of official Israeli recognition of the existence of the Palestinian people and their "legitimate rights and just requirements." In the English text of the agreements they are called "the Palestinian people," just as the Arabic translation reads *"al-sha'ab al-Filastini."* By contrast, as we have seen, the Hebrew version refers to "the Arabs of Eretz Yisrael"—a reference to a group of individuals who are not recognized as a political entity. It is true that the English word "people" is ambiguous, meaning both a nation and individuals, but the Accords go on to speak of negotiations with the Palestinians as a political unit even if it is limited to the "inhabitants of Judea, Samaria, and the Gaza Strip." This is the Hebrew version, of course, but semantics cannot change the reality of a Palestinian collectivity, and certainly cannot rescue a bankrupt policy.

Recognition of a collective Palestinian entity obviously has political implications—the demand that this entity have a political expression as well. Without this, there will be no settlement of the Arab-Israeli conflict. This does not mean that the solution must be a separate Palestinian state. Such a state would be landlocked and would need an outlet to the sea. There would, therefore, be a need to establish some connection between the Palestinian state and Jordan. Such a connection would certainly be welcomed by the Palestinians of the East Bank, who are Jordanians by citizenship but nevertheless identify themselves as Palestinians. It is no accident that both the Jordanians and the PLO recognize the need for a confederation between Jordan and the Palestinian region on the West Bank and the Gaza Strip. But any agreement on such a confederation requires prior Israeli recognition of the Palestinian state.

The attitude toward Jordan has been a bone of contention within the PLO. The radicals used to insist that the liberation of Palestine must be preceded by the overthrow of Hussein—"the road to Jerusalem leads through Amman." In recent years there has been a change in this position. Revolution in Jordan is no longer seen even by the radicals as a precondition for the liberation of Palestine. Only later will it be necessary in order to defend the Palestinian nature of the Palestinian region against the Jordanian regime, or at least from dependence on it. The moderates, on the other hand, hold that if a Palestinian state confederated with Jordan is established on the West Bank, over the course of time the Palestinians will stamp their image on it and ultimately become the dominant faction. As a first stage, then, confederation is needed to ensure the existence of the Palestinian state, while in the future it may contribute to the Palestinization of Jordan.

The Palestinians will certainly continue to long for the day that all the territory west of the Jordan will once again be "Palestine." That is the official position of the PLO. Its grand design envisions the liberation of the entire country—which from the Israeli perspective means the destruction of Israel—and is the central theme of the Palestinian Covenant.

It would be best for Israel and the PLO if the latter agreed to amend (or abrogate) the Palestinian Covenant; such proposals have even been raised within the PLO. But there is another way to detract from the status of the Covenant—to consign it to oblivion by ceasing to refer to it. In general, my impression is that the number of references to the covenant is on the decline. In the past the resolutions of the Palestine National Council and the communiqués issued at the end of its sessions always began by mentioning the covenant. But the resolutions of the seventeenth council, in November 1984, omitted this formula, and this may well not have been an oversight. The Palestinian radicals accuse Arafat of abandoning the Covenant, but in general the picture remains ambiguous, since references to the Covenant do occur in other official documents and communiqués, notably in the Resolutions of the Eighteenth PNC (April 1987).

It is difficult for the PLO to change its basic positions. It is difficult for the Palestinians openly to give up the principle of return—a collective return to the whole country—that has been sanctified as their prime national goal. It is difficult for them to abandon the extreme position that demands full attainment of their goal. Precisely because they define themselves in terms of territory, they find it painful to recognize that they will be the people of only part of Palestine. They also tend to ignore that their demand for self-determination is likely to imply a denial of the state of Israel's right to exist.

In an effort to find a way out of these difficulties, the Palestinians devote great attention to phraseology and their councils debate semantic devices at great length. For example, Security Council Resolution 242 was initially totally rejected by the PLO because it called for an overall political settlement with Israel. Later it was denigrated for ignoring the national existence of the Palestinians and referring to them as refugees without a collective self-identity. Opposition to Resolution 242 became a symbol, as if it frustrated all Palestinian aspirations—their grand design—rather than simply demanding that they make certain policy commitments. To get around this, the PLO eventually stated that it accepts *all* United Nations resolutions. One might understand this as a compromise—an indirect allusion to their acceptance of Resolution 242. But the formula also includes many other resolutions, e.g., the 1947 partition resolution; the 1948 General Assembly Resolution (no. 194) calling for the return of refugees; General Assembly Resolution 3236 of November 22, 1974, which recognizes the Palestinians' right of self-determination and the right to return to their houses and property; the 1975 "Zionism is racism" resolution, and many others. The vague reference to "all" United Nations resolutions thus equally implies that they have these other resolutions in mind.

The PLO's contention that it is withholding recognition of Israel for use as a bargaining card is disingenuous. A bargaining card represents something your adversary wants to receive, whereas the PLO's nonrecognition of Israel has benefited the extremists in Israel, who see no need to try to appease the Palestinians with concessions to gain their recognition. The recognition of Israel is in fact a necessity *for the Palestinians,* if they want to escape from the political bind in which they find themselves. The PLO leadership fears that either step—accepting Resolution 242 or even only recognition of Israel—would lead to no political results, and in the end they would be the only ones who yielded.

The precise definition of political terms is of paramount importance because the crucial ones have become so fraught with equivocation and ambiguity. For example, the PLO's position for settling the conflict is based on three rights: "Self-determination," "Return," and "Inalienable Rights" (which in Arabic means fixed and permanent rights). All three terms have been construed as negating the existence of the state of Israel. Thus, self-determination and inalienable rights have been interpreted as the demand to assume sovereignty of all of pre-Israel Palestine; the right of return has been understood as the right to flood Israel with repatriated Palestinians who have the right to repossess the property that formerly belonged to them. Hence any serious negotiation must begin by pinning down the concrete demands that follow from these rights and that can be made acceptable to both parties. Similarly, the demand that Israel must withdraw from "the occupied territory" must specifically mean the territory occupied in 1967 and not that of the previous borders of 1948–1967, which Arabs also refer to as "the occupied territory." It is not too much to say that the extremists on both sides have benefited greatly by using the maximalist meaning of these rights to thwart any movement toward negotiations.

The PLO comprises radical organizations that cling to the traditional position of merging grand design and policy and rejecting any settlement with Israel, alongside relatively moderate organizations, foremost among them Fatah, which is the largest and most important component of the PLO. But the PLO has always been terrified of schism and troubled by nightmare recollections of the internecine factional murders, within the Arab Rebellion (1936–39). The recurrent bloody struggles among its component organizations continue to remind it of the damage caused by internal disagreement. Several years after its founding in 1964, the PLO at its fourth and fifth councils (July 1968 and February 1969) became an umbrella organization of competing and warring Fedayeen (Commando) organizations. Nevertheless, it endeavored to maintain a facade of unity that would cover up the internal dissensions. Preserving this facade has always forced the PLO to adopt radical stands.

The moderate groups know that following the political path—a path involving the surrender of any possibility of attaining the official common goal of the liberation of all Palestine—would cause a serious split between them and the radicals. Such a split occurred at the 17th Palestine National Council meeting in Amman in November, 1984, which was boycotted by the radicals, whose organizations then seceded from the PLO. It was the growth in the relative weight of the more moderate Fatah within the PLO that allowed Arafat to pursue the policy that led to the split.

Although most of the constituent organizations seceded (only Fatah, the Iraqi-influenced Arab Liberation Front, and a section from the small Palestine Liberation Front stayed), the status of the PLO was barely affected because of the overwhelming predominance of Fatah. The secession did not detract from the prestige of the PLO in the eyes of most Arab states, foreign countries, and the Palestinian community at large, and did not deprive Yasser Arafat of his role as its recognized leader. Little was heard of the secessionist organizations that constitute the extremist Salvation Front (*Jabhat al-Inqaz*), as if the very secession relegated them to an inferior status. In the eyes of many and probably most Palestinians, the Salvation Front organizations were stigmatized as tools of the Syrians.

The moderation of the PLO's stand represented a willingness to become what we might call the "PPLO"—an organization for the liberation of part of Palestine. But such a change, with the associated perils of schism, would be perceived as worthwhile only if it became clear that it would realize the moderates' hopes of establishing a Palestinian state, albeit truncated, on the West Bank and in the Gaza Strip. The suspicion that even this limited goal might not be realized is a further factor discouraging the moderates from an unequivocal statement of their position.

As I write in 1988, twenty-four years have passed since the PLO was established. In any self-assessment it must confess that it has hardly come any closer to the goal of liberating Palestine. The contention of the Arab radicals that history favors the Arabs in their confrontation with Israel refers to the Arabs, not necessarily to the Palestinians. The blows they have suffered over the years, and more recently in Lebanon from both Israel and the Syrians, and the painful truth that no Arab state rushed to their rescue in their time of need during the Lebanon War—all of these cause many Palestinians to feel that time is working against them.

Basically, the Palestinians must wonder whether the choices facing them may involve the loss of a value they have exalted and gloried in: Palestinian independence of decision. Long ago, Ahmed Shukeiry, the founder of the PLO and its leader up to the end of 1967, wanted to place the PLO under the aegis of the Arab League in order to keep any Arab state from dominating it. Since 1982 the problem has become even more acute because the drastic effects of the Lebanon War have further restricted the PLO's options.

The decision of some Palestinian organizations to reject a settlement with Israel and continue the struggle against it meant accepting the patronage of Syria, which is the leading proponent of the radical line. The Palestinians involved thereby became tools for achieving Syrian goals, which are oriented toward the aggrandizement of Syria rather than the liberation of Palestine. Furthermore, Syria's leadership is known for its predatory nature and demand for absolute obedience. Thus PLO leadership will continue to resist being subservient to the Syrians as shown in Arafat's visit to Damascus in April, 1988. Going along with the Syrians means continuing the struggle indefinitely, and this process must eventually wear down the Palestinians. The Syrians give priority to their obligations toward pan-Arab and Syrian nationalism whenever a conflict arises between these interests and Palestinian interests. That is why the Syrians have supported rivals to the Palestinians, such as the Shi'ites, who are determined to destroy any independent Palestinian hold on Lebanon. For a long time the extremist organizations—Gibril, Habash, and al-Saika—cast their lot in with the Syrians, but many of their members too have doubts about their Syrian patron.

By contrast, following the political path has forced the Palestinians to entrust their destiny to King Hussein and to authorize him to negotiate in their name. For many years Hussein has symbolized repression of the Palestinians and a tendency to minimize their identity. Moreover, Jordan and Hussein also have been claimants for the allegiance of the Palestinians, and were thus at the same time partners and rivals to the PLO and its leadership. To the extent that the inhabitants of the West Bank are an important factor—and for the PLO mainstream they have become the main agents of the struggle, especially since the decline of the importance of the Palestinian community in Lebanon—a link to King Hussein has been essential. Maintaining ties with the large Palestinian concentration in Jordan likewise requires good relations with the Hashemite regime.

The PLO and Fatah mainstream therefore chose to cooperate with Hussein; their choice recognized that there would not be an independent Palestinian state. This was the main significance of the February 11, 1985, agreement between Hussein and Arafat. The agreement made no mention of an independent Palestinian state. Rather, it stated that "the Palestinians will realize their inalienable right in the context of an Arab confederation to be established between the Jordanian and Palestinian states." It is this relinquishing of the demand for an independent state that was the bone of contention between Arafat and Fatah on the one hand and the radical organizations that rejected it on the other. For Hussein's part, conducting negotiations with the Palestinians and moving closer to the PLO expressed his recognition that he could not negotiate for the West Bank without PLO approval.

The Palestinians demand that the arrangement be confederational (and not a merger) in order to preserve the separate identity of each of the two states. The Palestinians insist on maintaining the "Palestinianism" of their part of the confederation, and with equal vigor insist today on preserving the Jordanian nature of Jordan, in order to counter the idea put forward by some Israeli leaders of giving Jordan to the Palestinians as a "substitute homeland." They angrily denounce and reject this "plot," seeing it as the Palestinian version of Herzl's stillborn scheme to found the Jewish state in Uganda. Jordan is not to be Palestinized, and its Jordanian nature must be preserved to guarantee the Palestinian character of the West Bank. By a historic irony, the PLO has become a fervent supporter of a Jordanian Jordan, and Hussein has become no less a fervent supporter of retaining the Palestinian character of the West Bank. As Hussein has repeatedly said: "The Palestinian state is not an exclusively Palestinian option, it is also a Jordanian option."

To both Hussein and the Palestinians it is clear that a confederation, even if ostensibly a partnership between two states, will be an unequal relationship, between an established state possessing its own organs and army and a partner that is no more than the idea of a state carried aloft by a number of squabbling organizations. Hussein and the Jordanian authorities will have the upper hand, at least in the initial stage, which could last for quite a while. This is another factor that disturbs the radical factions.

Although it neither initiated nor directed the Uprising, the position of the PLO in the Arab world has significantly benefited from the insurrection in the occupied territories. Arabs everywhere have admired the audacity of the young Palestinians in challenging the Israeli army. As a result of this outpouring of public enthusiasm, which has repeatedly credited the young Palestinians with having done more for the Arab cause than any of the states, the Arab leadership has hastened to make up for its previous lack of support. Thus, an extraordinary summit meeting was convened in Algiers in early June 1988. Its main outcome was to pledge economic support for the Uprising and to give the PLO credit for it. The Algiers conference reiterated that the PLO is the sole legitimate representative of the Palestinians and reaffirmed their support of its goal of creating an independent Palestinian state. The Algiers Summit meeting once again called for the convening of an international peace conference with the five permanent members of the Security Council, but for the first time the Arab leaders specifically demanded that the PLO participate on an equal footing "with all the other parties concerned in the conflict."

Jordan, the PLO, and the Arab Countries

A significant change has occurred in the Jordanian position, which formerly viewed the PLO as an enemy. In the late 1950s and early 1960s Jordan did all it could to frustrate the creation of an autonomous Palestinian organization since such an organization would undermine its status as the heir to Arab Palestine. It finally acquiesced only when the establishment of the PLO in 1964 gave it no choice. It nevertheless continued to fight against the idea and endeavored to deny the PLO monopoly on the Palestinian issue. From a Jordanian perspective, the existence of the PLO meant that many of its own citizens felt their prime allegiance was to a foreign organization rather than to itself. Jordan officially abandoned this position, at the Arab summit meeting in 1974, when it realized that its policy was isolating it from the other Arab states. Nevertheless, Hussein still attempted to conduct negotiations with Israel while ignoring the PLO, and met several times with leaders of the Labor government. At the time, Hussein was prepared to reach a settlement with Israel on terms similar to those that Sadat obtained in the Sinai—i.e., Israeli withdrawal to the 1967 borders. But he was eventually forced to realize that there was no possibility of a deal between Israel and Jordan (i.e., excluding the PLO), because Israel demanded territorial concessions that he could not allow himself to make, both from the perspective of his national pride and from fear of pan-Arab accusations of treason. He could sustain a separate agreement with Israel only if it represented a complete victory for him—i.e., the recovery of all of the occupied territories, including East Jerusalem. The Israeli negotiators were impressed by King Hussein's personality, but at the same time held to a position that doubted his ability to conclude a separate peace and rejected his proposal of a return to the previous boundaries. So Hussein despaired of reaching any direct settlement with Israel, and the failure of the negotiations evidently left a residue of resentment.

Since then, changes have taken place both in Israel and in the Middle East. In Israel the Likud Coalition has been in power almost continuously since 1977. The Likud has never troubled to conceal its inclinations toward annexing the occupied territories. Some among its senior ministers declare that Jordan is Palestine, and that Israel should work to bring down the Hashemite monarchy and present Jordan to the Palestinians on a silver platter, as inducement to the PLO to relinquish the claim to the West Bank. In secret, however, Israel signaled to the king that he should not give any credence to these declarations. Yet at the same time, the accelerated pace of settlement activity signaled to Jordan no less clearly that the Israeli intention was to render impossible any political deal that would return the West Bank. If this is the Israeli goal, Jordan has nothing to negotiate about.

Jordan has enjoyed many years of prosperity, and has consolidated itself as a political entity. The scars left by the battles against the PLO in 1970–71 have healed. Even though the PLO was bloodied and driven out of Lebanon, that war proved to the Jordanians that Palestinian nationalism has the strength and will to continue its fight. The PLO is no longer a threat to Jordan. On the contrary, cooperating with the PLO on the West Bank has eased Jordanian relations with the Palestinian population of the East Bank as well, who are in any case for the most part loyal to the Hashemite regime.

Jordan was unable to cooperate with an extremist PLO whose declared goal was the destruction of Israel. This would mean sucking the region into the vortex of war—a danger that Jordan wants more than anything to avoid. But signs of moderation concerning a resolution of the conflict have begun to appear in the PLO. Its moderate wing shows signs of willingness to accept a mini-state on the West Bank—a change that has brought it close to Hussein's long-held position. If the PLO really aspired to take over the entire area between the Jordan River and the Mediterranean Sea, there would be no need to propose confederation with the Hashemite kingdom. Confederation is a necessity only if the independent Palestinian enclave is contracted to the West Bank and the Gaza Strip, since in such conditions the Palestinians need Jordan as an outlet and support.

The choice open to Jordan is not whether or not the West Bank will be returned to its sovereignty, but whether it will remain in Israeli hands or pass to the PLO. Jordan must choose between the lesser of the two evils, and leaving the occupied territories under Israeli rule is the greater evil. Jordan is afraid that Israel, in order to save itself from drowning in the increasing sea of Palestinians under its control, will expel the Arabs of the West Bank. The Arabs suspect that such expulsion would be achieved mostly by exerting enough pressure on the Palestinians to make their lives intolerable and expropriating their land. The continued occupation of the West Bank by its Palestinian inhabitants is a prime Jordanian interest. Their expulsion would flood Jordan, radicalize the entire Middle East, and could drive it to war. Jordan, or at least the present Jordanian regime, has a future in a calm Middle East, not in a tumultuous one. Since Israeli withdrawal from the West Bank is the only guarantee that expulsion of its population will not occur, Jordan's future depends upon a settlement.

Jordan has maintained close contacts with the Arabs of the West Bank and invests funds there as an incentive for them to remain on their land—a policy known in Palestinian jargon as "steadfastness." Jordanian assistance to the Arabs of the West Bank was not intended to lay the foundations for renewed Jordanian sovereignty but to prevent the establishment of Israeli sovereignty—although strengthening the Jordanian foothold on the West Bank would clearly be an advantage when a confederation is established and Jordan and the Palestinians have to jockey for power within it.

It would seem, then, that Hussein no longer dreams of recovering the West Bank. He is not interested in increasing the Palestinian element in his kingdom. It is not the expansion of his kingdom but its preservation that is paramount in his agenda. It is to Jordan's benefit for the Palestinians to remain on the West Bank, though they do so not out of loyalty to Jordan but as an expression of their national consciousness, which is represented by the PLO. Certainly King Hussein is aware that his drawing closer to the PLO strengthens the Palestinian consciousness of the Palestinians who reside permanently in Jordan. However, the 1987–88 Uprising in Palestine made Hussein all the more aware that the allegiance of the Palestinians of the West Bank is to the PLO and not to Jordan. Indeed, the Uprising may give him cause to fear that it may spread to Jordan. The debate in Jordan, and within the royal family, does not question Jordan's interest in the existence of a West Bank populated by Palestinians but examines the merits of cooperation with the PLO as the best means to guarantee this.

Israeli authorities delude themselves if they believe that an alternative Palestinian leadership can be called into being, and even more so if they believe that its demands will be smaller than the PLO's. Let us believe King Hussein when he emphatically reiterates that he can only be a *partner* of the Palestinians in negotiations with Israel and not a substitute or a proxy for them. His demands too will be no smaller than theirs.

The PLO has likewise changed its traditional position toward

Jordan. Previously, the prevailing view was that the Palestinians needed to gain control of Jordan as a necessary condition for regaining Palestine. Jordan was seen as the vital staging area from which the conquest of Israel would start; it was sloganized by Palestinian spokesmen that Amman should serve as "Hanoi" in order to get "Saigon," i.e., Jerusalem. Today the rejectionist organizations still adhere to this strategic principle. The PLO leadership, however, now considers that alliance with Jordan is a prerequisite for PLO action. This is, first of all, because Jordan serves as a link and provides access to the West Bank. Furthermore, in order to counteract the position held by some leaders in Israel that Jordan is the Palestinian state and should be offered to the Palestinians so that they will then be satisfied and relinquish their aspirations to areas west of the Jordan, the PLO now stresses the need to preserve the Jordanian character of Jordan. Such an Israeli proposal is considered a conspiracy against the Palestinians, denigrated as an offer of "a substitute fatherland."

Hussein has many grievances against the PLO, and is perhaps dismayed by some of its actions. Were he to perceive that the PLO is holding fast to its old rejectionist position, he would be likely to despair completely of cooperation with it. In such a case he would probably conclude that there is no alternative to allowing the present unresolved situation to continue, however it might develop. This is a bleak possibility, but it cannot be prevented, merely prepared for. He would seek to protect his own security and that of Jordan by entrusting its fate to God, and by searching for a way to resolve his differences with Syria. This would represent a victory for the Arab radicals and the conflict would once more become acute. Such a development is not in the interests of Jordan, the PLO, or Israel.

Hussein might have been ready for a first-step interim agreement with Israel without PLO participation, but only, first, if the agreement could be presented as a conspicuous achievement for the Arab side and, second, if there were clear guarantees that the agreement is not meant to be a final perpetuation of the status quo. Following the intention in official Israeli circles with regard to the autonomy plan foreseen in the Camp David Accords, Hussein would demand prior definition of the final arrangements to which the interim settlement would lead. The PLO might have given its blessing to negotiations that exclude it temporarily, but not for all time.

Hussein insisted that the PLO make itself eligible for the political process by accepting Resolution 242 and ceasing terrorist activities. However, the PLO disappointed Hussein by its unwillingness to accept Resolution 242 in a clear, straightforward fashion. From the perspective of Israeli interests it would have been better if the PLO and Jordan composed a joint delegation to negotiations. King Hussein, coming to the table alone, will adopt extremist positions that preclude any concessions to Israel. A joint delegation would be likely to be more flexible. This is apparently why Hussein himself has strenuously insisted on PLO participation in negotiations, so that it might share the responsibility for the concessions that Hussein understands the Arab side will have to make in order to obtain an Israeli withdrawal from the territories.

For Jordan, handing over the West Bank to the PLO may not be a heartwarming prospect, but it is incomparably preferable to Israeli annexation. After the bloodshed between them of 1970–71 it seemed that an unbridgeable gulf separated the Hashemite kingdom from the PLO. But over the course of time both parties seem to have concluded that their mutual benefit required them to forget the past and form a united front, at least as a temporary expedient, although the Jordanians are aware that the radical organizations support the confederation plan in the hope that such an arrangement will strengthen the Palestinian component on both banks and lead to the collapse of the Hashemite regime. However, the Jordanians hope that a confederation will give them significant influence over the West Bank and Gaza Strip and prevent the Palestinian enclave from becoming a center for plots directed against Jordan. It is true that Jordan and the Palestinians differ on the ultimate character of the Jordanian-Palestinian confederation, but this question can be deferred to the future and does not prevent cooperation in the present stage.

Even prior to 1985 some senior officials in the PLO such as Sabri Jiryes, director of the PLO Research Center, began to speak of the need for rational, realistic, nonrejectionist, nonnihilistic positions. Some explicitly say that the Palestinians will have to make significant concessions, and that they will have to concede some of their rights in order to obtain others. Refusing to budge from maximalist positions they say will be detrimental to the Palestinian cause; whatever can be saved must be saved. In their view, the Lebanon War made the Palestinian movement need to adopt a more realistic approach. The heady days of Beirut are over. The fall of the "Fakhani Republic" (the Beirut district where the PLO headquarters was located) brought the organization down to earth. The PLO, released from its dependence on Syria, can now perceive its true situation in a mature and realistic fashion.

Khaled al-Hassan, a senior figure in Fatah who has been close to Arafat and his special envoy for sensitive diplomatic tasks, and apparently also a leading political ideologue within the PLO, published a book in Amman in 1985 whose title translates as *The Palestinian-Jordanian Agreement for Joint Action.* In this book, which strongly attacks the radicals and defends the 1985 agreement, he surveys the development of the PLO's positions and the course of the negotiations with Jordan, presenting draft proposals for an agreement between them along the way. He continually stresses the ultimate goal of a democratic Palestinian state in place of Israel and affirms the PLO's commitment to the traditional anti-Israel goals of the Palestinians and Arabs. For him the grand design remains as before, but he expressed a readiness to modify PLO policy and stresses the need for negotiations and a political settlement.

This is a quite different line from the one that has formerly characterized Arab writings on the conflict—with the possible exception of Sid Ahmed's *When the Cannons Fall Silent,* published in 1975. Khaled al-Hassan remains loyal to the gradualism that underlies his conception, and also highlights the need for sophisticated and realistic thinking. He is afraid of the complications that might ensue should Israel force the Palestinians to emigrate, and this fear is the central motivation of his position. Probably as a gesture toward the Arab radicals, he asserts that any political settlement is a stage; but he does not specifically describe this stage as temporary. Thus, even though he does not explicitly say so, it seems that Khaled al-Hassan recognizes that a political settlement could endure. It is no wonder that the radicals have angrily rejected his approach as treason to Palestinian goals, and claimed that what he called "a stage" is in fact the final stage.

It is worth noting that al-Hassan does not base himself on the Palestinian Covenant. He argues against "radical rhetoric," which might be understood as including the covenant, and comes out explicitly against the absolutism that insists on full realization of Arab goals. Instead, he calls for the adoption of relative positions and relative solutions. He describes the ongoing conflict between the Arab *conscience,* which longs to achieve national goals in full, and *reason,* which demands that human beings settle for the possible.

In order to understand al-Hassan's position we should examine the grounds on which it is based. In his view, the rejection of a political settlement by the Arabs and Palestinians will lead to the annexation of the occupied territories by Israel. The weakened condition of the Arab states would not permit recourse to the military option to prevent this, and moreover would not permit the use of force to achieve their goals. The radicals are being irresponsible to place their trust in a violent solution, not so much because of the might of Israel, but because "the world, including Moscow and Washington, will on no account permit a military solution that will injure the Zionist entity within the pre-1967 borders, and in particular with the lines of the 1947 Partition Plan" (page 137). This obstacle is permanent. The existence of Israel has become rooted in the consciousness of the world and acquired international legitimacy, and the Arabs too must work within this context. Thus only one course of action is open to them today: a political settlement. Al-Hassan does express a hope that Arab aspirations will eventually be realized in full, but he does not make a settlement conditional on its including provisions that might lead to this.

The first clause in the Jordanian-Palestinian agreement spoke of "the territory for peace" as the basic principle of a settlement with Israel (even though Israel is not actually mentioned by name). Section 5 made explicit mention of "peace negotiations." No doubt certain clauses and phrases in the agreement were intentionally left vague and undefined, or may be suspected of concealing hostile intent. But, while such suspicions are appropriate, the agreement did represent a change of position; this was clearly demonstrated by the flood of condemnation poured on the agreement by Arab and Palestinian extremists. The agreement implied a readiness to conclude a settlement with Israel, albeit not on terms that the Israelis wanted.

Furthermore, the PLO has published in its official bimonthly the proposals it asked King Hussein to pass to the American authorities. The second proposal, in the official English version, reads as follows:

> On the basis of the Jordan-PLO Accord of February 11, 1985 and in view of our genuine desire for peace, we are ready to negotiate within the context of an International Conference with the participation of the permanent members of the Security Council and with the participation of all concerned Arab parties and the

Israeli government a peaceful settlement of the
Palestinian problem on the basis of the pertinent United
Nations resolutions including Security Council
resolutions 242 and 338.

The PLO declares its rejection and denunciation of
terrorism, which had been assured in the Cairo
Declaration of November, 1985. . . . The declaration of
the Palestine Liberation Organization of its conditional
acceptance of 242 is to be simultaneous with the
declaration of the United States' government of its
acceptance of the right of self-determination. (*Shu'un
Filastiniyya,* no. 158–159, May–June 1986, p. 74)

This version is far from ideal. It would have been preferable if
the PLO had expressed itself straightforwardly and not found refuge in devious phrasings that always raise suspicions of ulterior
intentions. The problem here is the phrase "pertinent UN resolutions," which they interpret as including the Partition Resolution
(November 22, 1947) which would further decrease Israeli territory, and the resolution identifying Zionism with racism—among
others. Nevertheless, one has to acknowledge that this declaration
represents a change for the better. The emergence of signs, flimsy
as they may be, that the PLO is prepared to try to reach a settlement of the conflict should be encouraged, and not nipped in the
bud.

For the PLO to acknowledge coexistence with Israel is tantamount to the negation of its entire *raison d'être.* The PLO, as its
name denotes, was meant to "liberate" *all* of Palestine. It is PLO,
not PPLO (Part of Palestine Liberation Organization). Even to
state that this change—to become the PPLO—is what is required
of the PLO, much less to harp on it, is likely to be counterproduc-
tive. The difficulties of such a change, or rather, transmutation,
should be appreciated. Of course it is the fault of the founders of
the PLO that their positions painted it into the corner from which
it has become such an agonizing affair to withdraw. They probably
expected that the indivisibility of their goal would constitute a
guarantee that the goal would be achieved in its entirety.

Suppose the PLO is defeated by U.S.-Israeli-Jordanian common
efforts with the support of other moderate Arabs, and a new representative of the Palestinians emerges. It is far-fetched to suppose
that it would forgo the basic claim of the PLO: that the Palestinians
deserve statehood. To atone for its participation in the burial of

the original PLO it may even resurrect the latter's demands in an extreme version. Thus the position frequently expressed in Israel of readiness to negotiate with Palestinian representatives who are not "members" of the PLO or were not active PLO functionaries ignores the possibility that the further they are from the PLO, the more subservient they may be to its commands. According to the PLO Fundamental Law, all Palestinians are its "natural members."

The ceaseless debate between Arab radicals and moderates is the best guide to understanding Arab positions, and the vehemence of the terms in which it is expressed demonstrates that the divergence is not over trivial details. The very existence of the debate disproves the conception, widespread in Israeli circles, that all Arabs share a common goal—the destruction of Israel—and that any differences among them are merely tactical. They may all dream or pray that Israel will disappear, but not all of them see this dream as realizable. Again, the moderates are willing to separate grand design from policy, whereas the radicals refuse to draw such a distinction. It is this distinction that contains the chance for resolving the conflict, a chance that Israel must exploit for the sake of its security and the peace of future generations—especially today, when the moderates still occupy important positions among the Arab states and the Palestinians.

Despite the signs of moderation in the PLO, its inclusion in a settlement is not a simple matter. The split within the PLO has always been a spur to extreme positions. The revolutionary pretensions of the PLO beget a style of thought in which compromise is disdained. The PLO has become accustomed to the fact that it is not a state and that the restrictions normally imposed on a state do not constrain it. Terrorism corrupts, and the practice of terror is no training for the diplomatic give-and-take of negotiations. The PLO's ideological heritage is a heavy burden. The PLO also has spawned many functionaries who have a vested interest in the conflict. A settlement would cost them their jobs, and they are therefore fearful of one. An educational system oriented toward preparing the younger generation for the struggle has endowed most of its members with a combative radicalism, hostility to Israel, and a conviction of the righteousness of their cause. Hence they are ready to battle Israel to the end, and if necessary to fight the Arab states as well. Generally speaking, the younger generation of the PLO is much more extreme than the older leaders. Aware of these trends, the latter are trying, with a certain amount of success, to rein them in.

The official common position of the Arab states, as expressed in the summits held by their leaders, has also changed. The twelfth Arab summit signaled the change. Held in Fez, Morocco, it stretched out over two sessions during the course of a year (November 1981 and September 1982) because its deliberations were on matters of principle. On the agenda was an eight-point plan, proposed by Prince Fahd of Saudi Arabia, which demanded an Israeli withdrawal to the 1967 borders, the establishment of a Palestinian state, but also affirmed the "right of all states in the region to live in peace." After protracted haggling, the resolutions passed at the summit were more guarded than the Saudi proposal. The demand for Israeli withdrawal to the 1967 borders, including Arab Jerusalem, remained; but the clause recognizing the right of all states in the region to live in peace, which might have been interpreted to include Israel, was modified: "The United Nations Security Council will give guarantees for peace that will apply to all states of the region, including the independent Palestinian state." Thus preserving peace is no longer an Arab concern, but a U.N. one, and the nonreference to Israel is evasive and suspect. Certainly this was not the sort of resolution that Israel longs for. But it was still a far cry from the former Arab proclamations calling for Israel's demise.

The Fez resolution also recognized the Palestinians' right to self-determination and the PLO as their sole legitimate representative. The original Saudi proposal spoke of United Nations supervision, whereas the resolution as passed gave the Security Council an active role in a settlement, which means that the Soviet Union would be included in its formulation. With the notable exception of Libya, all the Arab countries, including Syria (represented by President Assad), accepted this resolution.

King Hussein's basic stand on the Arab-Israeli conflict and the possibilities of a settlement thereby ceased to be out of line with the Arab consensus. The Fez resolutions also represented a change in Syria's traditional rejectionist stance. We can assume that Syria put its name to the resolution in order to draw closer to the Soviet position. True, Syria can and does see this resolution as one link in its theory of stages. Even though the Security Council would guarantee a settlement, this obstacle could be overcome, and even if Israel accepted it, a pretext could be found for reopening the conflict.

Despite these changes signaled by the Fez conference, the Jordanian establishment and moderate Palestinians are caught on the horns of a difficult dilemma. They desire a political settlement, and recognize that disaster impends without one, but at the same time they are afraid of initiating negotiations lest they lead nowhere. Such a failure is likely to be fatal to them and a triumph for the radicals. There is a political imbalance here: should negotiations, having once commenced, abort, the Israeli public would see this as a sign of their leaders' steadfastness and ascribe it to their credit. On the Arab side, however, it would be chalked to the debit side of the leaders' ledger, as proof that they had been foolishly tempted to follow the ineffective path of diplomacy.

Sadat faced a similar dilemma, but that was resolved by hints made to him before official negotiations commenced that they would be rewarded by positive results. Hussein, having met Israeli leaders, could not anticipate similar treatment. He was disappointed by the Labor ministers, and has no illusions concerning the Likud. His only recourse was preliminary negotiations with the Americans, which could give him a certain measure of security as to the successful outcome of later talks with the Israelis. From his point of view, the road to the government in Jerusalem passed through Washington. But if negotiations could not be begun without the United States, they could not be concluded without the Soviet Union, the only force that can counterbalance the American support of Israel and give weight to Arab demands. Moderate PLO leaders also fear that following the path of diplomacy might lead to a final and irreparable split in the PLO as a result of the opposition of more radical elements. The argument rages even within Fatah itself, which has its own rejectionist wing and does not unanimously support the political option.

The Rabin government scored a diplomatic coup when in September, 1975, Henry Kissinger appended a secret American commitment to the interim agreement with Egypt, promising that the United States would neither recognize the PLO nor negotiate with it as long as the PLO refused to recognize Israel's right to exist and accept Security Council Resolutions 242 and 338. Ever since, this commitment has tied the hands of the United States government in its contacts with the PLO. Nevertheless, King Hussein hoped that American fears of radicalization of the Middle East as a result of continued conflict and of the opportunities that the situation is likely to create for the Soviet Union would lead the United States to seek a settlement of the dispute despite its links with Israel. However, if attempts by the United States to mediate are frustrated, as they have been in recent years, the nonresolution of the Arab-Israeli conflict is more a nuisance than it is a life-threatening problem to the U.S. If both sides keep putting obstacles in the path of an agreement, the U.S. may simply leave them to their own devices, with all the dangers this implies for the region and its people.

The Evolution of Strategic Thinking: Terror or War

The Arab goal of destroying Israel took shape soon after the establishment of the state, but for many years the Arab leaders had no clear idea of how to achieve it. Many solved the problem with rhetoric, declaring that Israel would be strangled, that they would put an end to it, and so forth—but they did not say how. Professor Walid Khalidi, one of the most prominent and wisest of the Palestinian political thinkers, has noted that the Arabs lacked "applied thinking." A political position is hollow if it defines a goal without at the same time working out a plan of action to attain it.

When the question of a plan began to be considered in the 1960s, two possibilities emerged: the goal would either be achieved through a gradual, incremental, cumulative *process* or in a single decisive *event*. The dominant conception, supported by Nasser, was that of the event—the destruction of Israel in a brief, total war that would be over before Israel's allies, the United States and other Western countries, could rush to her aid. Destroying Israel by means of a protracted process did not seem reasonable because outside intervention was likely to frustrate it. Moreover, destruction of a state, by its nature, belies a process. On the other hand, the ability to deal a single mortal blow to Israel required massive Arab superiority, which could be attained only if the Arabs united, industrialized their states, and modernized their economies.

Nasser's basic position was self-contradictory: radical in that it sought the destruction of Israel in a total war, but moderate in that it deferred this war to the distant future. He explicitly told the Palestinians in 1962 that he had no immediate program to realize their dream of return.

The Palestinians, impatient, turned to guerrilla warfare as a way of destroying Israel through a process of attrition. According to one theory, Palestinian guerrillas would be the spark that would ignite the Arab states to wage war against Israel, even against their will. Given the stunning successes of guerrilla warfare in China,

Cuba, and Algeria, the faith in the potential of the guerrilla was so strong that important Palestinian circles thought that it could in itself destroy Israel.

The Six Day War, which demonstrated Israeli military superiority, disproved the Arabs' ability to defeat Israel in a conventional war. It therefore enhanced the status of Palestinian guerrilla fighters. But even among the Arabs there were those who were wise enough not to place too much faith in guerrilla warfare. By 1968 an idea had begun to develop that what the Arabs needed was perhaps not a total war, but a limited war and a "mini victory," which would be the first stage in a process that would change the confrontation with Israel. This was the strategy that guided Sadat in 1973.

Guerrilla warfare is not really appropriate for the conditions of Israel, as Arabs themselves, such as Mohammed Hasanein Heikal, a leading Egyptian journalist during the Nasser era, quickly discerned. Just as in other places where rural guerrillas failed, here too the Palestinians turned to what is euphemistically called "urban guerrilla warfare"—i.e., terrorism, which in many ways is easier to wage and less dangerous to its protagonists than rural guerrilla warfare.

I still maintain the opinion I first expressed in 1968: "Sporadic subversion may become a feature in our lives for a length of time no one can foresee; it might become like the toll in traffic accidents which modern societies have to pay. The challenge that Israel has to face does not lie in guerrilla warfare, but elsewhere. On the one hand in war. . . . On the other hand—the challenges lie in the complexities and dilemmas in which Israel finds itself enmeshed." I believe that Israel's overemphasis on terrorism is a mistake. It may be helpful in public relations, as a way to castigate the PLO, but Israel's major security problem is not that posed by terrorism.

By means of terrorist attacks the PLO has managed to draw world attention to itself and—though by no means only as a result of such attacks—has acquired international status and UN recognition. Its ability to provide services to terrorist organizations from all over the world—a haven, training, weapons, documentation, recourse to Arab diplomatic pouches, and money—has propelled it into a leading position in world terror. In exchange the members of these organizations have provided operational services—for example, those that enabled the PLO to launch terrorist actions outside Israel. However, such attacks were cut back after 1974, when the PLO discovered that they had a detrimental effect on its relations with world public opinion and foreign governments. Even the more radical factions have since mostly refrained from such external operations.

There is no PLO central command coordinating the operations of the various constituent organizations. The latter operate with a large measure of independence, but all of them seem to have come to recognize that guerrilla warfare and terrorism will not, as was once expected, lead Israel to surrender.

The radical factions practice terrorism in order to hurt Israel, to unsettle it, to deter Jews from immigration, to stir up internal dissent within Israel, and to lead the Israeli authorities to repress the Arabs of the occupied territories, which in turn leads to civil unrest that causes Israel more problems. Terrorism is thus intended to weaken Israel and to hasten the process of disintegration in preparation for an overt Arab offensive and full-scale war.

The moderates view terrorism as a way of forcing Israel to recognize that annexation cannot succeed because its price is too high, to demonstrate to both Israel and the United States that recurrent popular riots can be anticipated if the conflict is not resolved. Thus terrorism must hurt, and terrorist attacks must be impressive and of a kind that is hard to defend against. Even the moderates welcome actions that make Israel suffer. But at its core this terrorism is an attempt to pave the way to a settlement. Thus there are two sorts of terrorism: one is intended to further the destruction of Israel; the other hopes to hasten Israel's willingness to make concessions for the sake of peace. Even if they bring the same pain to the victims and their families, their cause is thus quite different.

These different perspectives on terrorism are also expressed by the fact that the radicals see no intrinsic limitations on terrorist activity, even if it harms the Arab population and worsens their lot to the extent of encouraging them to emigrate. The moderates, on the other hand, give priority to maintaining the Palestinian population on the West Bank; in their view terrorism must not be allowed to escalate to proportions that might endanger their goal. This attitude was responsible for the PLO orders broadcast once the 1987–88 Uprising began for the rioters to refrain from using firearms. They did not want to give the Israelis a justification for using more drastic means of suppression.

A new phenomenon is "freelance" terrorism, carried out by individuals, especially young people; it is not spectacular but wounds and incites just as much—such as random stabbings. Individual terrorism relies on easily acquired weapons, and is motivated by humiliation, hatred, and desire for revenge—by the residue of the past rather than a future goal, however remote. Although sporadic, it may become a considerable threat as Arab youth come to see it as a normal activity and proof of their manhood. This sort of terrorism is very hard to suppress. It has no command posts or headquarters to strike at, and attempts to counter it through increased repression and collective punishment are likely to lead only to an escalation in scale. It is neither controlled nor directed by the PLO, although of course the PLO leadership is delighted with such evidence of a nationalist fervor among Palestinian youth.

The new mode of Palestinian protest, which developed by trial and error, makes use of less-violent methods, typically stone throwing and tire burning. The principal advantage of this mode is that it brings the Palestinian masses into the struggle, making it more difficult to suppress.

Israelis tend to depict every act of terrorism as initiated by the PLO, partly for propaganda reasons and partly because it suits Israel's purposes to present resistance as a foreign import rather than as a spontaneous local reaction. But such a view is frequently mistaken, and erroneous perceptions lead to erroneous conclusions. Although it is not always possible to do so, Israel should attempt to distinguish between attacks that are directly initiated by the PLO and those that are not.

For the PLO, terrorism is also an organizational necessity. A conventional army can be maintained in the absence of operations by occupying it in training and exercises. But guerrilla organizations cannot exist unless they operate, even if only sporadically. We may assume that the operational circles within the PLO exert pressure to multiply and escalate the attacks as these are their *raison d'être*.

King Hussein frequently declares his opposition to terrorism, and has cooperated with Israel to prevent many attacks from Jordanian territory. However, it is unlikely that he sheds any tears over terrorist attacks against Israel, especially when there is no way that they can be linked with Jordan. He is probably more inclined to view terrorism and popular riots as a means of pressuring Israel and demonstrating that the present state of affairs is intolerable. However, he is likely to be concerned that the "Stone Revolution" can become contagious and spread to pockets of popular discontent in Jordan.

Terrorism and crime are close neighbors. Terrorist organizations often harbor criminals, and their fighters are likely to adopt some criminal traits. The mere involvement in random terror—attacking persons whose only sin is that they happened to be in a place selected as the target for an attack—is corrupting. Terrorists perform deeds that arouse revulsion. Nor can terrorism be precisely controlled, for an operation initiated by the higher echelons is liable to take a different route in the course of its execution. For example, the taking of hostages as a bargaining chip may end in their unintended death, due to a loss of control by the field agents acting under stress. The final outcome often does not reflect what the planners wanted to happen. The PLO has only a weak control over the attacks made in its name, both because of the weakness of its structure and the low degree of internal discipline. The level of communication and control has declined even further since the PLO's expulsion from Lebanon, with its various levels of command spread out in bases from Tunis to Yemen. Underground and terrorist organizations tend to split up into small groups, whose quarrels may spill over into violence. Groups like those of Abu Musa and Abu Nidal, which seceded from Fatah, see themselves as continuing the authentic path of Fatah; they see those signs of moderation that have established themselves in Fatah as a treacherous deviation from its historic course. They too continue to use the name Fatah. It should not be forgotten that much of Abu Nidal's terror has been directed against important figures within the PLO.

Abu Nidal's terror was also intended to embarrass the PLO, since public opinion has tended not to distinguish between attacks by the PLO and attacks by the organizations that have seceded. Even those who refuse to see the PLO as the representative of the Palestinians seem to blame it for every act of Palestinian terrorism. "PLO" has become a generic name applicable to everything in which Palestinians and their emissaries are involved. Abu Nidal thus wants his attacks to be as horrifying as possible in order to discredit the PLO as a partner for negotiations, thereby preventing what he sees as the greatest danger threatening the Palestinians and the Arabs—a settlement of the conflict. Israeli countermeasures against terrorism have been many times ill-advised, such as the killing of Abu Jihad in Tunisia in April, 1988. This is not to say he did not deserve a death verdict. No one engaged in lethal terrorism can claim immunity to retaliation. Repressing riots is invidious, but the IDF behaved with relative self-restraint.

As long as the Arab-Israeli conflict persists with no apparent chance of resolving it, both terrorism and civil insurrection will increase and will be even uglier and more painful than they are now. Throwing stones will not replace planting bombs. And, as the destructiveness and frequency increase, the possibilities of escalation increase too.

The wise conduct of policy requires an understanding of one's opponent's motives. Israelis should ask themselves what they would do if they were in the shoes of moderate Palestinians— unwilling to surrender completely to Israel, reluctant to disappear as a group from the stage of history, and seeking a national territory in the region where their largest concentration resides, even if they recognize that they will not return to all of Palestine and that Israel is a fact with which they must live. What policy would Israelis recommend that they adopt, given Israel's own policy in the territories? To deprive the Palestinians of a political course of action is inevitably to drive them to resort to violent protest in all of its forms.

As long as the conflict persists, even the moderates within the PLO, led by Fatah, will not desist from terrorism. But Israel for its part exploits terrorism as a justification for its refusal to negotiate with the PLO. Where is the escape from this vicious circle?

The riots in the occupied territories are too close to this time of writing to judge their long-term importance. Still it seems evident that they have opened a new chapter in the history of the conflict. Though they probably have not changed its basic structure, they have a good deal more significance than as the "media events" that Israeli officials have claimed were organized in order to put Israel in a bad light. The youths who began to throw stones and create roadblocks did so because of their outrage at Israeli domination and not to impress television viewers. Later, of course, the importance of the media dawned on them. But that, too, is still secondary. For the Palestinians the Uprising has taken on historical significance as a new source of pride to overcome their sense of humiliation. Even more importantly, in its modes of organization and cooperation it has become a nation-building experience.

Though the PLO did not organize the Uprising and though the demonstrations have made the Palestinian masses in the territories more prominent than the leadership in the Diaspora, they continue to recognize the PLO as their representatives. Even the fundamentalist "Jihad" circles in Gaza, who criticize the PLO for its moderation, emphasize that it represents them. The Uprising has only highlighted what was obvious long ago, that the PLO must be included in any negotiations concerning Palestine.

On the other hand, the Uprising is already showing the signs of its limitations. Palestinian workers and businesses cannot hold out indefinitely, whereas for Israel the impact of the disturbances seems to be limited to those sectors that employ Arabs. Indeed, as of May, 1988, there are signs that the Uprising is waning, at least for now. Nonetheless the fact remains that from now onward such prolonged outbreaks of protests will recur and likely become more intense. At the same time, the limitations of the Uprising may have the effect of proving to the Palestinians that there is no real remedy other than a political settlement.

A very impressive sign of this realization can be seen in the recent statement by Bassam Abu Sharif, an important aide to Arafat. Titled "PLO View, Prospect of a Palestinian-Israeli Settlement," it is the clearest expression to date of the PLO's readiness for peace between Palestinians and Israelis. It was included in an English language pamphlet, *Palestinian Dossier,* distributed at the Algiers summit meeting June 7–9, 1988, and extracts from it were published as an Op-Ed piece in the *New York Times* of June 22, under the title "Arafat's Aide on Israel."

Abu Sharif's statement is all the more significant in view of the fact that until a few years ago he was the editor of *Al-Hadaf,* the periodical published by the Popular Front, one of the extremist groups in the PLO. In 1985, however, he refused to leave the PLO with the seceding Popular Front and instead joined Arafat's inner circle. Abu Sharif's statement, written in sensible, humane language, is informed by the recognition that Palestinians and Israelis have a common fate and a mutual need for a political settlement: "We believe that all peoples—the Jews and the Palestinians included—have the right to run their own affairs. . . . The key to a Palestinian-Israeli settlement lies in talks between the Palestinians and the Israelis. . . . The Palestinians would accept, indeed insist, on international guarantees for the security of all states in the regions, including Palestine and Israel."

That the statement has been published as a personal one may somewhat dim its political significance. But we must bear in mind that it could not have been included in an official PLO pamphlet, particularly one circulated at the Algiers summit, without Arafat's endorsement. To be sure, it was immediately and vehemently rejected by the extremist groups, and it may also be repudiated by some Fatah leaders, as similar moderate statements have been in the past. Even worse, Israeli leaders have ignored or dismissed Abu Sharif's statement. Such rebuffs can only discourage Arabs from taking a moderate position.

2

The Arab-Israeli Conflict: The Israeli Position

THE FATHERS OF ZIONISM SOUGHT A GREATER ERETZ YIS-
rael that included most of Transjordan and parts of Lebanon and
northern Sinai. But the mainstream Zionist leaders among them
soon recognized the need to divorce the grand design from policy,
and settled for a much smaller territory. (It should be noted that
this divorce of grand design from policy was made possible also by
the fact that the Jewish religion was not then a factor influencing
Zionist policy.) They accepted the severance of Transjordan from
Palestine in 1922 and the UN partition scheme in 1947 and followed a policy that was compromising and modest in its demands.
Aware of the limits of their strengths and the constraints of reality,
their approach was pragmatic and conciliatory. The Jews of Palestine and then of Israel appeared as the side desiring peace, while
the Arabs presented themselves as uncompromising in their stand.
The moderation of Israeli policy won it friends among the Great
Powers and the support of world public opinion. Without such
support the impressive achievements of the Zionist enterprise
would not have been possible and the State of Israel could not have
come into existence.

The events that led to a change in Arab positions had an opposite effect on the Israeli side. The victory and occupation of territory in 1967 were taken to mean that the old policy that had put
the grand design to one side was erroneous in its minimalism, and
detracted from the ability to achieve loftier goals. This revised
outlook gradually led to a total revamping of the dominant ideology and a change in Israel's political culture and eventually (in
1977) brought Menachem Begin and the Likud to power.

This altered the character of the conflict. Just as the first signs of flexibility appeared in the Arab position, the Israeli position became absolute. The danger is that if the new Israeli absolutism persists it will lead to concomitant change in the Arab position. An Israeli demand for all the territory west of the River Jordan will encourage the Arabs to claim the entire area of Israel, thereby ending any incipient tendency to be satisfied by a return to the 1967 borders. The conflict will become an existential conflict, a fight to the death, and all possibility of resolving it peacefully will disappear. Moreover, the Arab stand will become much more extreme, since the negative and demoniac attributes that the Arabs have always ascribed to Israel (albeit sometimes with more rhetoric than conviction) will have been reinforced and affirmed by the positions and conduct of the Israelis.

Many Israelis do not understand the extent to which peace is in the Israeli interest. Continued conflict may doom the Arabs to backwardness and destroy part of their lands, but it threatens Israel's very existence. In making peace, including paying the price for peace, Israel would not be doing the Arabs a favor, but doing itself a favor.

Here, though, the Israelis confront a dilemma which parallels that besetting Arab moderates. Acknowledging its great need and desire for a settlement ostensibly detracts from Israel's bargaining power and increases the potential for Arab extortion. On the other hand, the failure to make the Israeli public aware of this problem can be even more damaging. For Israel, the best situation would be a national recognition of the need for peace without its being exploited by Arab diplomacy. This means that the Arabs must recognize the weakness of their own situation and what they are in fact suffering by prolonging the status quo: peace is essential for them too.

It is no secret that the crude balance of forces between Israel and the Arabs is evolving in the Arabs' favor. Even if today Israel is still stronger than the Arab armies, the Arabs' ability to absorb losses is ultimately likely to reverse the balance of forces. Let us not forget that North Vietnam defeated the mighty United States because of its superior capacity to absorb losses. Military might translates into the ability to create casualties, but the greater the adversary's capacity to endure them, the less one's capacity to inflict them is worth. Israel cannot absorb the magnitude of losses that the Arab societies can, both because its population is much smaller and its psychological and cultural sensitivity to such losses is greater.

Modern weapons have become more destructive and accurate; future wars, even those fought with conventional weapons, will not be "elegant." If Israel were to sustain high losses, especially in a war in which the home front suffered as well, the effect on Israeli society could be devastating—even if Arab losses were many times as great. The avoidance of war is a vital interest for Israel. Israelis must recognize that they cannot allow themselves a policy of maintaining the conflict, since to do so carries with it the danger of renewed and recurring wars.

Another difficult problem is that recognizing Israel's vulnerability in future wars is apt to undermine the nation's confidence in its might and its army. Some would say that this confidence is a national asset that ought to be protected. But it is better that words concerning the danger of war be spoken than that Israel be led astray by false illusions. Many of the mistaken political attitudes current in Israel rest upon the assumption that there is nothing to fear because the army will always come to the rescue. The Israeli army is seen as part insurance policy, part secular messiah. This concept is mistaken and could be dangerous.

This misconception has another guise as well. In order to raise morale, Israeli leaders emphasize the country's strength, resorting to the conventional formula that Israel can always deter Arab aggression, or, if the Arabs should be so foolhardy as to attack, can overcome them. The problem is that, if Israel is so strong, it can allow itself to follow any policy perceived as being to its benefit, while ignoring possible reactions in the world and among the Arabs. The emphasis on Israeli might is thus liable to be an impediment to rational thinking. The paradox here is that, in order to survive, Israelis must free themselves of the myth that their survival is guaranteed in all circumstances and conditions. A realistic policy must see the Israeli military capacity in more measured terms. From this perspective, it may be that the Lebanon War has been an invaluable lesson.

Arab leaders are also aware of the destructiveness of future wars, and this recognition may deter them from the military option. They fear not only the destruction that a war would cause but also the peril to themselves and their regimes. Wars do not break out automatically at the nadir of a deteriorating situation, but in accordance with decisions taken by political leaders. Such decisions often emerge in response to some difficult situation rather than because of a predetermination to wage war. It is not unknown for nations to go to war without wanting it or without its being in their best interest.

Conspicuous in any discussion of the Arab-Israeli conflict is the extreme nature of the Arab positions from the historical, cultural, and political perspectives. Arab utterances that truly and honestly accept coexistence with Israel are few compared to the number of bitter and sometimes venomous denunciations of Israel, some of which contain elements of anti-Semitism. Arab behavior—and it is sufficient to examine how Arabs conduct themselves toward Israel in the United Nations—would hardly seem to merit concessions. Likewise the ugly record on terrorism is not to the Arabs' credit. But what the Arabs "deserve" is beside the point: the real question is, what are the consequences of the various Israeli policy options? This is the pole around which the debate must revolve.

The riots in the territories have, paradoxically, humanized the Palestinians in Israeli eyes. What they see on their TV screens is people who are demanding their collective rights, who also have national grievances and aspirations, who are not merely subservient workers. To be sure, this response is accompanied by resentment at having their peace disturbed and the lives of their young men interrupted and endangered and by criticism of the Palestinians' "improper" use of children to throw stones. Among the Israeli soldiers the insurrection has tended to produce an ambivalent response: a hawkish anger on the personal level and a dovishness on the political one—i.e., "Let's rid ourselves of these territories." More generally, the disturbances have awakened grave doubts about Israel's ability to maintain control in the long run. The national debate has been provoked.

The Debate in Israel: The West Bank and Gaza Strip

The national debate in Israel concerning policy toward the occupied territories has led to the crystallization of two major options: annexation and withdrawal. The decision here is not between good and bad but between bad and worse. Decisions of this type require mature consideration. Any choice will have harmful consequences and each alternative has only relative advantages. The relationship between the advantages and disadvantages of the two possibilities is like that between concave and convex—the advantages of one option are the disadvantages of another. We can thus deal with them together.

A number of considerations weigh against Israel's withdrawal from the West Bank. First is the strategic consideration based on territory—namely, that hostile forces based there would be within artillery range of Israel's cities and airports. Second is the fear that the West Bank would become a base for terrorists. Third, Israel's living space would be cramped. Fourth, withdrawal would be a heavy blow to the nationalist ideology of Greater Israel, which has struck deep roots among the people. Fifth, withdrawal would be final and irreversible, but there is no guarantee that conceding the West Bank would satisfy the Arabs and put an end to the conflict. On the contrary, it might even whet the Arab appetite, since they would be able to use the West Bank as a base from which to prepare another attack. There is also the fear that Israel would be unable to control vital water resources. Border arrangements, including the disposition of Jerusalem, would be endlessly complicated, so much so that it would be almost impossible to arrive at a practical solution. Another fear is that opposition within Israel to a withdrawal might develop into a civil war. And, finally, the hearts of most Israelis must surely contract at the thought of parting with places to which the national memory is strongly linked, even if few among them have bothered to visit them recently.

Against these weighty arguments stands another consideration. By annexing the West Bank even only de facto, by continuing to rule it and to build settlements there, Israel increases not only its area, but also its Arab population. The settlement movement is not simply the establishment of new centers of population; rather its goal is to acquire property rights. The Hebrew word for settlement, *hitnahalnut,* implies political domination as well.

Were the Arabs of the West Bank to somehow disappear, Israel could annex the West Bank with equanimity. But the Arab population will not only not disappear, it will continue to grow. This being the case, annexation of the West Bank will create a strategic problem of demography more serious than the strategic problem of territory. In the stretch of land between the River Jordan and the Mediterranean Sea—Israel and the occupied territories—there are currently (1986 census) 379,000 Arab children below the age of four, compared to 370,000 Jewish children in the same age group. Extrapolating from present trends, the Demography Department of Hebrew University has calculated that by the year 2000 there will be 20 percent more Arab than Jewish children in this age group west of the River Jordan. The 1986 *Statistical Annual for Israel* informs us that in 1986 there were 24,241 births among Israeli Arabs and 58,224 among the Arabs in the occupied territories, or a total of 82,465 Arab births within Greater Israel, compared to 75,036 Jewish births. The ratio in the entire area today is 62 percent Jews to 38 percent Arabs, but the Jewish population is older.

An ostensibly decisive counter-assertion is the fact that during most of the period since 1967 the Arab population of the West Bank has not grown relative to the Jewish population. It should be remembered, however, that this has stemmed from Arab emigration in search of jobs in Jordan and other Arab countries that were enjoying an economic boom. But this boom has ceased, and with it the migration. In recent years the contrary movement, from Jordan to the West Bank, has actually increased. The fact that the population ration has so far not changed to the detriment of the Jews is no proof that it will not do so in the future. On the basis of current trends, it has been calculated that by the year 2015 Arab and Jewish populations will be equal, and thereafter the ration between them will continue to change to the disadvantage of the Jews.

The problem is not merely quantitative. One ethnic group can dominate another even when there is a significant qualitative gap favoring the ruling group. But the Arab population is advancing, its educated classes are increasing, and its demands are more assertive. It is thus more difficult to rule over it—and this even while the Arabs are still a minority. Moreover, so long as the Israeli occupation of the territories can be perceived as temporary, as indicated by the failure to apply Israeli law to them (Jordanian law applies in the West Bank), the situation is to some extent tolerable to the Arab population. But the more that Israeli control appears to be permanent, the less it will be acceptable—especially as the educational level of the Arab population rises.

A Jewish state with an Arab majority, or even near-majority, is not viable as a Jewish state. Annexation will lead to the realization of the PLO slogan of a democratic Palestinian state. Ultimately demography may have a greater influence on the future of the Arab-Israeli conflict than any other factor.

There may be some who scent racism in the position I am advancing here. They hold that the character of the state must be left open, to be determined by the majority of its inhabitants. As long as this majority is Jewish, Israel will be a Jewish state, and that is as it should be. But the possibility that the Arabs might become the majority, and would then impress their own stamp on it, must not be obstructed. I plead guilty; it is indeed my intention that Israel remain a Jewish state, for this is the purpose of Zionism. Thus, annexation of the territories is contrary to Zionism.

However large the settlement movement might be, and even if it were not limited by the financial constraints imposed by the economic crisis caused by the policies of the Likud government, it cannot change the Arab character of the West Bank. After more than twenty years of Israeli rule, including seven years when the Likud was in power, the Jewish population of the West Bank amounts to no more than 3 or 4 percent of the total. When determining sovereignty over a territory, the contemporary democratic world follows the principle of majority rule, or in diplomatic parlance, the right of self-determination. The British had to leave India because India is inhabited by Indians rather than Englishmen. Invocation of the principle of self-determination may sometimes involve hypocrisy and injustice; frequently it is not realized, and there are often disagreements regarding its application. But it is no accident that world opinion supports the application of this principle to the West Bank and Gaza Strip. The Arabs there are not orphans abandoned to their fate, and Arab forces and the international community will stand beside them in their struggle for political rights, including independence. Financial support from the Arabs and the PLO treasury will promote their capacity to carry on the struggle.

Israel's settlement movement has been a success in terms of housing and roads and cubic meters of concrete, but it has been a failure on the human level. The settlers have not been the harbingers of a national tide of migration. On the contrary, the human reservoir from which the movement is drawn has dwindled. Few of the settlers make their living in the towns where they live, despite their ideological motivations; most of those who do are employed as public functionaries and supported by public funds. In fact, the "towns" are in large part dormitory communities. This settlement activity is proudly acclaimed by its supporters as the continuation of the historical endeavors of Zionism, ignoring the fact that in the past the major accomplishment of settlement was to develop the agricultural sector, which provided a livelihood and a high degree of self-sufficiency. The pace of nonideologically motivated settlement on the fringes of the West Bank, which serves as a suburban hinterland for the cities of the coastal plain, has also dwindled. The acquisition of land has slowed down in the wake of revelations of many illegal transactions. The settlements may warm the hearts of Israelis traveling through the West Bank, but in their enthusiasm they fail to notice the expansion of Arab villages and towns. The yardstick for measuring Jewish settlement activity is the Arab settlement activity going on at the same time.

Some Likud politicians magnanimously declare that they will offer Israeli citizenship to the West Bank Arabs, as did Begin in his original autonomy proposal. This is a gesture in the spirit of the Jabotinsky tradition, but it is fraught with peril. Those who make the proposal do so from a conviction that the Arabs will refuse to accept Israeli citizenship, just as very few have accepted it in Jerusalem. But the comparison is misleading. Once the Arabs realize that becoming Israeli citizens will enable them to take over the country, their attitude is likely to change overnight. Why should they refuse? In combination with the Israeli Arabs they could elect fifty or sixty Arab Knesset members. In this light, the Likud proposal is seen to be totally irresponsible.

The demographic trends looming over Israel's horizon have not yet set off any alarms because alarms are set off by events, not by trends. So long as the trend has not been translated into an event one can close one's eyes and ignore it. It is true that understanding the danger of a trend requires a certain amount of sophistication, whereas an event has a direct impact; a trend is a matter for speculation, but an event is a fact. When the trend becomes a fact, however, when the Jews suddenly discover themselves a minority or close to being one, it will be too late.

As the Arab population of the occupied territories continues to be denied political recognition of its collective existence despite its continued growth, Arab reactions will become more extreme, as evidenced by the recent months of disturbances. The situation will intensify as the Arabs come closer to being a majority. The perpetuation of Israeli rule will worsen Israel's relations with the Arab inhabitants of the occupied territories, and Israel will find itself trapped in a vicious circle of repression and revolt. Arab terrorism in the territories will increase, encouraged by the example of Shi-'ite terrorism in Southern Lebanon. The deterioration of relations with the Arabs of the West Bank is likely to drag the Arabs of Israel into rebellion, creating a widespread and huge hostile camp. A Jewish state that is even 40 percent Arab, and in which the relative proportion of Arabs is on the rise, will be a very unstable country, a Belfast on a large scale.

As the response of the Israeli Arabs to the 1987–88 protest movement indicates, the continuation and inevitable intensification of the conflict will draw them further into it. This is so despite the fact that the Israeli Arabs have accustomed themselves to living in Israel, to the extent that a significant number of them are more familiar with Hebrew culture than Arab. The result is that many Arab Israelis say that even when a Palestinian state is created they will want to remain in Israel. Nonetheless, few of them can remain indifferent to the conflict, and as it goes on and becomes even more bitter, it will lead whether by personal identification or group pressure to their "Palestinization," producing an alienation from the state that is likely to culminate in a movement to secede from it.

Perhaps by the twenty-fifth century man will have attained sufficient wisdom for ethnic groups to live together in peace and friendship. Our century is characterized by the ethnic tensions that have erupted in various corners of the world. So long as a minority is small, it is likely to accept the domination of the majority for want of an alternative. But when the ethnic minorities in a country are larger, and all the more so when they approach numerical equality with the ruling group, tension is bound to grow.

Some Israelis believe that annexation will bring about a new flourishing of Zionism and awaken a fresh wave of Jewish immigration to offset the increase in the Arab population. But increased Jewish immigration would not affect the presence of a large Arab population, even if its relative proportion in the country was thereby decreased. Nor is there any reason to assume that Jewish immigration will increase. Jews may be attracted to a *Jewish* state, but not to a country with a mixed and unsettled population. No preaching about their obligation to move to Israel will help. Jews will prefer to continue to live with their peaceable Christian neighbors in America or Europe rather than to live alongside an angry Muslim population.

As far as immediate problems are concerned, annexationist policies have an advantage over withdrawal. Withdrawal will create difficult problems as soon as it is implemented. By contrast, the anti-withdrawal lobby claims, the problems of annexation are in the distant future, and something may yet happen that would change the parameters of the situation. Withdrawal requires a decision; continuing the annexation is the default option. Nevertheless, certain future calamity is not diminished by being distant.

A recurrent assertion is that the settlements, roads, houses, and Jewish population of the occupied territories have created an irreversible situation that leaves annexation as the only practical option. This approach, however, is simplistic and exaggerated. Our generation has seen the migration of a million Frenchmen from Algeria, after 130 years of French rule there; we can hardly be impressed by the argument that forty thousand Jews (or even more) on the West Bank constitute an irrevocable fact. If the national consensus in Israel comes to recognize annexation as tantamount to national suicide, it will not be influenced by a settlers' revolt or by the threat of civil war. Nor will there be a need to repeat the trauma of the destruction of the Yamit settlement in the evacuation of Sinai. If the West Bank is handed over to Arab rule, those Jews who live there should have the option of remaining there provided they agree to become citizens of the new state. There are Arabs in Israel; why shouldn't there be Jews in Palestine?

Nevertheless, severing the West Bank from Israel would involve great complexities. The economies of Israel, the West Bank, and the Gaza Strip have become integrated. Arabs from the West Bank and Gaza Strip are employed in Israel, and Israel needs them. There is no reason to end this mutually beneficial arrangement. Major problems—guarding the frontiers, customs, security, water resources, border points, and many others—will arise. The willingness to deal with these complex problems will be found only when the fearful consequences that will ensue if the conflict is not resolved are understood.

Jerusalem is a major problem. Anyone who believes that only Jewish aspirations focus on this city is living in a dream world. Arab aspirations will have to find some measure of satisfaction as well. One proposal would divide the city into boroughs, united within a Greater Jerusalem Municipality. The demand that Jerusalem remain undivided has wide support throughout the world, both in public opinion and in diplomatic circles—unlike the idea of annexation, which arouses strong opposition. The so-called Reagan Plan of September 1, 1982, says that Jerusalem "must remain undivided." The problem of the Jewish suburban areas beyond the 1967 borders, with a larger population than that of the settlements, will of course arise. This is one area where the Israelis can demand changes involving territorial compromise.

It will not be a simple matter. The Arabs too must make their contribution to a resolution of the conflict, and on this point Israel can enlist international support for its position. One must not make light of the difficulties involved in solving the problems of Jerusalem. Much talent, flexibility, and bargaining will be required. The negotiations over the city will be extremely complex and stormy, but let it not be said that the problem is a priori insoluble. The exact location of borders is also a matter for negotiations (according to Security Council Resolution 242 as well). The result of these talks will be influenced by the ability of the negotiators on both sides.

An apparently irrefutable claim is that the chances of reaching an agreement are frustrated by the absence of an Arab party willing to talk. This is a serious point. Arab rejectionism should not be treated lightly, nor should the Arabs be absolved of their part of the guilt for the tangle that has been created. But what was on the agenda then was not a leap directly into negotiations and an agreement, but a policy to prevent the erection of new obstacles (in the form of settlements) on the road to a future agreement. The English word "settlement" has neutral connotations; not so the Hebrew *hitnahalnut* (see p. 46), or the Arabic *istitan,* which is derived from *watan* (homeland). Israelis must realize that though the movement to implant settlements in the West Bank did not begin as a response to the Arab refusal to negotiate, its continuation reinforces this refusal. As long as the Arabs hear that "settlement" activity will continue, the very word tells them that the de facto annexation will continue: so what is there to negotiate about?

The United States did not determine the composition of the North Vietnamese delegation, nor the Soviet Union that of the Afghanistan rebels. So it is in international disputes. It is very strange, then, that Israel continues to insist on deciding who shall represent the Palestinians. There are Israelis who emphatically declare they are doves, that they disapprove of annexation and of the presence of the settlements, and yet argue that the PLO is not acceptable as a partner in the negotiations or that they cannot grant that it is because such a position "won't fly" in Israel. Thus, in effect, they support maintaining the status quo indefinitely and facilitate the process of annexation. They are self-contented doves who are in effect de facto hawks.

The feverish pitch of the national debate within Israel is reflected in its tendency to polarization, each side claiming that its opponent's path will lead to catastrophe. In most countries the national debate centers on what policy will yield the best results, whereas in Israel the debate is much more fateful: what policy is less perilous to the country's existence? Mr. Begin repeatedly said that if Israel withdraws it will find itself in "mortal danger." Only recently the Israeli ambassador to the United Nations, Benjamin Netanyahu, is reported to have said: "If we withdraw we will die." An argument based on the threat of death is primitive, but it is also the strongest one available to human beings; that is why Begin chose to emphasize it. His opponents did not dare to present their position in a similarly strong form: "If we annex we commit suicide." The Likud reaps the advantage of their temerity.

Israel must analyze and compare the dangers and possibilities of each course of action thoroughly and avoid focusing on the deficiencies of one while ignoring those of the other. There is a great cause for anxiety about a debate in which each side declares that the opponents' path is suicidal, the adversaries differing only on how Israel will destroy itself. The dangers that lurk ahead must be distinguished. Withdrawal will leave a state that will have to defend itself and live in difficult conditions. Annexation will lead to safer borders, but it is doubtful whether a state will survive to defend them. A state with bad borders can defend itself; it cannot defend itself if about half the population owe allegiance to its enemy. With all its nuclear arsenal the United States would have been undefendable if it had 125 million Russian inhabitants. The willingness to give up the West Bank does not stem from a lack of courage or of faith, from currying the favor of foreigners from national degeneracy or weakness, from leftist views or sympathy for the PLO, as Herut and its supporters would have it, but from a realization of the anticipated results of *not* withdrawing.

The case for a dovish position is very good, yet the doves fail. Why? One reason is their hesitancy to argue in an effective way that annexation will lead to disaster. Many doves present only one side of the problem. They say that annexation will lead to an "ugly" Israel, one whose democratic nature will be distorted and even undermined and whose character will be brutalized. They avoid dealing with the Arabs' position and hence with the actual problems and possibilities of a settlement. This is an arbitrary kind of dovishness: dovishness by assertion. It does not meet the main rebuttal, that there is no Arab partner to negotiate with. This omission forces it to remain uselessly on its high but vacuous moral plane.

Given the political predicament in which Israel finds itself, the question arises whether the two difficult alternatives of annexation and withdrawal can be avoided by means of some middle road that would convert the West Bank into a Jordanian-Israeli condominium. It may indeed be possible that in the distant future the Middle East will find it necessary to set up some kind of confederative economic and political arrangement, along the lines of the European Common Market nations. But we should remember that Europe's economic and political arrangements were framed against the background of a common Christian cultural heritage, whereas the Middle East is the home of different cultures and religions, whose common traditional unfriendliness toward outsiders has recently become more pronounced. One cannot switch directly from hostility to the intimacy required by an eventual common polity. It is hard to believe that an Israeli policy of settlement activity will be the meeting point from which a common political structure will emerge.

In any agreement, Israel will have to consider the possibility that some groups in the Arab countries will try to undermine and overturn it. The Arab dream that the entire region will once again be theirs will not vanish overnight. But it is in the nature of any agreement, as with any conflict, to beget parties with an interest in perpetuating it. The stability of a settlement will depend upon the arrangements made to shore up the peace and obstruct the return to a state of conflict. In its endeavors to reach such arrangements, Israel will be assisted by outside agencies as well as by the geopolitical world order, which is increasingly firm with regard to borders. Moreover, the Palestinians will have to cross through Israeli territory in order to get from the West Bank to the Gaza Strip, and this can give Israel leverage over them.

Any agreement with the Arab states or the Palestinians must deal with the difficulties created by the fact that, despite the abandonment of the Arab grand design of liquidating Israel and the adoption of a policy of coexistence as entailed by a peace agreement, various circles will continue to resort to anti-Semitic themes to vilify Israel in the Arab media. On the surface this is a nebulous issue of the sort that statesmen prefer to ignore; but in this case it is very important, and must be discussed with the Arabs with complete candor. The prevalence of such themes may justify Israel's demands for a guarantee against a return to old positions. To the extent that the Palestinians hold fast to the old phraseology in order to convince themselves that they are not giving up their ideal of turning all of Eretz Yisrael into a Palestinian state, Israel will have to demand practical arrangements that empty such rhetoric of any practical force.

A Summary of the Positions and Varieties of Peace

The irony of history produces strange bedfellows. Arab extremists and Jewish moderates share the belief that an agreement could end the conflict and lead to peace. By contrast, Jewish extremists and Arab moderates do not think that an agreement would necessarily be final; rather, the conflict would remain open. In other words, the arguments of Arab extremists tend to support the view of Israeli moderates that a peace agreement is likely to put an end to the gradualist program, so that Israel can risk a political settlement even if Arabs intend it to be merely a stage on the road to their final goal. Ultimately this interim stage will be revealed to be the final terminus of a lasting peace. The arguments put forward by Arab moderates tend to support Israeli extremists, namely, an accord need not frustrate the Arab strategy of gradualism and is therefore dangerous for Israel. All the same, the Arab moderates' analysis of the situation also causes them to recognize that an agreement could be permanent.

The Arab extremists suspect that the Arab moderates' separation of grand design and policy is strategic, and apt to become permanent, whereas, when the Israelis separate grand design and policies, the Arab extremists consider it merely tactical and are convinced that at the first opportunity the Israelis will revert to expansionism and renew their conquests.

Likewise, Israeli extremists suspect that when the Arabs separate their grand design of annihilating Israel from the policy of reaching an agreement with it this is merely a tactical ploy, and they will persist in their hostility toward Israel. On the other hand, the detachment of the grand design of a Greater Israel from the politic willingness to withdraw for the sake of an agreement is seen as strategic, a ploy that will write *finis* to the Zionist dream for all time.

The moderates on both sides have trouble in justifying their positions to the public, whereas the extremists have a ready audience. The moderates' desire for an accord is based on recognition of their own side's weakness and the damage that will be caused by a continuation of the conflict. Both sides fear that acknowledgment of their urgent need for a settlement is apt to be harmful. Extremists on the home front will attack them for impairing morale and public confidence in the capacity to endure, while the enemy will exploit any admission of weakness during subsequent negotiations.

In both camps the extremists have the easier task. It is always easier to preserve a status quo and flow with the momentum of continued conflict and no solution than to change direction. The moderate position, on the other hand, requires a conscious decision to modify the direction of the historic trend and embark on a new and untried course.

For clarity's sake I shall now summarize the various attitudes toward an agreement and peace presented so far in the discussion of the Arab position:

1. *No accord and no peace.* This is the position of the Rejection Front, which champions the refusal to divorce grand design from policy. This stance has an Israeli parallel. Each side continues to hold fast to its demand for the whole cake, with no inclination for compromise. The solution will come in the long term, through the total defeat of the enemy.

2. *A tactical agreement and a tactical peace.* This type of accord permits continued pressure for Israel to make further concessions until it is destroyed, and is compatible with the gradualist program. The separation of grand design from policy is temporary and tactical. Any agreement reached is meant to be broken. This was the position in the twelfth session of the Palestine National Council in 1974. This is what the Syrians are apparently still seeking.

3. *An open-ended agreement and uncertain peace.* This kind of accord is compatible both with a tactical settlement and temporary peace and with a final settlement and true peace. We can include a state of "nonbelligerance" which leads to interim agreements rather than peace treaties. Until 1977 this was the basic position of President Sadat.

4. *A permanent settlement and a true peace.* This is the kind of resolution that many Israelis long for—the conflict forsaken and the Arab grand design abandoned. This sort of peace is strengthened by the normalization of relations, which is intended to create

a permanent peace. Sadat's agreement to normalization was an indication of his willingness to bring about this kind of peace.

The Conflict Must Not Be Seen as Existential

There are some Israelis whose solution to the demographic problem would be to find a suitable opportunity to expel the Arabs. The idea of expulsion is a logical conclusion from the recognition that annexing the occupied territories with their Arab residents is likely to lead to national suicide. In the past, an important Israeli asset in the conflict was the lack of symmetry—the goal of destroying the enemy was found only on the Arab side. The call to expel the Arabs, however, is tantamount to calling for the de-Arabization of territories that are today Arab, and this makes the conflict symmetrical. For the Arabs, fighting Israel then becomes an existential imperative: the Arabs of the neighboring countries cannot remain apathetic in the face of a possible expulsion of Arabs from the West Bank, if only to prevent their countries from being flooded by Palestinians. The mere beginning of expulsion would cause Israel's peace with Egypt to collapse overnight. The conflict would become a matter of life or death, and this would impel the Arabs to unite despite all their divisions. Any attempt to expel the Arabs would result in international repercussions of unprecedented scope, and in all-out war on the part of the Arab states.

This trend toward making the conflict symmetrical is to be found not only in overt statements about "transferring" the Arabs, but also in threatening remarks about Israeli intentions to expand into the territory of Arab countries. Such utterances have appeared in Israeli publications. In a similar vein are expressions of Israeli intentions to impose a Pax Israelica on the Middle East, to dominate the Arab countries and treat them harshly. A gross example of this is an article entitled "A Strategy for Israel in the 1980s," by Oded Yinon, which appeared in *Kivvunim,* a journal published by the information department of the World Zionist Organization in February 1982. It is not surprising, given the auspices under which it is published, that Arabs attributed great importance to its content and assumed that it expressed the views of official circles with regard to Israeli policy and goals. The article had wide reper-

cussions in the Arab world, a fact that testifies to Arab feelings of
vulnerability.

Oded Yinon's generally correct analysis of the weaknesses that
characterize the national and social structures of Arab countries
leads him to the conclusion that Israel should work to bring about
their dissolution. However, that article conveys a certainty that it
is within Israel's power to do so: Israel has only to take measures.
But, if the dissolution of the Arab states is, as he maintains, inevitable, why must Israel get entangled in the repartition of the region?
Yinon goes on to describe in detail how to partition every Arab
country, according to geographical and ethnic consideration. One
wonders at the temerity of the editors who published an article in
the organ of the World Zionist Organization describing how Israel
will partition the Arab countries. Perhaps the failed Israeli attempt
to impose a new order in the weakest Arab state—Lebanon—will
disabuse people of similar ambitions in other territories.

Be that as it may, a symmetry has been created in the ideas of
the two parties to the conflict. The organ of the World Zionist
Organization presents a detailed plan for the destruction of the
Arab states, albeit in an elegant fashion, and presents this as a
prime strategic goal for Israel. In doing so it provides the Arabs
with retroactive legitimation for their goal of destroying Israel,
presenting their struggle against it as a life-or-death conflict.

A trend is apparent on both sides to regard the conflict as existential. This may be termed "hawkishness born of despair," that
is, adopting an extreme position from a conviction that the other
side's position does not allow any compromise solution. This claim
is made by extremists on both sides: Israelis assert that there is no
one to negotiate with in the Arab camp, and the Arabs continue
to plot to destroy Israel. Arabs assert that the Israelis are not
willing to make any concessions, even those demanded by the
moderate Arabs; that the Israelis will always refuse to recognize
the collective political rights of the Palestinians; and that the existence of Israel is a perpetual threat to the Arab countries. Both
sides should be more sensitive to the suspicions of the other side
and avoid pushing it, by word or deed, to this extreme position.
It should be noted, however, that the Arab extremists have a
stronger interest in turning the conflict into a fight for existence
than do their Israeli counterparts, because the former believe that
this is the only way Israel will eventually be defeated.

"Hawkishness born of despair" threatens even Israeli moderates
who have placed their hopes in a significant change in the PLO or

at least in the possibility of the imminent start of talks with Jordan. Their optimism was based on the perception that Israel would not have to make serious concessions in order to begin the process, so it would be easy for them to gain Israeli popular support for negotiations. King Hussein's refusal to negotiate under current conditions will then be interpreted to mean that the path to a settlement is obstructed by Arab intransigence, leaving Israel with no alternative but to persevere in the present policies.

Many Israelis are simply not alive to the depth of the sense of injury that Arabs harbor toward the establishment of Israel. To them, it is the greatest injustice in history. European nations that conquered a foreign land and subjugated its people still allowed them to remain in their homes and communities. Israel, then, is the worst kind of imperialism, what Arabs call *"Isti'mar Ijlayi"* (one that uproots the people). Whatever healing there may have been of this wound was terminated by the occupation of the territories and especially those areas that were heavily populated. Thus the settlements add insult to injury and become the incarnation of viciousness in Arab eyes. Maintaining the territories on the pretext of Arab intransigence has the effect of a self-fulfilling prophecy, in that it breeds the most intense form of hostility and the readiness to undertake even irrational actions as long as they may possibly inflict harm on the adversary. This, in turn, requires a response from the Israelis and so intransigence intensifies on both sides.

Both sides must be alert to a latent tendency toward radicalization and polarization that will convert the current situation into a total conflict. Radicalization of the conflict is so dangerous precisely because it is "natural," and follows from the severity of the confrontation. In a conflict of this sort it is easy to become fatalistic and adopt extremist positions "because there is no alternative." Moreover, extremism on one side fosters extremism in the adversary, and so on, in a vicious spiral.

Defining a conflict as "existential" derives from biology, from the competition among organisms for survival, and this metaphor is not appropriate to the realm of international relations. Organisms fight for their lives, whereas states compete for a *type* of existence, in wide borders that they believe they deserve. So long as annexation is described in Israel as a requisite of national survival, and so long as the Arabs see annexation deprive the Palestinians of the right of statehood and as proof that Israel is a dangerous neighbor avid to swallow up their territory, both sides will view the conflict as existential.

The major damage caused by Israel's settlement activity is that it reinforces the ethnic component of the struggle, turning it into conflict between peoples and populations rather than between states. It is in the nature of international conflicts to be resolved by some sort of compromise. In contrast, ethnic conflicts, by their very nature, are harsher. It is much more difficult to arrive at a compromise in them, and they are liable to deteriorate into unrelenting warfare. It is in Israel's interest to strengthen the international component of the conflict precisely at the expense of its ethnic component.

Settlement activities create humiliation, hatred, and a desire for revenge, not only among the Arabs of the occupied territories but among all Arabs. Each new building block in a settlement crushes incipient Arab tendencies to divorce grand design from policy, and unites the Arabs once more around the goal of destroying Israel. Emphasis on the religious aspects of the respective stands also make positions more extreme and make it more difficult to resolve the conflict.

Israelis argue that in Islam a peace agreement with a non-Islamic nation is considered to be no more than a ten-year armistice. They forget that this tenet has not prevented Moslem countries from living in peace with their neighbors. One must not dismiss lightly the harshness of Arab and Muslim positions toward Israel, but it would be a mistake to believe that the Arabs are different from all other peoples and are unable to live as good neighbors with a non-Arab state. Like all the world, they adapt to historic circumstances.

When an Arab leader such as King Hussein makes an announcement that implies a readiness for peace talks with Israel—even if his conditions do not satisfy Israel—and the announcement is totally ignored by Israel's leadership, it is reasonable to assume that the Arab extremists are right when they claim there is no possibility of making peace with Israel, and the only path open to the Arabs is that of total war to the end. The same reasoning applies to the Israeli attitude that fails to distinguish between moderates and extremists in the PLO, regards Arafat as no different from George Habash, and imposes a total ban on any contact with any element of the PLO. This approach tends to make PLO moderates believe that there is no advantage to moderation on their part, and leads them to support the extreme Palestinian position and accept the need for the PLO to close its ranks behind the radicals. This is certainly not in Israel's interest.

I reiterate: nothing can instruct us better about Arab positions than their disputes. The quarrel among them does not merely involve tactics, as is decisively proven by the amount of blood that has been shed because of it. This is a quarrel about political and strategic questions. There are important conclusions that Israel can draw from these disputes when shaping its policies as to what can be attained and what the Arabs, or some of them, are willing to agree to.

Turning the conflict into a zero-sum game, a struggle in which there must be a victor and a vanquished—whether intentionally as the Arab extremists wish, or by an unwillingness to compromise, as the Jewish extremists are doing—is fraught with danger. Israelis should consider carefully whether they will indeed prevail if the conflict is blown up into a war of life and death fought over a protracted period of time—a large-scale confrontation in which Israel will be opposed by the Arabs of the territories, by the Palestinians who live elsewhere, by the Arab countries, as well as by the Arabs of Israel, who in such circumstances will not be able to stand aloof.

The view that the conflict cannot be resolved, that the gap between the parties is so broad that it cannot be bridged, will perpetuate the conflict and make it both chronic and existential. Such a development is a disaster that must be prevented, since ultimately it will bring catastrophe to all, and first and foremost to the Israelis. Even if the parties prove incapable of resolving the conflict, they have a great capacity to create a hell for each other.

Promoting or Deferring an Accord

In the past it was in Israel's interest to defer an accord, since time appeared to be on its side. Thus a settlement along the lines of that proposed in the 1920s by Dr. Magnes and others—the Jews remaining an autonomous minority in an Arab state—was rejected by the Jewish leadership in Palestine. So was a binational solution; and the idea of a legislative council, which would have had an Arab majority and put an end to the Zionist enterprise, likewise fell by the wayside. In 1937 the Peel partition plan offered by Great Britain was rejected. In 1947, the Arabs rejected the United Nations partition plan. The war that followed resulted in Israel's increasing the territory of the UN partition by 30 percent. The following strategic question now poses itself: is this trend still operative, so

that rejecting an accord now will lead to boundaries later on that
will be to Israel's benefit? This is the question that leaders who
consider themselves capable of strategic political thought rather
than exclusively tactical calculations should ask themselves. It cannot be answered scientifically. The intelligence services cannot
provide an answer; they report on enemies, not on history. An
answer to this question does not depend on knowledge of what is
happening in any one section, but on an overall perspective of
historical trends. Statesmen will be judged by how they answer it.

To the extent that one can judge historical processes in which
one is personally involved, it seems to me that this trend has now
been reversed. The longer the conflict remains unresolved, the
worse will be the conditions that Israel can obtain. Negotiating
now on our own initiative will yield better conditions than if we are
eventually forced into them by the difficulty and danger of our
political situation or at the insistence of the superpowers. Arab
demands will increase in direct proportion to our inability to withstand them.

This is apparently the first time in the history of the conflict that
there is an impetus on both the Israeli and Arab sides to reach an
agreement. The cataclysmic vision of what is liable to happen if the
conflict continues is now perceived on the Arab side as well. Israel
and many Arab circles, including the mainstream of the PLO, are
allies against the continuation of the conflict, in view of the horrors
that otherwise await them. The desire for peace does not stem
from the delicacy and sensitivity of the parties involved, but from
their common fear of the horrible war into which continued conflict will cast them. It is this mutual specter of calamity that can
bridge the seemingly unbridgeable gap and bring the two sides
together in search of a settlement that will prevent it.

To summarize: From the Israeli perspective the following options are open: (a) A peace settlement, though one that contains
no ironclad guarantees of a final peace (no settlement has ever
implied absolute guarantees); the Arabs may still harbor vicious
intentions toward Israel. The only way to eliminate them is by a
settlement that gives them the opportunity to erode. Whereas lack
of a settlement will reinforce such intentions. (b) Annexation to
create a Greater Israel, which eventually will become an Arab state.
(c) Internal and external catastrophe caused by defending the borders of Greater Israel while struggling to prevent the Arab ascend-
ancy.

Since today the Arab countries, both individually and collectively, are beset by problems, it is almost certain that Israel can obtain much better conditions now than in the future. The Arab countries are encountering problems in modernization. Pan-Arabism, which called for political union, has failed, but the idea will not be buried and is likely to rise again. True, all recognize that political unity is hardly imminent, and that the present fractured structure of rival and even hostile Arab states will continue. In the Arab world this is a period of low spirits, of anti-heroism, of recognizing that the great hopes for a renaissance of Arab power and culture have failed, and, on the contrary, a nadir has set in. Arab periodicals repeatedly discuss the dejection of this nation or that, the acute despondency of its intellectuals at the vacuity of its cultural life, the decimation of political and social hopes. Fuad Ajami has aptly characterized the present malaise as "the Arab Predicament"—the sense of aimlessness and helplessness attendant upon becoming an object of history rather than an effective subject.

Iraq is entangled in a debilitating war with Iran; but it is in the nature of wars to come to an end, and the important question is how the war will conclude. At the time of writing, the war seems to have begun to run out of steam, and may end with a whimper. It is possible that after active hostilities are terminated the adversaries' forces will settle down to a long period of limited confrontation. Some sort of peace may even emerge. An exhausted Iraq may prefer to rest, or it may get entangled in disputes with Syria, or even combine with that erstwhile rival in a war against Israel.

The Gulf War has shocked the Arab states by demonstrating to them that Iran is a greater threat than is Israel. The ability of Arab countries to manipulate the international community through the price of oil has diminished drastically. The Arab countries must now deal with Islamic fundamentalism, a force that has developed from despair in the face of modernization and Westernization and threatens to return Arab societies to the Middle Ages.

There are even those who believe that Lebanon is not a unique case in the Middle East—in the words of Nagib Mahfuz, the prominent Egyptian novelist, Lebanon is a microcosm of the Arab world. The Arab weaknesses undoubtedly run deep, but it would seem to me a mistake to assume that the Arab states will disintegrate and Israel will be able to dictate any terms it desires. Lebanon is an anomalous situation and no simple analogies can profitably be drawn from it.

Some assert that just as the Arabs once rejected the partition-plan borders and the armistice lines whereas today they would accept them and even see this as an achievement, so too will they eventually accept the River Jordan as a boundary. This analogy is fallacious. The difference is that the international community endorsed the armistice lines, which is not the case with regard to Israeli occupation of the West Bank. The Arabs will not accept less than world public opinion, including the government of the United States, considers is due to them. On the other hand, the quarrels within the PLO, the decline in its international status, its terrorist tactics, and its emphasis on extremist positions all contribute today to greater international support for Israeli demands that the Arabs, too, including the Palestinians, must make territorial concessions, and that any settlement must be suitably buttressed to prevent the Arabs from easily renewing the struggle. But an Israeli stance that insists on holding fast to the present borders will annul these advantages.

Another important change in the conflict is that many Arabs have begun to recognize that the weakness and problems of their societies do not stem from the existence of Israel. The ideology that saw Israel as the nemesis of the Arab world created a direct link between all Arabs and the conflict and motivated them to join forces in the struggle against Israel. The understanding that this is not the case changes the ideological climate with regard to Israel and makes its presence more tolerable.

Meanwhile, Arab weakness fosters the erroneous impression in Israel that there is no need to reach a settlement and no danger in the continuation of the present state of affairs. Israel must recognize that if the Arab countries have been enfeebled Israel has been stretched thin. Israelis may be delighted at the sight of Arab weakness, but they should look at themselves in the mirror of history and recognize that strength does not last forever, and that in any case the massive and unprecedented numerical disparity between the sides will remain.

Certainly modern technology can change the situation, but it is doubtful whether it can alter basic political conditions. A qualitative gap can be closed more readily than a quantitative one. For example, China may develop industries on a par with Switzerland's, but Switzerland will never have a population like that of China. In addition to the numerical advantage already mentioned, it is precisely the backwardness of Arab societies that gives them the ability to endure, because one expression of underdevelopment is a decentralized society—a multiplicity of self-sufficient entities that are not strongly integrated. By contrast, the degree of concentration in modern societies makes them more vulnerable, since the disruption of one nexus is able to disrupt the entire network.

Any assessment of future developments must take into consideration humanity's generally poor track record in predicting the future. Frequently what actually happens was unanticipated, and the new developments significantly change conditions and problems. Nor do developments frequently correspond to what ostensibly follows from rational analysis of the present. Our analyses are not identical with the logic of history. Rational analysis may ignore a major factor that influences the future course of events. But this does not mean that an irrational outlook, such as the simplistic assumption that future developments will somehow favor Israel, is correct. Despite reservations about the human capacity for prophecy, if we want to formulate policies we have no alternative but to try to understand the current situation and anticipate future developments to the best of our ability. It is indeed hard to forecast future events, but it is relatively easy to anticipate trends such as those indicated by demographic data. I cannot imagine any event that will change the demographic trend in Israel's favor. Many Israelis find it difficult to accept this, but when pushed to propose a counter-measure they find themselves at a loss for words, or offer an irrational one, such as the large-scale immigration of Jews from the West.

I believe that the situation will not change in Israel's favor, and that Israel will not benefit from deferring a decision on such major problems. Refraining from a decision and leaving the situation as it is will only increase the danger and damage. Not deciding is to make a decision by default.

The perpetuation of the present state of affairs has a serious internal consequence for Israel: the increasing numbers of people who have a direct interest in continuing the conflict or who believe that there is no need to resolve it, that Israel should persist in the policy of annexation. (Recent studies show that the extremist position has been gaining ground among the younger generation.) This development will intensify the internal crisis in Israel when it becomes clear that Israel must nonetheless make concessions for the sake of an agreement, even if such conditions are imposed.

There is reason to fear that if negotiations do not get under way in the near future there will be a general hardening of Arab positions. Indeed, the trend toward radicalization is already evident. For example, Khaled al-Hassan, who was an ardent and influential supporter of the 1985 agreement with Jordan, has recently taken a significantly more militant line. Moreover, the inclination within the PLO to reach an agreement will wane with time. Today Arafat and his circle are restraining the extremist tendencies, but when these older leaders disappear and the young leadership inherits their place, the PLO will become more extreme. Moreover, as the Uprising in the West Bank and Gaza makes all too clear, the younger generation there is much more hostile and audacious and single-minded than their parents and likely to prove more formidable as time goes on.

Continuation of the conflict will lead to an escalation and hardening of the Israeli stand as well. Terrorism and civil insurrection will get worse, and consequently so will the repressive measures against Arabs on both sides of Israel's pre-1967 borders. Extremist Jewish religious nationalism, with its hostility toward non-Jews, will also intensify. World criticism of Israel will become harsher. Such developments will also affect how Jewish people everywhere see Israel.

Israel has taken the first steps toward resolving the conflict through its peace agreement with Egypt. If this movement does not continue, the peace with Egypt will collapse and Israel's situation will be drastically worse. For it is precisely Israeli unwillingness to make serious concessions in order to continue the peace process that may well turn the peace with Egypt into a disaster. The agreement with Egypt involved an explicit demand to move on to other peace agreements, and created a situation in which deferring such agreements is to Israel's discredit as well as disadvantage.

Even if talks with the Palestinians and the Arab states begin, there are likely to be crises in them, and they may even break down. The significant gap between the positions of the sides and the fierce differences within each camp make it very difficult to reach a modus vivendi. The extremists on both sides who oppose the concessions that will be required will almost surely attempt to torpedo the negotiations, and resort to violence—even to the risk of war—in order to do so. Successful negotiations would be a monumental accomplishment in view of the painful concessions that both sides would be asked to make. This miracle will only come about if both sides keep ever before their eyes the image of the calamities that await them in the absence of an agreement.

In order to restrain this escalation, both sides must make concessions. They will not necessarily be commensurate, but even if Israel will have to make more concessions, the Arabs too will have to pay a price to stay out of hell.

Each side can, as well as must, find ways to retreat from its established position. Israel can claim that a PLO that recognizes it and is ready to reach an agreement is not the same PLO that refused to recognize and negotiate. This point has already begun to be made by some Israeli leaders. For their part, the Arabs and Palestinians can claim—as some already do—that an Israel that withdraws from occupied territories and permits the establishment there of an Arab Palestinian regime is essentially different from the old enemy. For the essence of Zionism to them is expansion and the conquest of Arab land, so if Israel withdraws it is no longer "Zionist," in their eyes, and as such is a tolerable neighbor.

The assessment that henceforth any deferral of a settlement of the conflict is to Israel's disadvantage has major significance for Israeli policy. All other considerations pale by comparison. Israel must actively search out possibilities for an agreement, and even create them to the extent that it can, rather than wait in the hope that they will spring into being thanks to some change in the Arab stand or from foreign pressure. This must become the central imperative of Israel's foreign policy. Israel cannot adopt a neutral stance toward the various positions to be found in the other camp. It must work actively, to the best of its ability, and with full awareness of its limitations, to encourage developments among the Arabs that favor the possibility of an accord, rather than rejoicing over their negativism as a sanction for Israeli negativism.

Perhaps Israel will not be able unilaterally to advance the resolution of the conflict; but this does not absolve it of the obligation of endeavoring to do so, or of contributing to this end by offering significant concessions rather than sanctimonious declarations of its love for peace and its willingness to negotiate with the proper representatives. Such efforts are also important for its citizens' ability to endure in the absence of peace. Moreover, further degeneration of the conflict may lead to a concerted effort on the part of the superpowers, despite their many disagreements, to impose a settlement. The conditions of such an imposed settlement are likely to be less favorable to Israel than those that could be obtained by direct negotiations.

Finally, I should like to point out a common Israeli misperception of the conflict, which views the problem as at heart a social one—i.e., if Jews and Arabs continue to live together the political problem will disappear. Certainly it would be well if there were good relations between the Jewish and Arab communities within Israel. But the conflict is political and international. In such a dispute, social and cultural intimacy does not necessarily bring peace. There is no greater cultural closeness than that of religion, but nevertheless members of the same religion have fought each other mercilessly: French Catholics against Austrian Catholics and Spanish Catholics, Muslims against Muslims. The English and Americans fought two wars, even though they spoke the same language, had the same cultural heritage, and held similar political views. In international conflicts, improvement in relations between the people themselves comes after the conflicts are settled at the political and governmental level. It was not friendship between French and German youth that put an end to the centuries-old dispute between France and Germany, but a political settlement that permitted intimacy and friendship between the two peoples. The problem is not one of coexistence, or of tearing down social barriers. No solution of problems between Jews and Arabs in Israel will resolve the Arab-Israeli conflict, nor will the Israeli Arabs serve as a bridge between Israel and the Arab countries. On the contrary, the solution of the political conflict is a necessary condition for good relations between Arabs and Jews in Israel. The conflict does not have a social solution. The problem is political.

The Role of the United States

The question is frequently asked what the United States can and should contribute to the resolution of the conflict. I am loath to tell others what they should do. Still, I do not want to evade the question.

The American position has traditionally been against settlement and annexation. Until very recently, however, it has expressed this position, in excessively diplomatic and euphemistic terms—that settlement is "unhelpful" to peace, or as some have plucked up the courage to state, an "obstacle" to peace. It is not enough to have a policy or announce "peace plans" or "projects"; these should be buttressed by the rationale of why they are necessary, why without them calamity awaits us. What I ask of the United States is to be not diplomatic but *frank*. I consider that the U.S. has a stake in the conflict which gives it not only the right but the duty to speak out.

I have been told, recently, by officials of the Reagan administration that their evaluation of the situation is similar to mine. However, they refrain from expressing it so as not to hurt the Israelis, not only in public but even in private audiences with their leaders.

I fail to understand why they are so apprehensive of speaking out and saying that the present policy of annexation will miscarry, that it is bound to fail, that it will end in national bankruptcy or that it is suicidal—whatever is their evaluation. By such diffidence Americans do a disservice to Israel and to themselves.

I do not want America to exert pressure on Israel; precisely the position of not exerting pressure gives more weight to what America may say. A government may resent whenever a friendly government offers advice on policy, but may be much more receptive when friends make it privy to their worries about the situation and their evaluations. We all suffer from misperceptions and especially blind spots. A real friend is one who does not endorse all our views, but, on the contrary, despite the anger it may incur, draws our attention to our errors and insensitivities. Unreserved support by Imperial Germany for Austrian policy in the Balkans brought the First World War and was suicidal for the Hapsburg Empire. Paradoxically, U.S. friendship toward us can in this respect be no less harmful to us than Arab enmity. American leaders can be most effective if, after declaring their friendship toward Israel, their readiness to support it and to refrain from exerting pressures, they would publicly express their apprehensions that the continuation of the Arab-Israeli conflict and the current Israeli policies will in the long run be calamitous for Israel.

When the time for negotiations arrives, the United States will find itself demanding that Israel fulfill its obligation, set forth in Resolution 242 and reinforced by the Camp David Accords, to "withdraw," as called for by the central article in 242 and in the "Framework" of the Accords. As the United States will have already served notice that it opposed the settlements in the past, its stand will be irreproachable formally—though not morally, since its behavior in matters pertaining to this conflict has misled many in the Israeli public to suspect that its positions, such as criticism of settlements, should not be taken at face value. Instead of making its position clear and convincing, it spoke timidly. Thus it allowed Israel to become further and further immersed in the mire of the occupied territories. Moreover, its behavior was interpreted by many Israelis to mean that the annexationist policy of Mr. Begin was correct, leading them to idolize him and to vote for and support the approach of the Likud, Gush Emunim, and Tehiya.

Because of my love for Israel, I feel bitter about all of the factors that help it to go astray, first and foremost our own. The price will be paid by Israel and it will be exorbitant, as withdrawal will be very painful. At least some of this pain could have been spared.

3

The Two Streams of Zionism

IN ORDER TO UNDERSTAND THE RESPONSES IN ISRAEL TO
the present crisis, it is necessary to go back to their origins in the
Zionist movement.

Zionism raised serious political problems that had not previously concerned the Jews as an ethnic group. Jewish political experience was limited, especially in the international arena. It is no
wonder, then, that the Zionist enterprise that took shape after the
Balfour Declaration of 1917 sparked ideological confrontations on
two very basic questions: behavior in the political arena, and the
political principles that should guide Zionist activity. Two camps
emerged: the Zionist mainstream, represented by Chaim Weizmann, David Ben-Gurion, and the Labor movement (which I shall
refer to as Mainstream Zionism); and the "opposition"—Ze've
Jabotinsky's Revisionist movement, represented by the Zionist Revisionist Organization and later by Menachem Begin and the
Herut party (which I shall refer to as Revisionism). The persistence
of the confrontation between the two camps to this day attests to
the fundamental differences between them. True, the positions
taken by the Mainstream were not motivated only by ideology but
also by the needs of the hour, just as Revisionist positions sometimes stemmed from its role as the opposition to the Zionist establishment and later to the Israeli Labor government rather than
from its ideology.

The principles that underlie the confrontation are best seen by
presenting the positions of the two camps in their most extreme
form. In practice, of course, matters were less clear-cut; leaders on
both sides sometimes acted in ways identified with the rival camp.
Nevertheless, over the years certain basic differences between the
two political cultures became firmly entrenched.

What follows is not a comprehensive historical survey but an attempt to characterize each of the two ideologies and the respective ethos that animated it. To characterize a political movement, one must distinguish between enduring doctrines—that is, how its leaders customarily express themselves and behave—and exceptional utterances or deeds. In this way it is possible to identify the dominant thrust. My analysis therefore focuses on the basic, meta-ideological level of each political culture so as to uncover the ideas that motivate them—what modern French historians call *idées for-cées.*

Mainstream Zionism held that in order for the Jews to regain Eretz Yisrael as their homeland it must first be populated by a substantial community of Jews who would establish an economic and social base there. For peoples living in their homelands there may still be a problem of national liberation and achieving independence, but for the Jews the first task was *building* a homeland. Only by first accumulating the elements of an infrastructure would it later be possible to erect a political superstructure or state. Proclaiming a Jewish state in Eretz Yisrael would of itself avail nothing; the state would not endure if it lacked solid social and economic foundations. The first necessity, then, was to change the occupational structure of the Jewish people, to create an agrarian and urban working class who by their dedicated labor would build the homeland. Only after there was a Jewish homeland could it be turned into a Jewish state.

This school argued that achievements do not come as a dramatic *event,* but from a *process* of long struggle, of accumulating national assets (sloganized as "acre after acre, goat after goat"). Without abandoning the dream of Jewish independence, it stressed the need for realism. The feet of the people must be firmly planted on the ground, the constraints of reality always taken into account.

A major element in this approach was Jewish self-reliance. The British may have provided the possibility of a homeland through the Balfour Declaration, but the rest would depend on the Jews and particularly on their successes in establishing settlements. Consequently, the thrust of this school was directed inward, their approach toward the outside world was cautious, and they avoided making or provoking enemies or reinforcing their opposition. This caution grew out of a long Jewish tradition that goes back to the Bible and was reinforced by the Diaspora.

The second school, the Revisionist movement, saw the main problem as being that the Jews' long exile had enfeebled their collective will and made them politically weak and passive. In Eastern Europe, where this trend emerged, most of the Jews lived in small provincial villages and were unaware of the workings of international politics. They simply did not know that in the international arena decisions are influenced by the forcefulness with which demands are presented. The Revisionist movement therefore aspired to make the Jews part of a broader European culture and teach them the secrets of *Realpolitik*—that is, the nature and effectiveness of power politics. For the Revisionists, the Jews' weakness was psychological. What was needed was to strengthen their will, release them from their parochialism, and imbue them with a fighting spirit. Inspiring slogans must be impressed on the national consciousness so as to rouse the people to the bold deeds that make history.

This outlook is characterized by seeing achievement as the result of an *event*—for example, the evacuation of 100,000 Jews from Eastern Europe to form a new Hebrew army bent on conquest—an *event* that provides a solution once and for all, a historical big bang. It glorifies the heroism of the spectacular one-time deed for which the individual must be ready to sacrifice his or her life. Because of its power to change the course of history, such an event would obviate the laborious creation of infrastructure—an approach it scorned as overconcern with detail—and allow the Jews to proceed directly to statehood and power.

The very idea that it is possible to erect the superstructure without first putting down an infrastructure, to conquer without first building a demographic and economic base, to achieve a state before a homeland has been established required a romantic belief that it was possible to bridge the gap between reality and the desired goal by audacity. (The Zionist leader Nahum Sokolow [1861–1936] characterized this as a belief in "hocus-pocus.") The Revisionists accordingly elevated risk taking to the level of political strategy—"to die or to conquer the mountain," in the words of their anthem, as if only facing the danger of death could inspire the attempt to reach the summit and as if there were no intermediate achievements. As Jabotinsky himself said, "No national movement can exist without adventurism."

The Revisionist movement was intoxicated by the strength of the will. In their view, the bold will can shatter the fetters of circumstances and overcome all obstacles. The strength of subjective forces can overcome objective facts. The nation can rebel against its situation and determine its own destiny. Reality is protean stuff to be reckoned with as clay is in the hands of the potter. It is not a constraint to which one must submit.

The tendency to go straight for political results stemmed from a heroic view of history as well as from what may be termed a "Zionism of emergency": the economic situation of European Jewry was deteriorating rapidly in the 1930s, along with their security. There was no time to waste. In such an emergency, conquest must precede construction. The mass transfer of Jews to Eretz Yisrael could be accomplished with the aid of the European governments, which must be convinced that it was in their own interest to assist the great enterprise. The "evacuation" would simultaneously save the Jews of Europe and create a Jewish majority in Eretz Yisrael. The question of how this Jewish majority could hold its own without a social and economic network was never seriously considered.

Thus, even though the Revisionists stressed the values of Zionist nationalism, they were inclined to see the Zionist enterprise as less autonomous than the Mainstream Zionists, who simply did not believe that non-Jews would go out of their way to help the Jews. Revisionism, then, was a combination of maximalist national aspirations and a belief that Jewish will power could overcome any obstacle, as well as a paradoxical reliance on favors from the nations of the world.

The core of this outlook, the heart of its ideology, I call the "Jabotinsky-Begin ethos." In certain details the positions of Jabotinsky himself may have differed from the model I have sketched, but as with Marx it is not the teachings of the founder that matter but how they are interpreted. Just as Marxism is more important than Marx, so Jabotinskyism is more important than the details of Jabotinsky's actual doctrines.

The Jabotinsky stream is today represented by the Herut party, which has transmitted some of its views to its partners in the Likud governments (i.e., the Liberal party). In supporting its policies they adopted its ethos, even if unwittingly and only in part. Begin, the founder of Herut, often stressed that his policies were based on Jabotinskyism, and referred to Jabotinsky as his mentor. Some claim that Begin distorted Jabotinsky's views. This argument is not unfounded (see page 131), but it is irrelevant. From our perspective it is Begin's interpretation of Jabotinsky that matters, since that is what has had historical consequences. It is the policies *derived* from his teachings, especially during the period when Herut was in power, that today embody the Jabotinsky heritage. Nevertheless, the evolution of this heritage cannot be separated from its roots; the end bears witness to the beginning. That is why for the sake of precision I call this the Jabotinsky-Begin ethos—that is to say, a world view that includes the additions and amendments made by Begin to the master's doctrine. It is this world view that underlay the Irgun's struggle against the British Mandate before the establishment of the Jewish state as well as the positions taken by Herut after 1948. More especially, it was the world view that guided government policy during the period of Likud rule from 1977 and its sharing of power since 1985.

This view drew its inspiration from the heroic events of Jewish history, such as the Great Revolt against the Romans (66–70 C.E.) and the Bar Kochba rebellion (132–135 C.E.). Though such uprisings ended disastrously, it was the intention that lay behind them that mattered—revolt, the quest for freedom and independence.

Dr. Yisrael Eldad, the ideologue of Lehi (the underground group, also known as the Stern Gang, which seceded from the Irgun in 1939 and launched terrorist attacks against the British), calls himself a disciple of Jabotinsky. He told a symposium at the Hebrew University in 1984 that he felt at his best when facing powerful enemies. He seemed oblivious of the fact that the stronger his enemies the greater the chance that they will overcome him. As a typical representative of the Jabotinsky-Begin ethos, Eldad has convinced himself it was not the results of a struggle that count, but the intention behind it. This is expressed in the symbolic pose of standing against the great ones of the earth, thrilled by one's own daring. Reality is only a detail: glory, ceremony, style—these are more important than the result, or are themselves the only result that matters. This attitude is part of this school's proclivity for nationalist rhetoric, theatricality, and bombast. Jabotinsky himself said that man's superiority to the animals is ceremony.

A love of pomp indicates a tendency to what I call expressivity as opposed to instrumentalism. For the expressivist a deed has a value as a means of self-assertion, irrespective of its contribution to attaining a given goal. For example, heroic wars are fought for the sake of the self-gratification born of the display of bravery. Acts of retaliation are performed because of the sense that *something* must be done, not necessarily in order to deter the enemy. The instrumental approach, in contrast, evaluates a deed according to the degree to which its goal can be realized. The instrumentalist judges a war by its benefits, not by the satisfaction it provides. One fights bravely in order to achieve results and embarks on retaliatory actions for gains, not to feel better.

In the expressivist approach a *cause* pushes one from behind; in the instrumental approach a *reason* pulls one forward toward a goal. The line between the two approaches is not always clear-cut. In practice the expressivist approach can also have beneficial results. Nevertheless, the distinction is important and will recur in our discussion. Mainstream Zionism tends to the instrumental approach; Revisionist Zionism tends to the expressivist one.

One can understand the attraction of Jabotinskyism and the idea that great results can be achieved at a single stroke. What is more, there are indeed circumstances, such as the rescue of the hostages at Entebbe, where success can ensue from a single, daring effort. The problem with this approach is that such circumstances are rare. In real life it is a mistake to rely on a method appropriate for situations that occur infrequently. Moreover, one cannot take advantage of historical opportunities unless one has first prepared the means. Finally, there is a great difference between hoping for a favorable moment and clinging to the certainty that it will come.

The "event" approach to problem solving engenders the belief that the desired change can be wrought quickly, through violent and drastic action. Hence the connection between the "event" approach and militarism; for the Revisionists, the use of force is necessary and even laudable.

The Revisionist movement therefore advocated force in its struggle to gain leadership in Eretz Yisrael and a policy to take control of the land both east and west of the Jordan. Since it had nothing to contribute to building the land, it saw its contribution to the future Jewish state in events of terrorism that would drive the British out. (Terrorism is an activity with which even a small handful may achieve impressive results, for the Revisionists were very much a minority.)

The Revisionist movement bestowed on this activity the glorious title of "the Revolt," and later claimed that it was responsible for the expulsion of the British and the establishment of the state. The claim is at the very least exaggerated: terrorism generally strengthens the resolve of the enemy. In point of fact the reason for the departure of the British was essentially more prosaic: the British had come to the Middle East because it was the bridge to India; when they gave up India, the importance of the region to British strategy declined. It was primarily a revision of strategic considerations that motivated the British withdrawal from Palestine and elsewhere in the Middle East, although a number of other factors also played their part (see Chapter 6).

The Revisionists seceded from the Zionist Organization in 1935, establishing the New Zionist Organization (NZO). This rupture during a critical period in the Zionist effort produced great acrimony. It caused the Mainstream to treat the Revisionists virtually as pariahs during the next three decades. As the Herut party, the Revisionists and their followers remained bitterly alienated and antagonistic to the Labor government, and when it finally began to weaken in the early 1970s, this legacy of resentment contributed significantly to Herut's rise to power.

Both schools were aware that history is a combination of leaps and gradual developments—of revolutions and evolutions. But their emphases were different. To borrow a metaphor from the American diplomat and historian George Kennan, the Mainstream Zionists were "gardeners" who laid the groundwork and nurtured growth; the Revisionists were "mechanics," geared to dramatic improvements from a single, decisive move.

The Mainstream Zionists argued that political achievements depend on economic and social facts. The Revisionists countered that social and economic advances are ensured only by political achievements. With their belief in a redemptive event, they were disposed to believe that overcoming a perceived obstacle would achieve the desired solution. This readily led to a confusion of ends and means. The Revisionists were monists—fixated on one supreme goal (in Jabotinsky's slogan, "One flag"). They placed nationalism at the center of their ethos and gave it an absolute value; the achievement of social goals was relegated to second place. This inclination to absolute political positions is conspicuous in the Revisionist world view. Compromise was foreign to its spirit. They warned that concessions, even if merely tactical, were likely to become strategic and lead to full-scale retreat. Consequently, and to the extent possible, the Revisionists clung desperately to the goal depicted as the grand design and refused to trim their sails to cope with political exigencies.

The Mainstream Zionists were dualists—achieving statehood and developing the society were indispensable to each other. They espoused a more relativistic (and realistic) approach: not everything can be achieved, and sometimes one must compromise. One should of course strive to achieve the maximum, but when circumstances prevent this one must be prepared to distinguish grand design from practical policy. The overblown nationalism of the Revisionists is not peculiar to them, or to Israel. In this century it has appeared in other places, such as Poland and Italy, two countries that greatly influenced Jabotinsky. But such vehement nationalism has all but vanished from the developed world to which Israel belongs.

As an opposition movement the Revisionists had to compete for new supporters, especially after it seceded from the Zionist Organization. For those who were not inclined to the effort of the daily struggle needed to implement the practical step-by-step approach, the Revisionists' maximalist objective of a Greater Israel and promise of success in giant leaps was a most seductive idea. Whereas the Mainstream Zionists called for each individual to make a personal contribution to the realization of the Zionist enterprise, Revisionism, with its promise of great results from a bold move, a decisive intervention, was highly compatible with its tendency to court the favor of the masses. This populist tendency became even stronger during the Begin era, which was marked by a recourse to demagoguery—gratifying the masses with material rewards and exciting policies: the politics of bread and circuses.

There is a paradox here. The Mainstream Zionists were socialists with a proletarian orientation, but made élitist demands for pioneering and personal sacrifice. The Revisionist school, initially addressing itself mainly to the middle class and presenting itself as right wing, was populist. Both schools wanted to instill the nation with pride in itself, but their emphases were different. The Mainstream wanted to arouse pride in achievements as an impetus for continuing the effort. The Revisionists highlighted pride in the greatness of the Jewish people. They assumed that with the new self-confidence accomplishments would simply come of themselves.

The Mainstream accused the Revisionists of vainglory—being unrealistic and seeking unobtainable goals; by asking for too much they would end up with nothing. They also accused them of excessive provocation of the Jews' adversaries by their bombastic rhetoric. The Revisionists countered by accusing Mainstream Zionists of timidity—of pussyfooting because of their pathetic Diaspora mentality of underestimating the Jewish people's potential, of setting goals far short of what could be achieved and thereby missing opportunities for great achievements.

The two schools also differed with regard to the status of the leader. Jabotinsky had a much more central position in the Revisionist movement than did Weizmann and Ben-Gurion in Mainstream Zionism. Jabotinsky imprinted his own spirit upon the movement that he created. Begin, too, stood above his party. The

Mainstream had more of a collective leadership, even if one figure or another attained particular prominence from time to time.

Ideologies differ not only in their doctrines but also in their patterns of thought, or mindset. This is not surprising, since *what* one thinks and *how* one thinks condition one another. The combination of ideology and mindset create a disposition to a certain way of thought and behavior about a given issue. Of course this does not always determine how the group will behave, and certainly not how the individuals composing it will conduct themselves in every case.

Because human beings can escape the shackles of their ideology, one might conclude that ideology and other patterns of thought are unimportant. But this would be a mistake. When human beings assess reality, they perceive the possible goals, the available means, and the alternative outcomes. Ideology is a lens through which reality is perceived, and in this way can influence policy and deeds. In other words, an ideology and its dominant mentality generate attitudes that influence how people shape policies.

There is also the question of the relationship between the two ideologies and their adherents. Affiliation with a particular ideology is a matter of choice, and can be influenced by chance factors, such as the environment in which an individual grows up or finds his place in society. The division I have presented does not totally correspond to a party division, just as it does not apply absolutely to individuals. Some "gardeners" may also be disposed to rely on the "mechanics'" means, and vice versa. In addition, individuals adopt group attitudes more strongly in a smaller and more cohesive group, partly because in small groups the pressures to conform in thought and ideology are greater. As the group increases in size this homogeneity decreases. This can explain certain changes that occurred in Herut in the 1970s when it changed from a small party to a mass movement.

The characteristic weakness of the Revisionist movement was expressed in its failure to identify the major historical challenge that had to be coped with. Jabotinsky initially saw the British as an ally and savior; in time, however, the Irgun regarded the British as the enemy and fought against them. Moreover, the Irgun was not prepared for the real threat to the Jewish community of Eretz Yisrael on its way toward statehood—invasion by Arab armies. It was the Mainstream who stressed the importance of the workers and labor and established a people's army. The Revisionists set up terrorist units. The contribution of the Jabotinsky school, both from the Irgun and Lehi, to Israel's War of Independence was marginal: the State of Israel was born of Mainstream Zionism.

Once the state was established, the Revisionists bowed to the inevitable and accepted the state institutions and the democratic process. The transition from underground to political party, Herut, was reasonably smooth, thanks in large measure to Menachem Begin, who understood the requirements of statehood.

It should be emphasized that both movements had the best intentions. They both wanted to realize the Zionist idea and establish a Jewish state. But this does not mean that they should not be held responsible for their deeds and judged accordingly.

Until the mid-1970s the Labor party, Mapai, succeeded in persuading broad sections of the public that Herut was proposing unrealistic policies. In consequence, Herut was regarded as irresponsible and unfit to lead the country. But, despite the long years in opposition, Herut did have its faithful followers, a hard core that cherished the memory of their leader Jabotinsky and his teachings.

As times change, the ideological baggage of political parties, in part or in whole, becomes irrelevant to the new challenges. As an ideology ages, what remains is the mentality that has accompanied it. Jabotinsky's doctrine became outdated, but left in the minds of its adherents the sediment of a disposition to certain kinds of policies and methods. This legacy is the Jabotinsky-Begin ethos.

The ideas of the two schools were shaped during the period of the British Mandate over Palestine, when the major question was how Jewish independence could be achieved. The establishment of the State of Israel changed the situation completely. Once the state was a fact, the new challenge was to stabilize and develop it. In these circumstances the ideology of *process* was more suitable than the ideology of *the event.* "Emergency Zionism," heroic evacuations from Europe, conquest of a Greater Israel by war—these ideas were no longer appropriate. They were replaced by the challenges of absorbing the massive immigration of diverse peoples and building the economy. Israel's wars were great events, but generally these were imposed rather than sought out.

The new circumstances rendered the Revisionists' ideology obsolete. In opposition, however, Herut had less need to come up with new ideas than the government did. The long period of opposition also increased the tendency to extremism. Herut's activities acquired an even stronger tinge of incitement and destructiveness. Populism came hand in hand with demagoguery. A long stay in opposition can corrupt any group, especially an élite that claims to have been chosen to rule, as Herut's slogan would have it. Time also eroded the ideology of the Mainstream Zionists of the Labor movement. The more solid the state became the less the challenges of the pioneering ethos were perceived as relevant. The call for personal effort and sacrifice was replaced by an emphasis on going along with the system. One important legacy did remain, however, and this was the attachment to realism. In part this stemmed from the responsibility of its long years in power, and from the fact that for many years Mainstream Zionism was favored with leaders like David Ben-Gurion, Moshe Sharett, and Levi Eshkol, who were endowed with a realistic understanding of historical processes.

The Labor movement must be credited with important achievements during its long rule. This does not mean that there were only few mistakes or failures, or that it was free of personal and party conflicts. On the contrary, eventually it was undermined by the arrogance, complacency, and self-interest that long-standing regimes are prone to. These led to its downfall.

The Coalition

Historic changes generally take place from the convergence of a number of factors. This was the case with the change in the political climate that began in 1967 and led, by 1977, to the decline of Mapai and the rise to power of the Likud. The central partner in the Likud coalition that formed the government was Herut, under Begin's leadership, and it was Herut that determined their image and policies. The great change occurred when there began to be widespread popular support, particularly from the Sephardic masses, for the Likud. The National Religious party, which had always achieved its objectives by joining forces with the ruling party, accordingly changed its policies and joined the Likud government. But, while this change was principally from coalitionary calculations, it is important to remember that it was also because of the change in attitude among the religious Jews that began with the victory in the Six Day War. The same applied to the even more orthodox Agudat Yisrael party, which joined the parliamentary coalition but not the cabinet.

Many reasons have been offered for the political reversal of 1977, when the Likud took power after thirty-odd years in opposition. In the present context, though, it is pertinent to point out that the political climate changed in Israel after the Six Day War no less than it did elsewhere in the Middle East. In the Arab countries the war led to some movement toward divorcing grand design from policy. In Israel, by contrast, it fostered a belief that Israel could allow itself more ambitious political goals now, including the occupied territories. Thus the old Revisionist grand design of a Greater Israel became policy.

The change was gradual, since it takes time for historical changes to assert themselves. It extended to sections of the population that traditionally belonged to the Labor movement and influenced their thought as well. The Six Day War lent credence to the Jabotinsky-Begin ethos by demonstrating that great achievements can be produced by a spectacular, one-time event. Although not planned, the war proved not only that bold leaps are possible but also that they can reap great political gains: all that is required to expand the political domain is sufficient strength. The attitude toward force started to change from defensive to offensive. Moreover, Israel began to be seen as a Middle Eastern power; this newfound recognition was also a source of national pride. Through concentrated military effort, security problems that had weighed heavily on the Jewish state at last seemed to have been overcome. The victory had been achieved by a Mapai government; the grateful public continued to support it, but in consequence of that victory the political climate began to change.

The shock of the Yom Kippur War in 1973 proved to be a decisive factor of change because it stood in glaring contrast to the victory of 1967. In the past the Labor government had been seen as the bulwark protecting the state against its enemies; the events of 1973 revealed an unreliability on security matters. If powerful Israel was surprised by an attack, the government must have been guilty of negligence.

Large segments of the Israeli public were delighted by Begin's attacks on the Mainstream. He expressed their outrage at the negligence of 1973 as well as their economic and social frustrations. Begin's attacks on the government and the Labor party, delivered in his grandiloquent rhetoric, made many of his more ardent supporters hail him as "King of Israel," a leader whom they could rely on. His speeches about Israel's greatness and his overt hostility toward non-Israelis, especially Arabs, found a sympathetic echo among the masses, many of them recent victims of Arab repression and discrimination. The election campaign in 1977 highlighted the public admiration for Begin and his personal style as well as his values. His subsequent attacks on foreign leaders, which were seen as displays of personal and national fortitude, also received widespread acclaim.

The wars of 1967 and 1973 demonstrated the advantages of force. If 1967 showed that Israel had the might to expand territorially, 1973 underlined the importance of territory for the country's security. Activist circles formerly within the Labor movement began leaning toward Herut because the Labor party's limited position on using territories to set up a handful of strategic settlements, mainly along the Jordan, now seemed hesitant and meager, whereas the Likud's support for widespread settlement activity was reminiscent of the days when Mainstream Zionism had seen settlement as a major component of their strategy. In more populist circles, support for annexationist policies stemmed not so much from an ideological identification with the Begin-Jabotinsky ethos as from hostility toward Arabs, and from the gratifying feeling of flexing one's muscles.

Many commentators have stressed that it was not ideology that attracted voters to Herut—that, in the popular phraseology, ideology no longer sells. But this view is based on an erroneous image of what ideology is. It does not necessarily have to be a detailed structure of codified ideas like Marxism; it may be nothing more than a few strongly held, if weakly related, concepts and perceptions. In its broad sense, ideology is the dialogue of a group with itself as it operates in history, and is therefore a permanent manifestation of political life.

The political adoration of Begin and support for the Likud were not merely a reaction to the leader's personal charisma. Those who voted for him explained that they liked his "attitude." But "attitude" belongs to the ideological realm. In other words, Begin's admirers were expressing their support for his political perceptions and expressivity. It is possible to absorb the principal ideas of the Jabotinsky-Begin ethos and repeat its slogans without becoming familiar with the details of Jabotinsky's doctrine. At the same time, the election of a leadership is never detached from the attitudes and beliefs it represents. Those segments of the population who voted for Herut because they liked Begin's approach later began to adopt certain principles of Herut's mindset, even if only partially.

Jabotinsky was a secular Jew. His traditional Jewish education was superficial. Moshe Bella wrote that when he was planning his anthology of Jabotinsky's thought Jabotinsky's son Eri wrote to him as follows: "Don't make my father into a religious man, as the fashion of recent years would have him. He was not that at all. If you cite passages that express a sympathetic attitude towards religion, please also cite those that are anti-religious." Bella himself wrote: "At times he expressed bitter criticism of the rigidity of the Jewish religion and its official standard-bearers and of their uncompromising adherence to outdated customs." But Jabotinsky also expressed a sympathetic attitude toward the Jewish religion and tradition as the central cultural values of the Jewish people and as the active agency that had preserved them as a people. For him, religion was ancillary to nationalism. His doctrine, especially as expressed by Begin after 1977, contained elements that were likely to attract religious people: ethnocentrism, hostility toward foreigners, an attachment to the land for historical reasons based on God's covenant with the Biblical Jews. Moreover, as we shall see in Chapter 4, Jabotinskyism's attribution of supreme value to Jewish nationalism was compatible with the religious concept that stressed the uniqueness of the Jews as the Chosen People. In addition, reliance on an event is compatible with the religious expectation of divine intervention in a world-shattering act. Begin had a positive attitude toward the Jewish religion as the carrier of Jewish nationalism, and his frequent use of expressions such as "with God's help" shows that he certainly knew how to put it to good advantage to win support from religious Jews.

Thus, in the Likud led by Begin, a new coalition was created. In coming to power Begin was supported not only by the veterans of Herut who had been educated in the Revisionist ethos but also by broader segments of the public, including the Liberals and the religious parties, as well as other smaller groups that had crossed the aisle from the ranks of the Labor movement. Israel had entered a new era.

4

The Likud in Power

Failure: Essence or Continuation?

Until 1977, the Revisionist movement and Herut had minimal influence on Israeli policy. While in opposition, Herut was never able to implement its ideas and proposals; it was only after it took power as the leader of the Likud coalition that one could judge how the Revisionists' concepts translated into political action.

The Likud government presided over a series of great failures: the peace treaty with Egypt, which loomed initially as a great achievement; the Lebanon War, which turned into a fiasco; which has become a quagmire; de facto annexation; Israel's economy, which nearly collapsed; the conduct of politics that degenerated into demagoguery; the worsening in the relations between various segments of the population—those of North African and Middle Eastern origin (the Sephardim) against those of European backgrounds (the Ashkenazim), as well as religionists against secularists. Generally, the national confidence was undermined by this widespread deterioration of Israel's situation. What caused all these failures? Were they purely accidental and unrelated, or were they all of a piece? Were they the result of unforeseen problems and bad luck, or were they built in? Did they have a common denominator in some erroneous policy? Were the failures rooted in the personalities of the leaders, in their lack of ability or unsuitability for office? Or did they result from a political philosophy, aspects of these leaders' mentality and basic concepts that influenced both their personalities and their policies?

My answer is that there was a common denominator: a misperception of reality or an insufficient regard for it. The accumulation of failures cannot be explained in isolation from the Jabotinsky-Begin ethos. They all stemmed from a pattern of thought that was influenced by this ethos: a superficial approach that searched for shortcuts to great accomplishments by means of a single dramatic event or policy, a focusing on intentions instead of outcomes and an exaggerated belief in the power of the will.

Taken in the aggregate, these failures constituted a veritable national tragedy, since they critically worsened Israel's condition and weakened the basis of its existence. Many Israelis have begun to wonder whether their country can endure, whether the nation can climb down safely from the slippery cliff face to which successive Likud governments have led them. This will depend on recognition by both the public at large—and not only by a minority within it—of both the severity of the situation and its causes. Recognition that Israel's problems were intensified by its leaders' errors and not by unavoidable circumstances will bring energy for change. On the other hand, refusing to recognize the severity of the situation will encourage the mindset that brought these calamities upon Israel and pave the way for further disasters.

(The initiatives of the Labor "Alignment" in the National Unity Government, constituted in October, 1984, have since alleviated many of these failures. The Likud record should be evaluated for the period—1977–84—when it alone was in power, before the establishment of the government of national unity.)

Some argue that, although error does lie at the root of all these failures, they are not peculiar to the Likud but have always been present in the Israeli polity. This excuse, generally voiced by members of the Likud in an effort to deflect censure from themselves, sees continuity between the problems of the present and the failures of the past (implicitly, the failings of Mainstream Zionism). Accordingly, they themselves are no more blameworthy than anyone else.

This explanation is not totally without foundation; there is no doubt that past Israeli governments were guilty of mistakes, faulty assessments, deficient thinking, and improper conduct. But in assessing failures one must go beyond the observation that they are recurrent: an analysis that fails to consider the degree of failure will naturally lead to obfuscation on the intellectual level and nihilism and decadence on the moral level. For example, if we say that taking life is always a sin, then we are equating a child who steps on an ant with the vicious commander of a Nazi death camp. Even though there is no human being without sin, not all sinners are equal. In the same way, in judging the actions of governments, are we not to consider the weight of their errors? Is there really no difference between the failures of the Likud government and those of its predecessors?

Another explanation used to blur the differences between the government of the Likud and that of its predecessors is that the recourse to violence that found expression in the Lebanon War was not peculiar to the Likud, but is an essential part of practical Zionism. This explanation juxtaposes Herzl's "political" Zionism, which labored to persuade the international community to grant a homeland to the Jews, and "practical" Zionism, which turned to independent action to achieve its aims and was not adverse to employing force when it encountered difficulties. But if "practical" Mainstream Zionism accepted the use of necessary force (how else could Israel have survived?), it did not advocate a policy of force. The distinction is important.

To see the whole of Israel's history in a militaristic light offers too simplistic a solution. Can it really be said that the Lebanon War was not exceptional in Israel's security policy? Was the outcome similar to those of previous conflicts? Were the goals comparable? Were Arab civilians harmed to the same extent? Was there a comparable split within the nation? Were the same accusations concerning the conduct of the war made about previous military campaigns?

It is frequently asserted today that the rot that has set in is a general and unremitting phenomenon; it does not matter which government is in office. The Likud is bad, Labor is bad, there is no difference between them. The establishment of the National Unity Government in the autumn of 1984 undoubtedly facilitated the spread of this way of thinking because it made it possible to sew the Labor label onto failures tailored by the Likud government. The danger of this attitude is that it can lead to a general despair that typically supports extreme nationalistic solutions.

Some see the solution to the problems besetting the Jewish state in raising the level of its morality. The remedy they put forward is to establish in the tumultuous Middle East an island of liberal Jewish ethics. Though taking an opposite tack, their course is similar to the Revisionists' in its preference for the subjective over the objective, its proclivity to ignore the reality determined by other people and the challenges they pose. This is a mistake. If Israelis adopt an unrealistic attitude toward the outside world, they will be unable to act ethically internally. A country's domestic morality depends on its foreign relations as well.

Clearly, not all the evils began in the Likud period. Right after

Israel's victory in the Six Day War in 1967 the Arab countries seemed to be clinging to their old design of liquidating Israel, so Israel had no choice but to continue strengthening itself in anticipation of the next war. The situation was changed by Egypt's readiness to make peace with Israel. This change made all the previous policies toward the Arabs outmoded. Let us see what the Likud did with this opportunity.

The Peace with Egypt

Peace with Egypt, the largest Arab country, was Mr. Begin's and the Likud's greatest achievement. It may well be true that no other prime minister could have achieved it; history will undoubtedly credit it to his favor. But at the same time Begin cannot be absolved of blame for the deterioration in Israeli-Egyptian relations that has since cast a shadow over this achievement.

The peace with Egypt was based on two "Framework" agreements concluded at Camp David and signed on September 17, 1978, and on the peace treaty itself, signed on March 26, 1979, which was a continuation of the Framework agreements. The text of these Accords is short, but one sentence recurs five times (four times in the "Framework Agreement for Peace in the Middle East" and once in the "Framework for the Conclusion of a Peace Treaty Between Egypt and Israel"), to the effect that *the agreements were signed as a means to implement Security Council Resolution 242.* This repetition is no accident: it was the central point on which the negotiations were conducted and on the basis of which the Egyptians signed the Accord. The preamble to the peace treaty also mentions the need to establish peace in accordance with Resolution 242. A central clause of Resolution 242 calls for "withdrawal of Israeli armed forces from territories occupied in the recent conflict." Further, the Framework agreements repeatedly speak of "all parts" of Resolution 242 and "all of the provisions and principles" in it, apparently to reinforce the point made in the preamble to this resolution, which asserts "the inadmissibility of the acquisition of territory by war." In August, 1970, Mr. Begin had resigned from the first National Unity Government because it had accepted the principle of withdrawal, whose source was Resolution 242. In his speech to the Knesset on August 4, 1970, he explained the damaging significance for Israel of this resolution and its preamble. Yet he was later to sign the Camp David agreements, which were based on Resolution 242. What he had formerly objected to so strongly now became the cornerstone of his policy. He was never to explain how he came to make his shift.

The accord with Egypt is only one of the outcomes of Resolution 242. The preface to the "Framework Agreement for Peace in the Middle East" specifically states that it applies to all agreements with Israel's other neighbors and reads: "The agreed basis for a peaceful settlement of the conflict between Israel and its neighbors is Security Council Resolution 242, in all its parts." And further: "To achieve a relationship of peace, in the spirit of Section 2 of the United Nations Charter, future negotiations between Israel and any neighbor prepared to negotiate peace and security with it, for the purpose of carrying out all the provisions and principles of Resolutions 242 and 338 [calling for an Israeli-Egyptian cease-fire and immediate initiation of negotiations under appropriate auspices]." And again: "Taking these factors into account, the parties are determined to reach a just, comprehensive, and durable settlement of the Middle East conflict through the conclusion of peace treaties based on the Security Council Resolutions 242 and 338, in all their parts." It should also be remembered that, whether Resolution 242 is obligatory or merely a recommendation, the fact that the parties accepted the resolution obliges them to implement it as if it were an agreement between them.

Legal experts may say that the preamble to a resolution has less force than the resolution itself. The preamble sets forth an intention; but is it merely a summary for rhetorical purposes, obligating no one? Resolution 242 is mentioned twice in the preamble to the "Framework Agreement for Peace in the Middle East," but it is also mentioned twice in the body of the agreement. It seems to me that, legal opinion notwithstanding, the preamble of the resolution has real meaning; most certainly it has a political and historical significance. In his resignation speech in August 1970, Mr. Begin even stressed that there is an essential linkage between the preamble to Resolution 242 and the body of the resolution.

There is a dispute as to whether Resolution 242 refers to withdrawal from "*the* occupied territories," as the French text would have it, or from "territories occupied" as in the English version—i.e., not from all of them. Both versions are binding, but there is basis for the claim that the English text should be preferred because the draft resolution was prepared and submitted in English, and the negotiations that preceded its passage were conducted in English. It can be argued that, even if the resolution did not require withdrawal from all the territories, the intention was for more than symbolic withdrawal, and almost certainly *from most of the territories.* Thus Resolution 242 applies to all borders; it cannot be interpreted to mean that the scale of withdrawal in Sinai was sufficient to compensate for a lesser or no withdrawal on other borders. It was, as it were, only an advance payment, and did not absolve Israel of the obligation to follow through in the other occupied territories.

Those Likud leaders who opposed the Accords, such as Yitzhak Shamir and Moshe Arens, understood correctly that it contradicted Herut's desire to maintain Jewish rule over the West Bank. Today, however, these two erstwhile opponents of the Accords are their fervent advocates, again without explaining their *volte face.* Yet, while clinging to it in their arguments, they distort its meaning, as if it were now miraculously compatible with their policy of settlement and eventual annexation.

One can argue that the concept of a five-year period of autonomy to be followed by negotiations separates the agreement from the stipulations of Resolution 242, that is, that the negotiations to be conducted between Israel, Egypt, Jordan, and representatives of the residents of the West Bank and Gaza Strip can determine the final arrangement in the territories without reference to Resolution 242. However, the first Framework explicitly states: "The negotiations shall be based on all the provisions and principles of U.N. Security Council Resolution 242. The negotiations will resolve, among other matters, the location of boundaries and the nature of security arrangements." Thus the Camp David Accords and the prospective autonomy negotiations were not meant to supersede Resolution 242, but only to spell it out in concrete terms. The demand that the precise boundaries be determined in negotiations does not contradict the idea that the boundaries should be drawn in accordance with Resolution 242. It is true that Resolution 242 did not call for withdrawal precisely to the old borders, and a demand for such phrasing was rejected in the Security Council debates that preceded passage of the resolution. President Sadat himself, in a speech on July 24, 1972, acknowledged that Resolution 242 does not unequivocally require withdrawal from all the territories. But Sadat's demand for full withdrawal in Sinai was accepted, and one may assume that the complete withdrawal from Sinai will serve as a precedent for Arab demands with regard to the delineation of other borders.

A plausible interpretation of the Camp David Accords was provided by the right-wing Likud and Tehiya leaders who opposed them. Precisely because they support annexation, their arguments that the agreement rules out annexation are persuasive. Professor Yuval Ne'eman, one of the founders of the Tehiya party, was right when he claimed that autonomy as envisaged at Camp David could not be a transitional stage in a process that would ultimately lead to Israeli sovereignty, since the decision on the fate of the territories was explicitly given to the Palestinians, Egypt, and Jordan, as well as Israel. In reality, autonomy can only be a transitional stage toward more autonomy, culminating in Arab sovereignty.

With regard to the negotiations at the end of the autonomy period, the Camp David Accords stated that representatives of the Arabs of the territories would participate. Earlier, it was asserted in general terms that "The negotiations [would be] among Egypt, Israel, Jordan, and the elected representatives of the inhabitants of the West Bank and Gaza to agree on the final status of the West Bank and Gaza." With regard to negotiations concerning the autonomy regime, the Accords explicitly state that "the delegations of Egypt and Jordan may include Palestinian Arabs from the West Bank and Gaza or other Palestinians, as may be mutually agreed." In any case, the final arrangement must be accepted by Israel, Egypt, Jordan, and the Arabs of the territories together. True, each of the three other parties can block a settlement which does not authorize Israel to perpetuate its domination over the West Bank. Sadat did recognize a legitimate Israeli interest in the West Bank but not that Israel alone can determine its future.

I am not a legal expert, but understanding such texts is not a lawyer's monopoly. The agreement was phrased ambiguously in an attempt to find a compromise between the contradictory positions of the negotiating parties. I find it worrying that Israel signed the Accords despite declarations by Herut and Likud leaders that make it a matter of principle to maintain Israeli rule on the West Bank and ultimately annex it. An agreement based on the principle of withdrawal is incompatible with settlement activities, which aims at annexation of the territories.

Gush Emunim, the spearhead organization for settlement in the occupied territories, which is more qualified than any other group to explain the intention behind settlement activities, has actually proclaimed that its settlements are intended to render the autonomy plan obsolete. It was thus disingenuous of Israel to invite Egypt to negotiate about autonomy while simultaneously supporting settlement activities intended to rule out any possibility of autonomy.

I do not disqualify schemes and stratagems simply because they may infringe the bounds of morality if they in fact lead to political benefits. I want Israel to be a moral state, but I do not require it to be more moral than other countries—only that it be realistic. Great powers may allow themselves to renege on their signatures; Israel cannot. The historical truth is that in the Camp David Accords Mr. Begin conceded that the West Bank and the Gaza Strip would not be part of Israel. Or, put another way, as some of his aides remarked on the spot, at Camp David Mr. Begin founded the Palestinian Arab state. Israel will yet be called upon to pay the debts, and the United States *will* be the first to demand payment.

Israel does not bear sole responsibility for the deterioration of relations with Egypt. True, the Egyptians did not make peace in order to abandon it; they assumed that it would evolve as described in the Accords, alongside the negotiations on autonomy, in a process called "normalization" that would lead to mutual cooperation and commercial and cultural ties. But the Egyptians did not envisage normalization within the context of a separate, autonomous Israeli-Egyptian peace agreement. Rather, real normalization could result only from other peace agreements with other Arab countries, for which the peace with Egypt was merely the first step. Accordingly, when the autonomy negotiations aborted in 1982, the Egyptians began to use "normalization" as a stick with which to beat Israel and reneged on other, more minor conditions of the Accords. As relations worsened, anti-Semitic utterances directed against Israel surfaced more vehemently in the Egyptian press.

Another question that historians will debate is whether Israel obtained the best possible conditions at Camp David. Those who took part in the negotiations have asserted that many mistakes were made. In initiating negotiations one should consider how to produce a climate that will mellow the position of the other side. The Camp David negotiations, however, began under the cloud of increasing quasi-settlement activity in the Yamit district in the Sinai, which undoubtedly hardened the Egyptians' stance. There are well-informed Israelis who believe that, if the negotiations had begun in a better mood, Israel could have obtained better conditions, such as allowing some settlements to remain in the Sinai under Egyptian sovereignty. Professor Yoram Dinstein, then Dean of the Faculty of Law of Tel Aviv University, and an expert on international law, commented, "The way in which the negotiations with Egypt were conducted raises many trenchant questions. It is almost impossible to imagine such an unremitting sequence of errors in judgment." (*Ha'aretz*, December 1, 1978)

Sadat's peace initiative was revolutionary in that it contradicted basic trends not only in Arab policies but also in the Arab political culture and religion. Sadat dared to take this road because he assumed that the Egyptian public's war-weariness would generate support for his move. But peace is a fragile plant, and if not tended carefully, it is likely to wither.

Egypt was impelled to make peace by considerations of interest, mainly to remove the economic and political burden of maintaining a state of conflict and a legacy of defeat with respect to Israel. However, as the peace remained a separate one, distancing Egypt from the rest of the Arab world and leaving Egyptians with the bad conscience of abandoning the Palestinians, the legitimization of Camp David by the people was stymied and old sentiments of enmity toward Jews and Israel reappeared. Though governments make peace, only its people can accord it normative meaning as the beginning of good neighborly relations. Egypt keeps the peace now only from considerations of interest, the reluctance to go back to the warlike relations of the recent past. Moreover, peace is considered a condition for the continuation of the vital assistance Egypt receives from the United States. Once the growth of real peace was halted it has degenerated to a nonaggression pact of sorts.

The Camp David Accords and the peace treaty are significant for Israel in that they were intended to be a first step toward a peace agreement with other Arab states. I am deeply troubled by how evasively Israel has conducted itself in its first agreement with an Arab state. On the basis of this experience, why should other Arab countries want to conclude agreements with Israel? Mr. Begin once said that the entire future of a small nation depends first of all on the credibility of its word. He apparently has disregarded his own counsel. Moreover, if the goal is continued rule over the West Bank—that is, no agreement, no peace, and ultimately more wars—the peace treaty with Egypt cannot endure. It is irresponsible to assume that Egypt can stand aside in the event of a war between Israel and other Arab states and not join in the fray. If this is what the future holds, Israel's situation would have been better if it still controlled Sinai.

The Lebanon War

Israel has experienced several wars. All of them brought it benefits, with the exception of the Lebanon War. The principal damage was to Israel's strategic situation.

According to Yaakov Shavit's study of the Revisionist movement, the Lebanon War was a classic example of Irgun's ideology
and mindset. To return to the analogy used earlier, a war is generally perceived as a drastic event, run by "mechanics." This war was
to lead to a peace agreement with Lebanon and end missile attacks
on Kiryat Shmona in northern Galilee; it would also destroy the
PLO and defeat the Syrians, thus changing the political structure
of the Middle East; it finally would erase the trauma of the Yom
Kippur War. The attitude was that these objectives would be
achieved in one decisive stroke.

In fact, however, a war is not an event, but a process; a battle is
an event. On the Israeli side the Lebanon War was typified by a
tendency to wage the war as if it were a battle. This tendency to
"tacticize" strategy is frequently found among officers, Ariel
Sharon and Rafael Eitan, whose most memorable experiences
were incidents at the tactical level, in which daring action in battle
led to gains and victory. On the strategic level, however, a single
battle is not conclusive; even if the enemy is defeated he can
recover, reinforce his contingents, and continue to fight, thereby
robbing the victory of significance. Thus tactical gain in a battle
does not necessarily mean gain in a war.

The "tacticization" of strategy on Israel's side was conspicuous
throughout the Lebanon War. It was likewise apparent in the Israeli conception that defeating the PLO and Syrians in battle
would enable Israel to win the war and dictate a new order in
Lebanon—tantamount to changing the face of the Middle East and
the conditions of the Arab-Israeli conflict. At the tactical level it is
unnecessary to conquer the enemy's entire territory; it is enough
to dominate a wide area from a number of strategic strong points.
But this tactical approach does not work on the political level.
Occupying one-third of Lebanon was not enough to impose a new
order in all of its territory. That required the conquest of every
inch of Lebanese territory and holding on to it for a long while,
until the new order took root.

The tacticization of strategy has affinities to the perception of
war as a competition between two powers. A war becomes a sort
of scale; each side places its forces on its pan until one outweighs
the other and that side wins. The image is appropriate for a battle,
but not for a war. In a war, the larger fighting force does not always
emerge victorious. Historically the power at the disposal of colonial peoples was immeasurably smaller than that available to the
colonial powers; nevertheless, the latter were compelled sooner or
later to withdraw. Historical and political factors influence the

result of contests no less than military ones. In the Lebanon War, Israel's tactical perception of war led to the simplistic error that an unprecedented concentration of forces would guarantee victory. Its outcome demonstrates that it is historical circumstances, rather than military factors, that more often determine the final outcome. The Lebanon War was guided by a more grandiose political conception than any other Israeli war, but historical factors ignored by Israel's leaders frustrated its military gains.

As Clausewitz explained in his treatise *On War,* "No one starts a war—or rather, no one in his senses ought to do so—without first being clear in his mind what he intends to achieve by that war and how he intends to conduct it. The former is its political purpose, and the latter its operational objective." The idea here is simple: one must first articulate the political gains to be achieved by the war, that is, the intended outcome. These are the goals of the war. They are translated into military objectives *within* the war. The Israeli planners of the Lebanon War had a number of goals in mind: expelling the PLO from Lebanon; expelling the Syrians from Lebanon; and imposing a new political order on Lebanon that would lead to a peace treaty with Israel. There have been attempts to deny that the planners envisioned such far-reaching goals, but the documentation exists that they did. The incompatibility between the war's political goals and military objectives is striking. True, the military objectives were not achieved; but nothing would have been different even if they had been, because they were simply inappropriate to the political goals of the war, which were impossibly grandiose and detached from reality. Furthermore, Israeli goals were mutually inconsistent: for example, peace between Israel and Lebanon could only exacerbate the hostility among various Muslim, Druse, and Christian groups and, in turn, destabilize the already precarious regime and prevent it from guaranteeing peace.

Similarly, expelling the Syrians from Lebanon would have necessitated occupying the entire country, since the tactical gain of Syrian withdrawal from districts occupied by Israel could not produce the strategic gain of their expulsion from areas that were not conquered, which remained the majority of the country.

The course of events in the Lebanon War was not inevitable. True, chance and unforeseeable occurrences influenced it, such as the murder of President Bashir Jamayel on September 14, 1982. But this does not mean that had it not been for his assassination the goals of the war would have been achieved. It is almost certain that, given the historical circumstances, he would have had to take the same pro-Syrian policy his brother came to.

Military actions require military knowledge and military understanding, whereas conducting a war on the political level requires no special military knowledge—merely simple, common-sense understanding of the major problems of political significance that will arise. Ben-Gurion said when he accepted the defense portfolio in the Jewish Agency that he did so "not because I am a general proficient in military science, but because decisions in military matters are made not by technical experts but by those whose eyes are wide open and who have common sense. These are attributes every normal person has, to one degree or another." (Ben-Gurion's speech to the Mapai Council, June 19, 1948). It is enough if the political level knows how to ask the right questions and give general guidance. In deciding whether to order the army to advance and confront the Syrians, Israeli statesmen did not need to know the range of the cannon on the Merkava tanks. The problems to which the statesman must give his attention are of the sort that later figure in the criticism of the war by historians: failure in war (not in battle) is related to failure to pay attention to major factors—historical circumstances, not small technical and tactical details. The statesman's task is to anticipate the historian's criticism and intervene to preempt it.

Mr. Begin's apologists explain that he failed because he was improperly advised. This claim is spurious because the entire government and military apparatus exist to inform the prime minister of the alternatives. The problem was inherent in the way of thinking that corresponded to the ethos.

Given the fiasco of the Lebanon War, Mr. Begin's attempt to present himself, at a graduation lecture at the National Defense College, as the innovator of a new theory distinguishing between "wars of choice" and "wars of no choice" is strange indeed. A war of choice is what is generally called a preventive war, and many have dealt with this problem. The war of no choice, as described by Mr. Begin, is a problematic concept because, as Clausewitz explained, even the reaction of the victim of aggression who strikes back against the aggressor involves a decision, a choice. It is always the side that defends itself that starts the war, since without that decision there would be no war, merely an unopposed walkover.

For the conduct of war to be strategically successful there must not be a gap at the interface between the political and military.

Rather, the political leadership must guide the military on major questions, explaining the strategic goals to them as well as how the planned operation fits in with the historical circumstances and with other political and diplomatic activities it is undertaking. It must likewise provide direction as to what should be achieved and what avoided, foreseeing any difficult situations that may be created and how best to handle them.

In the Lebanon War, the scenario was very different. Israel's ministers gave the impression that they were merely rubber-stamping a decision that had been made for them without guidance or comment on their part, as if they had no choice. But the political echelon, which in Israel is the entire cabinet and not just the minister of defense, cannot content themselves with encouraging words. Both before and during the hostilities they must continue to think about the political significance of military events and issue commands in accordance with the changing political considerations. Yet, as published reports make clear, in the Lebanon War the functioning of the political leadership was decidedly passive and remiss. One could say that the fiasco of that war was arranged at the cabinet table.

The Lebanon War, as I have said, was conducted as a campaign, not as a war. Sharon, the minister of defense, served as the supreme chief of staff, operating from the forward command posts. When the supreme command focuses on the tactical level instead of the strategic, tactical operations also suffer.

Errors and deceptions. A number of spurious claims have been put forward in Israel with regard to the fiasco of the Lebanon War:

1. *"Our failure to crush the Syrians robbed us of victory."* Some contend that the Syrians could have been dealt a massive defeat; had this been done, the outcome of the war would have been favorable to Israel. Such a development was prevented by criticism of the war on the home front and American hesitancy. This argument transfers responsibility for the failure to the opposition, such as the Peace Now movement. But suppose that Israel had routed the Syrians and forced them to withdraw from Lebanon. Ultimately nothing would have been different, since Israeli forces would have had to remain entrenched along the Syrian border indefinitely to keep the Syrians from returning to their former positions. Significantly, a Soviet diplomat, openly hostile to Israel, expressed the hope that the Israelis would enter Damascus. The conquest of Damascus, seemingly the greatest military triumph Israel could

have over Syria, would have been a pyrrhic victory. The Syrian government would have retreated to Aleppo in the north and continued to direct the struggle from there by means of popular resistance and terror. Israel would have suffered the inevitable heavy losses of urban fighting, and in the end would have had to pull back without achieving anything. An Israeli advance into Damascus would have been like Napoleon's conquest of Moscow. Furthermore, there would undoubtedly have been a strong Soviet reaction.

The Lebanon War revealed an ongoing Israeli limitation: no matter how complete Israeli military triumph, the strategic results will prove to be limited. Ben-Gurion understood this when he said that Israel could not solve its problems once and for all by war. But this view is in stark contradiction to the spirit of the Jabotinsky-Begin ethos. It is no wonder that those who adhere to it cannot accept that the great event is of no avail. Begin's proclamations of the prospective grand achievements of the Lebanon War indicate his inability to understand this.

2. *"The problem was the lack of consensus."* This claim explains Israel's inability to achieve the goals of the war by the absence of a consensus in the army and among the general public. Even some of those who supported the war have been critical of the failure to ensure such a consensus in advance, as if this was an unwitting technical error. Can one create a consensus under all circumstances? Is the public at large unable to think for itself?

This argument is ultimately directed against those who opposed the war, who were described as "defeatists" and "backstabbers." My recollection is that most of the criticism of the war originated in the army, whence it spilled over into the general public. Military men recognized the problems of the war before they were understood on the home front.

Consensus makes it possible to exploit a nation's might to the full, but it does not create this might. There was a broad pro-war consensus in Germany and Japan during the Second World War, but nevertheless the Axis Powers were defeated. A consensus cannot change the fundamental balance of power or the basic constraints of the battlefield and the political situation. The results of the Lebanon War were determined by these basic conditions, not by a lack of Israeli public support.

The importance attributed to consensus seems to have deep roots in Jewish culture. The Jewish sages of old said that Jerusalem fell to the Romans in 70 C.E. because of "senseless hatred," and this saying has become part of the Jewish folk ethic. The sages' moral reproof of internecine squabbling was justified, but it should not be taken as a serious explanation for the failure of the Great Revolt. Had the Jews been united, Jerusalem might have held out six months instead of four.

A closely related mistake attributes great importance to will power as a factor in attaining victory. This approach is called "voluntarism," and is found in abundance in the Jabotinsky-Begin ethos, although not only in it: witness the famous remark made by Theodor Herzl that inspired much of the Zionist spirit: "If you will it it is no dream." In this remark, though, the sublime meets the stupid, as we may will all we can to no effect. The defeat of the Germans and Japanese was hardly caused by a failure of will. Both sides want to win a war, but wars are not decided merely by the stronger will.

Some Israelis claim that the Arabs' quantitative advantage is countered by Israel's will power and dedication. It is easy to make this mistake from looking at past wars. But Israelis hold no monopoly on will and faith; the Arabs possess these traits as well. The conflict with Israel has compelled them to increase their forces quantitatively, but it has also inspired them to strengthen their devotion to the struggle.

The supreme danger in the assumption that only the lack of consensus deprived Israel of victory in Lebanon lies in its encouraging the delusion that there was a real possibility of winning. A consensus is useful when it supports a good policy and harmful when it supports a bad one. In the latter case it is precisely a lack of consensus that is apt to improve the situation. A consensus supporting an ill-conceived policy is likely to lead to steadfast popular attachment to it, such as happened on both sides in World War I, prolonging the useless bloodshed and agony. The mistake in launching the Lebanon War was that there never was any possibility of Israeli victory.

3. *"The problem was 'security arrangements' and the delay in withdrawing."* Even when it became clear that the Lebanon War had failed and that Israel would have to withdraw, the move was delayed for more than two years by the assertion that "we cannot withdraw without adequate security arrangements." In the meantime, Israel sank deeper into the morass of Lebanon, continued to suffer heavy losses, and antagonized ever larger sections of the

Lebanese population. The mistake of remaining in Lebanon even after Ariel Sharon was removed from the ministry of defense was no less critical than that of launching the war in the first place. The withdrawal was an admission that the war had been a failure, so it should not surprise us that those who instigated it tried to delay it. Perhaps they were praying that some miracle would change the parameters of the problem.

Israel leaders spoke repeatedly of "security arrangements," but what security arrangements could defend along the northern border and with whom should they have been made? With the Lebanese authorities, who had so little control over the anti-Israeli factions? An Israel-Lebanon agreement was precisely what the Syrians had stubbornly worked to prevent. In some respects Israel had done their work for them, because the war it launched had served to strengthen the Syrian influence in Lebanon. It therefore did not require great effort by the Syrians to prevent the Israelis from arriving at security arrangements with the Lebanese government.

4. *The wages of deception.* The Lebanon War was accompanied by lies and deceit at the highest political levels. Defense Minister Sharon has been repeatedly accused of having misled Begin and the cabinet. This explanation was disseminated not by the opposition but by sources within the Likud who are close to Mr. Begin. The accuracy of official announcements by Israel's military spokesmen, which had always been considered trustworthy, now became suspect. The Israeli Army is a people's army, and the home front soon became aware that army and government communiqués contradicted what the public learned from first-hand observers.

To provide a justification for the war the Likud government also lied to the public by grossly exaggerating the terrorist acts conducted from Lebanon. Responding to a question in the Knesset, Defense Minister Rabin said that during the eleven months of the cease-fire that preceded the war the northern settlements were attacked only twice, and that during this period Israel had suffered a total of two killed and six wounded from terrorist attacks. Moreover these attacks were preceded by Israeli air force strikes in response to the planting of a bomb on a bus and the attack on the Israeli ambassador in London, Shlomo Argov. It was distortion at the highest political level to present terrorism as Israel's chief problem, when the major threats are in fact the demographic balance and the menace of war. Even the official pretext for the war, the attack on Ambassador Argov, was at bottom a lie, since it was not carried out by the PLO, but by the secessionist faction of Abu Nidal that had also assassinated PLO leaders.

Nor could the war destroy the "terrorist infrastructure," as its proponents claimed. Terrorism's greatest advantage is that it needs no infrastructure. Terrorists require only a few weapons; even knives will do. This lesson should have been evident to the Likud from their own experience as an underground force with a minuscule number of weapons. The PLO sought to convert its forces into a conventional army and deployed its units in the military structure of battalions and brigades. It might have been possible to strike at this deployment, but not at the PLO's capacity to launch terrorist attacks. The same applies to statements about deterring terrorism. One can deter an organization whose agents it can send out or restrain at will, but given the extent to which PLO groups are dispersed and autonomous and the fact that many terrorist acts result from local and individual initiatives, no threat can have a significant impact. Announcements by organizations that they were responsible for some attack or other frequently proved to be empty boasts.

Terrorism is grist for the demagogue's mill, the perfect topic for inciting public opinion, arousing popular fury, acquiring popularity. It is all too easy to harp on motifs like "the right of Israelis to live in peace," "we must use strong-arm tactics against terrorism," and so on. As I have already said, the problem is that there is no quick fix for terrorism; no military operation can put an end to it.

Israel should certainly strike at terrorists whenever and wherever possible—but on the condition that such strikes are effective. The task of hurting terrorists, whether by preemptive strikes or by reprisal raids, is not at all simple. The vast experience that Israel has accumulated in this field since the reprisal raids of the 1950s seems to have been ignored. While the simplest course seems to be to send planes on bombing raids, this is not always the most effective method. Destroying buildings used by terrorist organizations in Lebanon generally has little real impact on their operations. Very few terrorists are killed and casualties are not a serious loss, because the organizations do not lack manpower. Indeed, the way in which the air force has been employed in Lebanon gives the impression that the missions were intended to display the government's will to the Israeli public rather than to achieve some real goal.

It is true that Begin's principal motive in launching the war was his fear of the momentum of the peace process—that he might yet be called upon to honor his signature to the Camp David Accords and withdraw from the territories. Calling the Lebanon War "The War for the Peace of Galilee" is more than a misnomer. It would have been more honest to call it "The War to Safeguard the Occupation of the West Bank."

There is an evasion of responsibility in the claim by Likud members that if Israel had known then what it knows today it would not have started the Lebanon War. This transfers the onus from the political leadership to an echelon that can always be blamed—military intelligence. New developments always make us aware of aspects we did not perceive before; we always understand more on the morning after. A large quantity of information was placed before the leaders, but they did not pay attention to it. No information drove them to war or could have held them back, because their enthusiasm for battle, based on their magical faith in the single world-changing event, dominated their thinking.

5. *"Criticism is unfair as it is based on hindsight."* This argument implies denial of the right of criticism, as all public criticism is always retrospective. Historians do not anticipate the events they chronicle; but no one would disqualify their critical judgments for this reason. Are we forbidden to criticize government decisions because we do so after they are taken?

6. *"It wasn't Begin's fault."* In view of the fiasco of the Lebanon War, many of Begin's apologists, such as Arye Naor, claim that he was led astray. Is this possible? The plan that underlay the war was presented to him and the other ministers at his house on September 20, 1981, and Begin himself asked them to approve it. He knew what Sharon's intention was. How can a prime minister be deceived on so large a matter as the goals and course of war? These are not insignificant technical details. Moreover, we know that Begin did not have confidence in his defense minister; he even said that Sharon might station tanks in front of the prime minister's office. Begin's intimates, facing a difficult dilemma, prefer to present him as if he was misled by Sharon, even if this necessarily diminishes his stature as a prime minister. The question remains: Why didn't he oppose Sharon? If Sharon was the cause of the disaster, how could Begin let him continue as defense minister? To me it seems that Sharon simply knew what Begin wanted in his heart of hearts; as the Talmud puts it: "A person proceeds on the path he wishes to be led."

The results of the Lebanese War. According to Clausewitz, in strategy there is no such thing as victory. The result of a war is assessed according to whether it achieved the goals for which it was launched, or whether it improved the situation of its initiator. Victory or defeat on the battlefield may be irrelevant. The United States was not beaten on the ground in Vietnam, but all the same it lost the war. Since the Lebanon War worsened rather than improved Israel's position, it was an Israeli defeat. Admitting this may hurt, but ignoring it is even more perilous.

Syria is Israel's bitterest enemy, and it is certainly not in the Israeli interest to strengthen it. Yet the Lebanon War strengthened Syria and increased its influence in Lebanon. It also taught the Syrians many lessons about the weaknesses of their army and how to improve it. The Soviet Union's commitment to Syria increased, and this too is not in Israel's interest. Furthermore, from the Syrian point of view, Israel's attack was unprovoked. So the war increased Syrian hostility toward Israel, its urge for vengeance, and perhaps its lack of respect for Israel's political skill, as well as its belief that its own goals would yet be achieved.

An agreement was signed between Israel and Lebanon on April 17, 1983. One may well wonder at the value of an agreement with Lebanon to which Syria, the major force in that country, was not a party. Israel made its withdrawal from Lebanon conditional on a Syrian withdrawal, but without asking the Syrians what they thought about the matter. Why should the Syrians comply with an agreement from which they were excluded? It is hardly surprising that they ignored it and made fools of the Israelis and Americans.

Whether Israel's deterrent capability declined remains in dispute. In proving Israel's ability to choose the military option and to strike deep inside an Arab state, and even to occupy its capital, the war certainly reinforced the Arabs' fear of Israel. On the other hand, some Arabs believe that Israel's experience in the Lebanon War is likely to deter it from aggressive action in the future, or at least make it more cautious about going to war. In Arab calculations the Lebanon War is perceived as having increased Israel's unwillingness to act, thereby also impairing its ability to deter the Arabs. The Lebanon War detracted from Israel's military status, although I suspect that the Arabs have more respect for the Israeli military machine than for the strategic thinking of its military and political leadership.

The Lebanon War did wipe out the PLO's deployment on Israel's northern border. It did not put an end to terrorism or to the threat of Katyusha missile attacks on Israeli settlements. Begin's proclamation, "no more Katyushas," resounds as an empty boast. The war severely damaged the PLO's institutional infrastructure in Lebanon. This was a real achievement for Israel, but terrorist activities can be directed from other places as well, even from within Israeli territory. On the other hand, the war also provoked Shi'ite terrorism, which, if it grows, is likely to be much worse than the PLO version. The war inflamed the Palestinian desire to avenge the ravages of war on them and their families. It increased the pressure of Palestinian refugees because many who had made their permanent homes in Lebanon were uprooted. Israeli interests were at cross-purposes to those of their supposed allies, the Lebanese Christians. The Christians wanted to expel the Palestinians from their midst, and would have been very happy to send them all to Israel.

To the extent that the goal of the war was the destruction of PLO artillery emplacements, it was a response to a real problem. But countries should not go to war to escape an intolerable situation or even because their cause is just, unless there is a reasonable chance of a favorable outcome. Many Israelis do not understand this and argue: "We had no choice but to go to war," and ignore the truth that wars should not be started for expressivist reasons—anger, ambition, national pride, a show of decisiveness, or the like—but only for instrumental reasons: from calculations of benefit. What is the point of waging a war for even a just cause if one will be worse off as a result? Sometimes it is better to live with an injury than to take too drastic measures to remedy it.

Whatever the cause of the Lebanon War, it became clear that the destruction of the PLO artillery would not be complete until its command center and major concentration in Beirut had also been hit. To ensure that the PLO would not return to its bases in Southern Lebanon, it was necessary to set up a new regime in Lebanon, and this was possible only if the Syrians were defeated. In other words, the progress of the war was subject to a domino theory: before making a move, Israel should have given more thought to where the developments might lead, how war aims might get out of hand, and whether the process being initiated might ultimately do more harm than good.

The Lebanon War is ample illustration that Israel is not merely the victim of others, as Mr. Begin claimed, but is also the victim of its own illusions, and more particularly of the leaders it has chosen for itself. There are situations for which there is no military solution. A historical example of this is the situation of Germany before the First World War. Bismarck understood the bind in which Germany would find itself if forced to fight simultaneously on two fronts—against both Russia and France—and therefore attempted to apply political means to prevent a military alliance between them. The Lebanon War is an example of the problems that the continuation of the Arab-Israeli conflict can cause; because there is no military means for dealing with them, a solution must be found on the political level.

Economic Deterioration

It is no accident that Revisionist thinking in the field of economics was very limited. The movement focused on political events, but a national economy and society cannot be achieved through events; they must be built up by careful attention to infrastructure. Revisionism always invested more resources and effort in gaining populist support than in building infrastructure. It never encouraged the sacrifice of narrow, individual interests and personal pleasure in the interests of the welfare of society as a whole. This failure to set national challenges brought Israeli motivation and initiative to an unprecedented low.

As prime minister, Mr. Begin championed a populist belief in "giving the people a good life" *(lehetiv im ha'am)*. On the face of it this is an admirable goal, but in practice it meant profligate consumption of national resources. Stock-exchange fever now infected wide circles of the population, who took Begin's slogan as moral justification for easy riches; VCRs became commonplace in a society where only recently phonographs had been a luxury. The problem was that "giving the people a good life" was a short-term objective aimed at gaining popular support for the Likud, and was implemented without any regard for the consequences in the intermediate and long term as national resources dwindled and inflation soared.

In modern parlance, "rational" has inherited the significance of "good," but a rational choice from the short-term perspective of individuals is not necessarily identical with the collective good. For example, people who want to ensure that their money retains its value may attempt to smuggle foreign currency abroad, but the state suffers as a result. The issue of individual versus collective welfare is central to all political and social thought. A leadership that pretends to represent the "general will" or the "public interest" may well be on its way to an authoritarian or totalitarian regime that claims to know what is good for everyone and so need not hold free elections to discover what public opinion is. On the other hand, deferring to what the people want is apt to lead to populism: adopting policies that will win the public's approval even if in the long term they will work to its detriment; exploitation of the impulses and yearnings of the masses, and demagogic manipulation of public opinion. A democratic system requires mature thinking to identify the public interest. The greatness of democratic leaders is their ability to persuade citizens to choose what is good for the community as a whole—that is, to place the public interest ahead of their private interests.

The tension between the individual and the collective welfare is fundamental to human life and may manifest itself in political corruption. More serious than the petty financial corruption of office holders is corruption in the name of an ideology, since the latter is "justified" as the means to attain a hallowed end and becomes institutionalized. It is no secret that the attempts of zealous champions of Greater Israel to acquire land on the West Bank soon developed into unscrupulous profiteering.

Economic policy is based on concepts that are meta-economic and meta-ideological. The decline of the Israeli economy during the Likud government stems from populist and grandiose policies. Of course phenomena like inflation, corruption, election economics, and demagoguery existed in previous governments as well. But they were accompanied by demands, if not always sincere, that Israelis keep the collective welfare before their eyes, even if only as an ideal, and restrain their appetite for personal gains. Egoism was bidden to bow before civic virtue. Under the Likud all such barriers were breached and the disposition to seek easy gains spread rapidly. Such a fundamental change will not easily be reversed.

The new tendency to self-delusion was translated into a grandiose economic policy that squandered resources on misconceived projects, aspired to short-term political and party gains, and plunged the state into a deep crisis. The high cost of the Lebanon War and resultant budget deficit caused further deterioration. What the Likud minister of the treasury called its "correct economics" came to be an oxymoron.

The champions of the "event" mentality are oblivious of the

dangers of squandering the nation's wealth and driving it into debt because the consequent damage is not immediately translated into an event. Moreover, for all their failings and deficiencies, the Labor-led governments had a certain sense of responsibility toward the state and society that many of their members and supporters had worked hard to build. Those who have toiled to accumulate public assets are loath to dissipate them. The Revisionists of Herut had no such commitment. On the contrary, their long period in opposition generated a desire to control the public purse strings in their own way, and perhaps also to engrave their term in office in the public memory as a carefree time. The frame of mind that connects greatness with achievements creates a tendency to husband resources and postpone gratification, whereas a frame of mind for which greatness is a matter of essence or gestures will tend to be more profligate. The nature of a state is reflected in the character of its citizens. An annexationist state produces greedy citizens.

The feeling of national grandiosity spread from the politicians' rostrums to the business world. The ideal of the small entrepreneur making profits from investing his efforts in his own business gave way to an ideal of quick revenues from using borrowed money to make large profits on the stock exchange.

As with the Lebanon War, the Likud has made all sorts of attempts to throw sand in the eyes of the public and explain away its responsibility for the economic mess. As with the security situation, they claim that the failures have their roots in mistakes made long ago. It is true that there was inflation in the past, but it never reached three digits. All governments err, but not to the same degree. Likewise, Likud supporters frequently use the formula "Israel found itself in a crisis"—as if this were the result of anonymous forces or a world-wide recession. But let us not forget: Israel did not "find itself" in a crisis; it got there because of the direction taken by its leaders.

After the havoc wrought by the Likud government, even more competent leaders have found it difficult to rescue the country. It is not easy to wean a people and a country from populist habits.

The Decline of Israel

In recent years Israel has experienced massive decline: a worsening of the public mood, the vulgarization of political thought and language, a degeneration of norms of public conduct, permissiveness in state affairs, demagoguery—the good of the country shunted aside in pursuit of short-term party gains—the domination of mediocrity, the proliferation of falsehoods and rampant deception of the people by their rulers, a magnification of domestic tensions. The responsibility for this decline belongs to a great extent to the Likud government. This is the most serious result of the Likud's misrule, much more serious than either the economic crisis or the Lebanon War.

Renaissance philosophers believed that the success of states—their rise, their flowering, and even the deferment of their decline—was influenced by the spirit of their public: the virtu that beat within them. On the collective level this attribute is translated into a readiness to prefer the common welfare over narrow egoistic interests, into steadfastness, internal unity, resourcefulness, and immunity to corruption. Within the limitation that no human society has ever been perfect and devoid of flaws, Israel used to be a paragon of this virtu. Israel was never perfect, but nevertheless it earned a reputation as a symbol of cultural and social innovation; even its military excellence was attributed to its citizens' public-spiritedness.

Today, however, unethical conduct in public life arouses no surprise in Israel; it has become the normal state of affairs. Brutal criticism of governmental activities in the press makes no stir in the public, as the written word has been greatly devalued, along with everything else. When a responsible newspaper like *Ha'aretz* can open its editorial column with the statement "The fraudulent acts of Ariel Sharon and Menachem Begin dragged the country into the Lebanon War on the basis of a false claim" (May 27, 1985) without a political earthquake's ensuing, the national conscience is clearly deadened, and perhaps dead.

Some veteran Jabotinskyites claim that were Jabotinsky alive everything would be different; he himself, they say, would have come out strongly against Begin. They may be right—but where is the consolation in that?

In the first years of statehood, a conspicuous fact influenced Herut and the positions it could adopt from the political sidelines to which it had been banished: the War of Independence was the triumph of the Haganah, which they had opposed, and of Ben-Gurion, who had extremely harsh things to say about Jabotinsky. It is no coincidence that a large proportion of Herut voters belong to ethnic communities that came to Israel after the War of Independence. They do not understand that Herut and its satellites made little contribution, in thought or deed, to the massive enterprise of establishing the state. Everything that was attained in that period—the absorption of immigrants, the construction of settlements, the establishment of an army, and the establishment of a state apparatus were all made possible by the legacy of Mainstream Zionism.

As Raymond Aron put it, in *History and Policy,* a measure of "moderate Machiavellianism" is imperative in political life, and particularly in confronting large tasks: "In order to save his nation the statesman must sometimes sacrifice his soul." Bismarck would not have been able to unify Germany—a national goal of the first order—without instigating wars by schemes that were at odds with moral standards. De Gaulle concealed his thoughts about Algeria and rode to power on the shoulders of those who demanded that Algeria remain French. Some three and a half years later he betrayed his supporters and granted independence to Algeria. Aron concluded: "I do not believe it is possible to avoid saying that in this event there were elements of Machiavellian policy. I do not denounce it, because I do not know whether France could have extricated herself from this crisis without General de Gaulle, and I am not sure that General de Gaulle could have succeeded in what he did had he refused to be devious."

As long as we stick to absolute standards, judgment becomes simply a matter of black or white. Once we allow that a measure of moderate Machiavellianism—dishonesty, demagoguery, schemes to win favor with the voters, flattering them and soliciting their votes—is a part of political life, then our delineation of the boundary between the tolerable and the intolerable becomes blurred. But, even so, not everything is permitted. One may accept the recourse to populist schemes in order to gain power and even in order to retain the public's allegiance, but still there have to be reasonable limits. My argument is that Mr. Begin and his government went far beyond what reason can allow.

The difficulties inherent in Israel's political situation ought to motivate its leaders to raise the level of national discussion. Only through the course of conducting a searching examination can the public be brought to the awareness and resolution needed to cope with the critical problems. Instead of enabling the alternative outcomes of withdrawal and annexation to be fairly and fully presented, Prime Minister Shamir, like Begin before him, employs demagoguery to warn the public only of the dangers of withdrawal; he glosses over the dangers of annexation. When the national dialogue does not include a full-scale analysis of the advantages and disadvantages of the available options, but focuses instead on the disadvantages and dangers of one option only, the level of discussion becomes dangerously simplistic and emotional. Instead of stimulating a debate on the real issues, Begin and Shamir consciously exploited antagonistic sentiments.

A further manifestation of this trend has been the focusing of attention on Palestinian terrorism, as if this were the main challenge to Israel. Begin spoke incessantly of terrorism, creating the impression that the only enemy was the PLO and the PLO was only a horde of terrorists. Israel's strategic status was thereby inflated because the obstacle facing it was diminished. Annexation also became easier as the adversary was defined as "only a bunch of terrorists." The "terrorization" of the conflict encourages rather than deters terrorism by revealing Israel's sensitivity to it. The emphasis on terrorism also distorts the Israeli view of the Palestinians by presenting them as the perpetrators or encouragers of despicable acts. In this view, the Palestinians do not have a national movement with legitimate goals and grievances; their movement merely expresses a lust for murder. This dehumanization of the Arabs reinforces Israeli self-righteousness and the "terrorization" of the Palestinians negates any possibility of negotiations to resolve the conflict.

Let us briefly review some other examples of the national decline:

Delusions and impotence. When Israel's self-importance is exaggerated beyond proportion, every attack becomes a humiliating blow to the national pride. Israel can stand resolute in the conflict with the Arabs only if Israelis understand that terrorist attacks will occur from time to time, and that these must be seen in a balanced perspective. Fostering expectations of radical and ultimate solutions, in the spirit of the final event—"no more *Katyushas*"—is an invitation to disappointment. The Begin government did not imbue the nation with the strength to stand firm or the vision to control its own destiny. On the contrary, it produced a people ruled by its destiny, a people inclined, after a terrorist attack, to emotional outbursts and immoderate reactions.

When a problem arises to which Herut's leaders have no answer, the frequent response is "We have to confront it." After chanting this magic formula they can continue on their way and ignore the problem. For example, "We have to confront the demographic problem on the West Bank"; but what in fact can we do about it? There is no answer. Problems are not solved, only "confronted."

Moral permissiveness and self-righteousness. The Holocaust must never be forgotten, but it must not be trivialized by being exploited for political gains as Mr. Begin has done. The Jewish people have suffered terribly at the hands of non-Jews, but this suffering cannot today serve as a licence to contravene established norms. In order to strike at a terrorist headquarters located in an apartment block in Beirut, Israeli bombers destroyed the entire building, causing hundreds of casualties. What would Israelis say if a similar thing were done to them?

The Jewish people has traditionally seen itself as a chosen nation, but generally understood this to mean additional obligations, not as permission for immoral behavior. The new moral permissiveness breeds self-righteousness and self-congratulation. But self-righteousness is a main source of national mistakes. Dazzled by its self-righteousness, Israel cannot see the case of the other side. Self-righteousness encourages nations no less than individuals to absolve themselves of every failing and shake off guilt for every mishap. When everyone is guilty except them, the very possibility of self-criticism and self-improvement vanishes.

Self-righteousness leads Israeli spokesmen to explain any criticism of Israeli policy by neutral governments, and even more so by friendly governments, as having been coerced. In the past, "Arab oil" was the magic phrase that provided an infallible explanation of foreign support for the Arabs; but this explanation was correct in only some cases. Moreover, whereas political moves against Israel are explained as motivated by opportunism and narrow self-interest, support for Israel is always seen as a manifestation of conscience and morality.

The greatest damage wrought by Likud rule and Mr. Begin's leadership is the decline of self-criticism in Israel. This poses a greater menace to Israel than any of the other factors.

Incitement and hatred. No Israeli government has ever incited hatred both domestically and abroad, as Mr. Begin and Herut did. Polls show that hatred of the Arabs has risen significantly in Israel. Part of the problem is that hatred directed outward is wont to boomerang and strike internally. Within Israel, factionalism has increased. Political controversies have always existed, but only under Likud rule has there been a conspicuous tendency to describe adversaries as "traitors" or "PLO supporters."

The tension between religious and secular Jews has reached new heights, and the Begin government and Mr. Begin himself cannot be absolved of responsibility for this. This tension, as we shall see, is ominous.

Deceit. Every human being, and especially politicians, lies. But lying in public life became much more frequent under the Likud. There are several possible explanations. First, it is part of the demagogue's style to believe that they have a dispensation to manipulate the public. Second, when leaders who follow unrealistic policies are slapped in the face by reality, they are likely to try to extricate themselves by deception and lies. A policy that fails because it ignores reality is apt to lead to stratagems intended to cover up the failure by false information, as was done often in the Lebanon War.

It is banal to say that politics makes strange bedfellows, but seldom have there been such contradictory ones as Herut, which pretends to represent the poor and downtrodden, and the Liberal party, which represents the high bourgeois. Does not this imminent merger represent the summit of cynicism and deceit?

The Lebanonization of Israel. In the Middle Ages princes and groups frequently waged private wars. One of the characteristics of the modern state is that it reserves for itself a monopoly on warfare and the means of warfare. When segments of the population no longer rely on the state's authority and establish overt and covert military organizations to promote their own political ends, the state begins to crumble. This is what happened in Lebanon. Under Likud rule a similar process has become apparent in Israel. This "Lebanonization" of Israel began when settlers on the West Bank declared that they could no longer depend on the state to impose order on their Arab neighbors and must take matters into their own hands. True, some of the settlers denounced this subversive activity as a matter of principle, but even they supported its practical results. They have also arrogated to themselves the right to distinguish between "legitimate" government policies, which must be obeyed, and "illegitimate" policies, which must be resisted, with violence if necessary. The Lebanon War generated an antipathy in Israel to the factionalism of the Lebanese. However the seeds of Lebanonization are already to be found in Israel, for instance, in pronouncements that, were the Israeli government to decide on withdrawal from the territories, civil war would ensue. Lebanonization is also expressed in the tendency of certain groups to present their demands and rights as absolute, to be fulfilled *in toto,* with no possibility of compromise, just as the various ethnic groups in Lebanon did.

(One outcome of the Uprising is that the settlers now feel a greater dependency on the Israeli army and therefore are less inclined to threaten a civil war.)

The relationship of Israelis to their country. One achievement of the Likud government was a rapprochement between the state and certain groups such as the Morrocan Jews, who, on account of their estrangement from the Labor government, had previously felt alienated from the state itself. At the same time, however, the Likud succeeded in alienating other groups that had previously identified with the state—notably the intellectuals and members of the kibbutzim. It is no accident that emigration from Israel has increased. Paradoxically, it appears that many of the emigrants are Likud voters.

The principal and seemingly only value in Herut's ideology is a militant nationalism. Its nationalism is not an aspiration to improve the Israeli society and is expressed chiefly as hostility toward strangers and domestic foes. This has led to a nihilistic Zionism (formerly an oxymoron): the spirit of national mobilization for the collective welfare is displaced by ethnocentric extremism. The idealism directed at the establishment of a just society gives way to factional selfishness and anomie. These concepts weaken the restraints on what people are ready to do for gain, since the greater the disappointment with the collective, the stronger the inclination to seek personal monetary gains, even at the price of dishonesty and disobedience of the law. A corollary development has been the growing tendency to shirk responsibility, popularly called "the small head phenomenon."

The diminishing status of Zionism. In the past Israelis always scorned non-Zionists as being morally, ideologically, historically, and practically wrong. I suspect that today there are some in Israel who feel that perhaps the non-Zionists were not all that foolish. Articles in the Hebrew press now frequently discuss the failure of Zionism and no longer pass judgment on those who emigrate.

THE LIKUD IN POWER   113

We are facing the painful spectacle of Zionism, once a sacred value, becoming for young people a target of derision. Leaders of the extreme nationalist camp claim that this is the result of the educational failures of their predecessors and refuse to consider how large is their own share of the blame. National ideals will be held in esteem only if they are seen as a vision that can be realized and not as bombastic fantasies.

The Coming Crisis in the Occupied Territories

The greatest crisis of all for Israel has yet to come: the evacuation of the West Bank and the Gaza Strip. Many Israelis are unaware that Israel has already relinquished the right to control these territories in the Camp David Accords. Some argue that the Arab inhabitants of these areas need not be granted Israeli citizenship. But how long can a large population live in the territory of one state and be citizens of another? And what if an Arab majority should come into being west of the Jordan River? These questions are shunted aside by the supporters of the Likud as they indulge in the hope that some event will magically change the parameters of the problem. True, unforeseen events frequently do change things, but what revolutionary event can change demographic trends? Will the Palestinian Arabs stop having children? Will they emigrate en masse? They have nowhere to go. What happened to the Palestinians in Lebanon at the hands of the Syrians, Lebanese Christians, Shi'ites, and Israelis will cause them to think twice about leaving.

Some Israelis forget that the problems of the Jews before the Second World War have changed and that the impoverished Jewish masses of Eastern Europe who needed a new home are no more. Some predict, and perhaps even hope, that the condition of Jews abroad will deteriorate, forcing them to immigrate in their millions. There are no signs to confirm this forecast. No one predicted that the Germans would annihilate the Jews. But the fact that the Holocaust was not foreseen in the past does not mean that another Holocaust can be expected in the future. The major concentrations of Jews live comfortably in the Western countries. Their occupational patterns, many of them being established business owners and professionals, make them less prone to emigrate.

Also many of their children have all but given up their Jewish identity. Finally, we have to remember that in the 1920s and '30s the numbers of Jews and Arabs in Israel were small. Thus, a small Jewish immigration could have a significant effect. Nowadays Jews and Arabs are nearing six million and even an immigration of sixty thousand would only produce a one percent change.

It is simply untrue that the demographic threat is the same whether only the Israeli Arabs are included within the borders of the state or whether the Arabs of the West Bank and Gaza Strip are also included. Demographers estimate that if current trends persist, Israel's Arab minority, today 18 percent of the population, will reach 23 percent in the year 2000. However, within Greater Israel, including the West Bank and Gaza, they are expected to constitute 45 to 50 percent by the year 2000 or shortly thereafter. The natural increase of Israeli Arabs has declined, but on the West Bank and in the Gaza Strip it remains very high. It may yet start to decline, but by then the ratio of Arabs to Jews will be an ineradicable fact. A Jewish minority will not be able to rule over an Arab majority for long.

There are some Israelis who in their hearts pray for a development that will make it possible to expel the Arabs. Rabbi Meir Kahane, leader of the extreme right-wing Kach party, recognizes the demographic threat; to, as he puts it, sit back with arms folded and allow the Arabs to grow and destroy Israel from within is irrational. He adds that he wants to prevent Israel becoming a Jewish State with an Arab majority. From this he derives the idea of expulsion. He hints that he is not alone in thinking this way and repeats his familiar slogan: "I'm only saying what you're thinking."

One suspects that manifest annexationist positions conceal a desire to expel the Arabs. For example, Professor Yuval Ne'eman, of the Tehiya party, says that Israeli citizenship must not be granted to the Arabs in the territories, except for those "who are willing to identify with the Zionist State of Israel, to be examined in Hebrew and Zionism, to do national service, and to pay taxes." Thus "some of the Arab population (350,000–400,000 in Judea, Samaria, and Gaza) who hold refugee documents . . . will have to find themselves a permanent home. . . . This home will not be here, and just as we absorbed Jews from the Arab countries, the Arab countries will have to absorb the refugees" (*The Policy of Sobriety*, 1984, pp. 168–169). What is meant by "will have to find themselves a permanent home"? This can only be outside Israel, of course—

but who will "persuade" them to embark on this course, and how? And what if they refuse?

The case for continued occupation. There are a number of arguments put forward to support Israeli control of the West Bank and Gaza Strip. Let us consider each in turn:

1. *"We have no intention of annexing them: all we want is to ensure they do not fall under Arab sovereignty."* This argument is first of all absurd because it contradicts the established world order, which is based on dividing the planet into sovereign territories. The only exception to this is Antarctica, where sovereignty is suspended. But Antarctica is not the West Bank, and the Arabs will never acquiesce in being deprived of sovereignty; moreover, as their numbers grow and their strength increases they will apply greater pressure, as has become dramatically evident in the recent months of riot, and eventually will receive active support from the Arab countries and political support from the rest of the world. Second, is this claim that no annexation is intended honest? What is the meaning of slogans about "ancestral heritage," "settlement," "you can't annex what already belongs to you"? "We shall not make any territorial concessions" (Shamir). Are these merely rhetoric?

It is true that Israel has not yet dared to assert sovereignty over the West Bank and the Gaza Strip, out of fear of the international reaction to such a step. Nevertheless, this apprehension only proves the weakness of Israel's political claim in the territories.

Likewise, despite the two decades that have passed since 1967, Israeli governments have not dared to change the legal system prevalent in the West Bank, which remains Jordanian. Thus Arabs on the West Bank are tried according to Jordanian law, but Israelis who live there have the right to be judged according to Israeli law. This causes complications, for example, in mixed litigation disputes between West Bank Arabs and Israelis. The settlers, recognizing that the present arrangement is unstable, press for the application of Israeli law for all in the territories. The legal absurdity again demonstrates the untenability of Israel's hold on the territories.

2. *"The West Bank cannot be 'returned' because it did not belong to Jordan."* Some argue that since Jordan's 1950 annexation of the West Bank was recognized only by Great Britain and Pakistan (some say also the United States) there is no need for Israel to

relinquish control. But is Israel's title any stronger? No country has recognized Israel's right of sovereignty over the West Bank, and this applies to the application of Israeli law to Jerusalem as well. Moreover, Israel's signature to the 1949 Armistice Agreement can be taken as de facto recognition of Jordanian control of the West Bank. If Jordan's title has lapsed, one can readily argue that sovereign rights have reverted to its Palestinian inhabitants, in accordance with the principle of self-determination.

3. *"Jordan is the Palestinian state."* Some Israelis support Ariel Sharon's proposal to "hand over Jordan to the Palestinians," thereby satisfying the demand for statehood and allowing Israel to hold on to the West Bank. Jordan, however, is Jordanian, and the Palestinians who live there have become increasingly "Jordanized," not the other way round. Many Palestinians express allegiance to Hussein and his dynasty. (Although it is perhaps true that if a Jordanian-Palestinian confederation was created the Palestinians might ultimately stamp their imprint upon it.) Furthermore, giving Jordan to the Palestinians would not eliminate the Palestinian concentration in the Gaza Strip and West Bank, and the demographic time bomb would continue to tick. This argument is harmful as it antagonizes the Jordanians and King Hussein. Latent in this proposal is a recognition that the Palestinians *do* constitute a political entity and have the right to self-determination. However, if Arafat's claim to Jordan is better than King Hussein's, given the number of Palestinians who live in the Hashemite kingdom, should the same principle not be applied to the occupied territories and eventually to Israel proper as the number of its Arab inhabitants increases? Likud leaders like Sharon and Moshe Arens have not recognized the PLO; nevertheless they want to rush into a political transaction with the PLO in a common collusion against the Jordanian regime.

4. *"There is no obligation to return territory conquered in a war of self-defense."* This argument was frequently put forward by Mr. Begin. But, when the Security Council debated Resolution 242, its members knew the rights of a state to defend itself and called for withdrawal nonetheless. International law does permit a state that has been attacked to demand border rectifications in order to ensure that the aggression will not be repeated. Accordingly, Resolution 242 does not require withdrawal to the old borders, but neither does it permit annexation.

5. *"Peace for Peace."* This slogan is ostensibly the resolute counter of Mr. Shamir to the formula of Arab moderates—"peace for the land." Neither side owes anything to the other; all that need be done is to freeze the current situation and confirm the annexation. It seems that the Likud definition of an "Arab moderate" is one who is prepared to hand over the territories and their Arab residents to Israel without protest.

The situation between Israel and the Arabs is not comparable, and no slogan will make it so. There are no Jews living in Jordan; nor will the Arabs of the territories be charmed by the slogan "peace for peace" and resign themselves to Israeli rule. Jordan is not imperiled by a potential Jewish majority. Resolution 242 did not demand a Jordanian withdrawal from Jordan; it did, however, demand Israeli withdrawal.

To the Arabs, the slogan "peace for peace" sounds like a cynical ploy to sanctify the conqueror's appetite for the territories he has conquered, ignoring the will of its inhabitants. Occupation does not acquire moral force because it is an established fact. The Arabs have a counter-slogan—"a just peace." To the extent that Israelis fail to display a sensitivity to the problematic nature of their demand to rule the occupied territories, they are morally bankrupt in Arab eyes.

The Israeli claim that they want a peaceful solution impresses no one except themselves. Throughout history countries have claimed to aim to achieve peace, but wars have erupted because each side had its own image of what peace meant. Countries go to war to attain the peace that will ensue. The problem with this slogan is that it increases Israelis' self-deception and self-righteousness and clouds their view of themselves and of the circumstances of the conflict. Significantly Mr. Begin did not present Sadat with the slogan "Peace for peace" but agreed to follow the principle of "land for peace" and gave Sinai, a territory almost devoid of population, which would have been much easier to annex than the highly populated West Bank and Gaza.

6. *"Autonomy for the inhabitants, not for the land."* Another Israeli suggestion is that the Palestinians living in the West Bank and the Gaza Strip be granted full civil rights but only as individuals: the *people* would be autonomous, not the land, as if people somehow float free on the surface. It is at variance with the world order, which is based on the principle that ownership of territory devolves on those who live there. Furthermore, it contains an innate

contradiction: Jewish settlement activity is based on the assumption of a political connection between human beings and the land on which they live. Does this attachment disappear when the settlements are Arab?

Autonomy is an anachronistic revival of Jabotinsky's idea from the 1930s about granting autonomy to large ethnic minorities within European countries. Autonomy, he thought, would satisfy them, and they would be able to live with the majority in peace and harmony. History has refuted this idea—for example, the Sudeten Germans in Czechoslovakia. Begin attempted to adapt this concept to Israeli circumstances, where its chances of success are even less.

Presumably Mr. Begin intended that his version of autonomy would become a permanent situation, an escape from his concession of the West Bank in the Camp David Accords. But this is a delusion. Autonomy must ultimately become Arab sovereignty.

7. *"We have to explain."* The Herut party has a magic prescription against the world's unwillingness to acquiesce in annexation: we have to explain things to them! It is not the policy that is flawed, but other people's lack of understanding. For every political failure, for every rejection of the Israeli position, even by the Americans, the answer is always the same—"we have to explain it to them," as though the other side's powers of comprehension are deficient. Once enlightened, they will accept Israel's view, and the problem will vanish.

This approach emphasizes public relations: "We have to explain things to the gentiles"; "we have to tell Jews to come and live in Israel"; "we have to conduct an information campaign"; "we have to make an effort to educate them"; and so forth. The *content* of the message to be thus conveyed is a secondary detail. The problem is presented as one of salesmanship, irrespective of the nature of the commodity for sale or whether there is anyone interested in buying it.

8. *"Settlement activity is beneficial, because that is what forces Jordan to want an agreement."* This is a specious argument meant for the outside world. Settlements are a ploy intended to pressure Jordan to begin negotiations with Israel; without the settlements and the threat of annexation Hussein would have no interest in reaching an agreement. But is this truly the goal of settlement? Are the settlers aware that Likud propagandists are playing with their fate? Are Jews settling on the West Bank only in order to promote negotiations that will put an end to Israeli rule in the territories

and perhaps to the settlements themselves? And if the ploy proves ineffective and Jordan does not come to the negotiating table, will settlement activity be terminated?

9. *"Settlement is a major national task, in the present as in the past."* Here the assertion is that history proves that the achievements of Zionism resulted from the settlements it established. There is historical irony in this, since in the past the Revisionist movement attributed little value to settlement activity, even derided it. Yet in the words of the Psalmist, the stone rejected by the builders has suddenly become the cornerstone.

In the past, settlements had political importance as a means to expand the Jewish foothold in the land; but at this point in history, are we interested in more territory if this means facilitating an Arab majority in the country?

An opposite argument also based on analogy is the fact that until 1967 Israel managed within the old borders proves that those borders were good. This argument is not persuasive either.

10. *"The demographic problem is not a threat today."* This argument implies that the demographic problem *could* be a threat. But if so, when? When the Arabs are a majority or nearly so? A threat is a threat when one can still do something to ward it off; after that it is a reality. The attitude of Herut and its allies to the demographic threat is the height of irresponsibility. In closing their eyes to reality they hope to evade it. The "event" mentality dismisses the importance of the harmful process. The Likud and Herut have no solution to Israel's foremost problem.

11. *"Annexation is a security imperative."* Some assert that Israel cannot be defended without the West Bank. But as Brigadier General (res.) Aryeh Shalev pointed out in *The Defense Line in Judaea and Samaria,* time is not working in Israel's favor, so from the Israeli perspective it is harmful to defer dealing with this problem in anticipation of more favorable political and military conditions than those existing today. Moreover, even if it is possible politically to maintain the status quo, it perpetuates the risk of further wars that will not necessarily improve political conditions. An attempt to perpetuate Israeli rule on the West Bank is liable to provoke the Arab countries to war, undermine the Israeli-Egyptian peace, and even drive Egypt back into the enemy camp. Shalev believes that a Jewish presence on the West Bank has a security value; but to the extent that settlements imply annexation, the security gain is ne-

gated by the fact that the risk of war grows almost to the point of certainty.

Shalev examines the contribution of kibbutzim and moshavim in war. During the War of Independence no settlement, except for Nirim, a kibbutz near the Egyptian front, withstood the onslaught of a regular Arab army without the aid of the Israeli army. Even with regard to day-to-day security, settlements are more of a liability than an asset because they require forces to guard them and because they are a provocation to the Arab population. The settlements increase rather than decrease the need for Israeli military efforts. This applies to the war on terrorism as well. Their very presence magnifies the incentive for terrorism, and actually facilitates terrorist acts because their proximity to centers of Arab population makes them easy targets.

During the riots of 1987–88 Minister of Defense I. Rabin called the settlements a "burden." If they had not existed, it would have been much easier for the Israeli Defense Force to control the occupied territories. For example, if a child from a settlement needs medical treatment outside of it, a military convoy may have to accompany him.

The settlements are not important in their contribution as observation posts against Arab invasion. Sophisticated intelligence-gathering methods are increasingly able to provide Israel with warning of an Arab invasion long before settlements could sound the alarm. The ability of new military intelligence technology to observe and target far beyond the horizons and of tactical missiles to destroy these targets have much improved Israel's ability to defend itself once the occupied territories are relinquished. This is true even if the same technologies are used by the attacker's forces.

12. *"An iron wall."* Herut asserts that Israel must remain steadfast on the present borders. Just as the Arabs acquiesced in the armistice lines and have virtually given up the demand that Israel return to the 1947 partition plan, ultimately they will accept the boundaries created in 1967. The contest is a war of attrition in which Arabs will be worn down first. This argument shows how unaware Israelis are of the extent to which Arabs are convinced that historical justice is on their side—and of their consequent resolve to pursue the conflict.

The idea of standing fast reflects Jabotinsky's position in his essay "The Iron Wall," where he argued that the Arabs must be countered inflexibly until they come to terms with the existence of the Jewish state. But what if the Arabs, too, erect an iron wall? The Jews have no monopoly on this device. This error is typical of one-directional thinking, which ignores the possibility that the other side is just as determined. The analogy with the armistice lines is misconceived. The international community accepted the armistice lines, and this agreement influenced the Arabs. But no political power in the world recognizes the boundaries created by the Six Day War. Any expectation that the Arabs will accept these borders is a delusion. Furthermore, the Arabs of the West Bank and the Gaza Strip will not be abandoned by the Arab states, which eventually will fight for them militarily as well as politically. Demographic problems cannot be solved by the iron-wall mentality.

13. *"Negotiations without prior conditions."* This demand is in itself a prior condition on Israel's part—just as Israel's settlements in the territories, by their very existence, most certainly are. Did Sadat negotiate without prior conditions? True, it would be nice if King Hussein and the PLO were willing to begin negotiations without ado, but they have good reason to believe that Israel's demands would be unnegotiable.

Likud spokesmen rebuke the moderates who try to formulate a negotiating position by insisting that Israel should not disclose its demands and concessions. To do so, they say, is to betray the national cause by giving up "bargaining chips." The demagogues of the Likud act as if only they understand the craft of bargaining, which requires one to be firm and persistent. It is as though diplomatic negotiations are similar to those in a Levantine marketplace. In the end, though, their approach is intended to throw dust in the eyes. Diplomatic negotiations usually follow after the parties have agreed on the principles that will guide them and after they have declared their positions. Furthermore, are we to conclude that the Likud position on the occupied territories is only so many bargaining chips? Do the settlers know that? Refusal to declare one's positions is not a productive way of preparing for negotiation but of forestalling it.

14. *"There is no one to talk to."* Israel has long claimed that there is no one on the Arab side to negotiate with. But while at first sight this seems valid, it immediately raises the question of what would happen if there *was* someone to talk to? Would Israel give up Greater Israel and the historical and religious claims it makes? Is the absence of another party to negotiations justification for taking

positions that would put off such a side and make an agreement impossible? The lack of a negotiating partner is not a *reason* for annexation, merely a pretext. The merest hint that negotiations might be possible causes panic among Herut and its allies. They know that a peace accord is not possible if the present situation is frozen and no concessions are offered. Thus any sign of moderation on the Arab side is depressing, while the frequent manifestations of Arab extremism are seen as a heaven-sent blessing that proves the point. But, while Arab extremism makes Israeli propaganda efforts abroad easier, this is a marginal consideration. The main point is that any increase in Arab extremism also increases the number of Israeli casualties in the short term, and in the long term reduces the chances of resolving the conflict and achieving peace.

An Israeli position that exploits Arab extremism tends to encourage it, because by its actions and slogans it provides the Arabs with pretexts and justification for adopting extreme measures. The extremists in both camps are *de facto* allies, and mutually reinforce each other. In denying the possibility that the Arabs may have partial or limited goals, Israel is propelling them to the absolute position that demands the entire country. Furthermore, why should Palestinians moderate their position if the messages they get from Israel leaders are that, whatever they do, Israel is not going to make any territorial concessions? The extremism on both sides blocks the way to a settlement.

15. *"Conceding the territories will not satisfy the Arabs."* The radicalization of the Arab world will not change, it is asserted, and every Israeli concession will only generate fresh Arab demands for territory; they will not be satisfied with Nablus, but will demand Jaffa and Haifa as well. This argument has some truth to it; I have no illusions about Arab ambitions. But one must also consider that any agreement reached will create parties with a vested interest in maintaining it. As described in the second chapter, there are Arabs in the neighboring countries as well as many Palestinians who are haunted by the nightmare of an endless struggle and the vision of recurrent, destructive wars. The fear of the inferno that has already begun to smolder as the conflict continues is shared by many thinking people on both sides. The radicalization of the Arab world is not inevitable; the conflict itself encourages it. Israel will not disarm after signing a peace agreement. Moreover, the prospect that the Arabs might exploit Israeli concessions and continue the struggle from a more advantageous position must be compared with what is likely to happen if there is no agreement. Is the

vision of an Israel with an Arab majority more comforting? On the other hand, an effort to establish measures in a peace settlement that would prevent a renewal of the conflict is likely to win support from the international community.

What will satisfy all but the most extremist Palestinians is a peaceful life. In the course of pursuing their livelihoods, interests, of raising their children, and engaging in all of the other activities that give a life its meaning, the Palestinians will deepen their stake in the settlement. Moreover, many will continue to work in Israel, and trade relationship between Israel and the Palestinian State will further cement the adjustment. So, too, will tourism become an important source of revenue for the new state as it has been for Israel and, as Israel has already learned from the Uprising, tourism depends upon domestic tranquillity.

16. *"There must be a middle ground between annexation and withdrawal."* Herut leaders and others, in order to keep their position plausible, formulate solutions that evade the realities. "We shall keep control of the territories but we do not want to rule the residents." How? "The Palestinians will live here but exercise their rights in Jordan." Is such an arrangement possible? Or again, "Other alternatives besides annexation or withdrawal may emerge in the foreseeable future." But no such alternative has been found after years of searching for one. All of these slogans ignore the reality that a settlement cannot be dictated by Israel.

When the Zionist enterprise was in its infancy, Palestine was underpopulated, and it was generally not difficult to find uninhabited areas for Jewish settlement. Land could be purchased because Palestinian national awareness had not yet crystallized, and organized Arab opposition to land sales to the Jews was weak. Israel's War of Independence led to an exodus of Arabs to the West Bank and Gaza Strip, which became extremely overcrowded. Conditions have changed completely, and no analogy can be drawn from the situation in the past. The establishment of agricultural settlements in the territories occupied in 1967 is difficult because there is little cultivatable land that is not utilized by the local population. The claim that public land can be expropriated is also problematic, since Israel has not asserted sovereignty over the territories, and without sovereignty it is not the proprietor of these areas.

For Herut the Israeli claim to the occupied territories is first and foremost ideological, a direct continuation of the basic position of the Revisionists, which demanded both banks of the Jordan. As we have seen, the security argument is no more than auxiliary; the fear of the threat to Israel's existence is genuine, but it is not the main issue. In the anthem Jabotinsky composed for his movement he wrote: "The Jordan has two banks—one is ours, so is the other. . . . Let my treacherous right hand forget its cunning if I forget thee, left bank of the Jordan." Despite Jabotinsky's rousing proclamation and the logic of the "iron wall," the Revisionist movement swallowed the bitter pill of giving up Transjordan—the East Bank. If the West Bank were to be abandoned what would then remain of the Jabotinsky ideology? This could be a mortal blow to the Revisionist movement and the Jabotinsky-Begin ethos.

In order to prevent the nightmare that a political settlement would wreak on the Herut ideology, its leaders and allies seek to "establish facts" that will make withdrawal and compromise impossible, by linking the Israeli hold on the territories to the very existence of the state. If withdrawing from the territories would leave Israel in an untenable situation, Israel will refuse to withdraw. Nonwithdrawal will become an existential imperative for it. Moreover, if Israelis, foreign governments, and world public opinion discover that the price of withdrawal is Israel's destruction, the result will be twofold. First, Israelis will mobilize en masse in a refusal to withdraw. Second, Herut leaders cling to the forlorn hope that foreign governments will desist from pressing Israel to withdraw if they understand that such a withdrawal will undermine Israel's existence, and may even prefer to sacrifice the West Bank with its Arab population in order to guarantee Israel's continued existence. In any case, Herut wants to create a situation in which the refutation of its ideology with regard to the territories would be tantamount to "refuting" Israel, thus saving Israel and the ideology at a single stroke.

This discloses a readiness to gamble on Israel's existence. The State of Israel has become a pawn to guarantee that the vacuity of Herut's political line is not exposed, its ideological bankruptcy not revealed.

An Israeli withdrawal from the territories would be a terrible blow to the settlers. Their world would collapse. It is readily comprehensible that there is almost no limit to what they would be prepared to do to prevent this. For them, withdrawal in the wake of a peace treaty is certain spiritual defeat, whereas the calamities that accompany no political settlement of the conflict are merely potential. For them, the Zionist enterprise loses all justification without the territories. Consequently, they identify withdrawal from the territories with the destruction of Israel.

It may be that some members of Herut admit that historical

circumstances made the relinquishing of the East Bank inevitable. With regard to the West Bank, however, they recognize that the chances of its remaining under Israeli control may not be good but argue that the best course is to defer a decision until it is absolutely unavoidable. Such an approach is based on the assumption that postponement will have no effect on the conditions Israel can eventually obtain. But what if every deferral of an accord makes these conditions worse, or even endangers the chance of peace? Is it better for Israel to wait until it is compelled to withdraw and is unable to demand any quid pro quo? Does Herut believe that Israeli rule on the West Bank and Gaza Strip can be perpetuated until the State of Israel has an Arab majority, and that then Israel will give up the territories?

Some of the settlers seek to exploit the hostility of their Arab neighbors as an excuse for severe repressive measures. But increased repression will intensify Arab rebelliousness. The damage to Israel from Arab civil unrest will be much greater than the damages from terrorism. This is already being clearly borne out by the Uprising. The lives of the Arabs cannot be made a hell without Israel's also being sucked into the pit. This is in addition to the harm that such a policy would cause Israel in the international arena. Some Israelis may hope that a repressive regime will lead to the flight of the Arabs from the West Bank, thus solving the demographic problem. This policy, too, is likely to end in catastrophe for Israel. An attempt to expel the Arabs will remedy nothing; it will merely propel the region into an escalating cycle of violence and warfare.

So long as the hope remains that an Israeli agreement to withdraw from the territories could lead to a peace accord, Israel must distinguish between the fate of Herut's policy and the fate of the State of Israel. There is no cause to assume that the two are inextricably linked. Rejecting the Jabotinsky-Begin ethos has become imperative for Israel's survival.

An Evaluation of Menachem Begin

Menachem Begin impressed his personal stamp on Herut, the Likud regime, and its legacy to the extent that one cannot evaluate them apart from the man and his role in the events that have brought Israel to its current position.

Since Begin retired under cloudy circumstances several years ago, no successor has emerged who resembles him in stature, force, and influence. His ostensible successor, Yitzhak Shamir, is a pale shadow of Begin, who obediently follows the Jabotinsky-Begin ethos in general and Begin's policies in particular. In other words, the spirit of Begin still rules Herut and therefore we can best understand present Israeli politics by scrutinizing Begin's legacy.

An evaluation of Begin's activities in the pre-state period must be linked to an assessment of the Irgun and the "Revolt" that he led. Historians may credit his role as leader of the opposition in restraining antidemocratic tendencies among his followers. Menachem Begin, both in the opposition and as prime minister, made an important contribution to the institutionalization of Israeli democracy. His legalistic approach helped strengthen the rule of law in Israel. Historians will note his ability to attract followers and to garner enthusiastic mass support; they will see this as his special talent, but will perhaps also note the dire public consequences.

A first attempt at a conclusive assessment can be found in Teddy Preuss's book *Begin, His Regime,* published in 1984, which has not received the public attention it deserves. The popularity of Begin inevitably provokes comparison with Ben-Gurion. Preuss's verdict was severe:

> Ben-Gurion stood with his face to the future, looked ahead and was ready to pay with earnings from the past. Begin behaved quite the opposite: he stood with his face towards the past, looked backward, and was ready to mortgage the future for it.

The book concludes on this note:

> Ben-Gurion's apocalyptic prophecy, found in a letter he wrote to Moshe Sharett on May 21, 1963, resounds today like a heavenly voice from beyond the mountains of darkness: "I have no doubt that Begin's rule (Mapai is bringing his rule of Israel closer) will lead to the destruction of the state. In any case his rule will turn Israel into a monster." After six and a quarter years of his rule, Ben-Gurion's warning is not far from realization. The peace treaty with Egypt—his one and great accomplishment—was emptied by Begin of all content and squandered through settlement activities and the Lebanon War. With the erasure of this accomplishment from the balance sheet, Prime Minister

Begin's resignation remains the sole service that he performed for his country.

Begin's great tragedy, as a man and as a leader, is that by temperament he was not suited (and here his long period in the opposition may have had its effect) to the role of the energetic "mechanic" for which the ethos designed him. Despite his prestige and his ministers' willingness to accept his every word, he was a weak premier, keeping his ministers in tow rather than leading them. Generally he lacked the strength to reprove them. He had little but scorn for those around him, intimates and Herut activists alike. While in opposition he was not called upon to perform any political function, and had only to react verbally to the deeds of others; his voice was his major instrument. As prime minister, however, he had to show some sort of administrative capacity and aptitude for political planning. Here he did poorly. Populism disposes a leader to demagoguery, and so in some respects makes him the slave of his followers. True, there were also occasions when he rose to the task and took dramatic decisions in accordance with the ethos he professed; we know for example, of the decision to bomb Iraq's nuclear reactor, against the advice of most experts. This was certainly a courageous decision, which as of now seems to have been a success.

How will historians evaluate his resignation and withdrawal from public life when he realized that he had failed in the Lebanon War? Will they see this as the pangs of a stricken conscience, a "sobering up from illusions," as his personal secretary said, a fear of the results that his policy might have? Or was it merely the manifestation of a profound emotional collapse? To paraphrase Jabotinsky's ringing words, having failed to conquer the mountain (Lebanon), did he choose political death, an emotional response when he could no longer bear the burden of his role? In sum, did his collapse have mainly personal significance, or is it symbolic of the entire movement and its ethos?

At a symposium on the National Unity Government held at the Hebrew University of Jerusalem in May, 1985, Professor Shlomo Avineri noted that Begin had become hated throughout the world, despite his having received the Nobel Peace Prize, and that this was the result not so much of his deeds as of his words, for example, his attacks on foreign leaders such as Helmut Schmidt that so delighted his own followers. The hostility of politicians and public opinion toward Begin was translated into criticism of Israel.

Human beings have a tendency to believe, erroneously, that a country always gets the leader it deserves. It is difficult to estimate how far Israel's status in the world declined because of foreign distaste for Begin. The support of foreign governments and world public opinion will be of prime importance for Israel in any future negotiations with the Arabs.

It should be noted that the deterioration of Israel's reputation came during a time of extremely favorable international circumstances. Begin was lucky in the historical developments that occurred during his term of office. The status of the Arab countries declined and rifts appeared among them. The oil weapon, which had formerly held the nations of the world at ransom, lost its potency and oil prices fell. Iraq got itself entangled in a war with Iran and attracted much of the attention and concern of the Arab countries to its war. Saudi Arabia was revealed to be not so much a country as a family afraid of its own shadow, which under the cloak of hesitancy adopts extreme positions. The threat that the Arab countries would attack Israel decreased because of their disunity and lack of preparedness, and the internal strife within the PLO following its defeat in Lebanon. In the West the ideological pendulum swung toward conservatism, which tended to view Begin favorably; and an incomparably pro-Israeli president, who appreciated Begin's fierce anti-communism, took office in the United States.

Begin was aware of the sensitivity of Israeli public opinion to continued American support for Israel. Consequently, he presented every disagreement with the Americans as a tactical dispute or family spat. To prove this he would demonstratively embrace the American ambassador, especially in front of the television cameras. The United States, although opposed to his annexationist policy, did not want to provoke a crisis, and muted its expressions of opposition to the feeble line that "settlements are unhelpful in promoting peace." The United States evidently preferred that Begin, who had signed the peace treaty, remain in office until the withdrawal from Sinai was completed in April, 1982, as a guarantee that its terms would be honored. Many in the American administration believed that Israel would ultimately withdraw from the West Bank in accordance with Resolution 242, but premature emphasis on this demand seemed unnecessary as it might be viewed as an anti-Israeli step that would provoke a furor among American Jews. As Arab positions seemed intransigent and the difficulties of the decisions confronting Israel were recognized, so too the

Americans became more inhibited about taking a clear-cut position.

Occasionally the Americans protested some Israeli action, and even temporarily halted arms shipments in order to express their displeasure. But the Israeli public learned that American opposition or criticism need not be taken seriously, and that in the end the Americans would come around. In Israel the idea gained currency that it was a security asset for the United States, and Begin carefully nurtured this perception. Hints were also dropped that the services Israel provided were so important that the United States had no choice but to support it. This was widely believed in Israel to be the reason for the continuation of American support despite Israel's conduct. The idea was harmful, especially once it took root in the popular mind, for it created an erroneous perception of what Israel can allow itself to do in its relations with the United States, and thus provided indirect support for annexationist and other extreme policies. Begin was increasingly perceived in Israel as knowing how to handle the Americans, which further increased his public support.

The U.S. reluctance to make Israel clearly aware of the inevitable bankruptcy of its policy in the territories will ultimately harm the United States, too. But, as the former American ambassador in Israel Samuel Lewis put it, for a great power a mistake is an episode: for a small state like Israel it is a tragedy. Had the United States called Begin to order over the failure to stand by the obligations following the Camp David Accords or Israeli policy on the West Bank, his emotional collapse might have come earlier and Israel might have been spared much suffering. But, even if the Americans displayed short-sightedness, they certainly do not bear all or even most of the guilt. It may sound as if I hope that the United States will distance itself from Israel; that is not the case. But only a candid public discussion of this issue may prevent such an estrangement.

Begin had some negative influence on Diaspora Jewry's attitude toward Israel, both because of the antipathy his style aroused in the world at large and because of internal developments in Israel as a result of his policies. Most Jews are inclined toward liberalism and are therefore influenced by liberal opinion about Israel; when this becomes more critical, many Jews feel uncomfortable. Israeli populism repels educated Jews in the Western world. As one American acquaintance said to me: "In the past, when I came to the office I was proud to discuss Israel with my colleagues, but

when the topic comes up today I slink off into a corner." This is
a serious development, whose consequences have not yet been
felt, and may be directly attributed to Begin.

Even those American Jews who have reservations about Israel's
policy have usually constrained themselves not to air their criticism, lest it hurt Israel's position and help its adversaries or even
anti-Semites in general. They feel they have a duty to defend Israel
and its policies. Repeating the arguments of Israel's spokesmen,
they themselves become convinced. For many American Jews,
Begin's becoming prime minister was an embarrassing development, but in time the more conservative and even middle-of-the-
road American Jews identified with the strong positions he
adopted. He became the symbol of Jewish toughness and pride,
and initiated a trend that has produced a partial "Herutization" of
American Jewry.

The Abandonment of Herut's Thinking

Those who reject the currents of thought that brought Herut to
power are inclined to justify the ensuing disasters that beset Israel
as the price the people must pay for their errors. This attitude is
too severe: the public cannot be cleared of its liability, but one
must take into account that people may vote for a political concept
without fully identifying with it.

It is most worrisome that, despite the evident failures of Herut
and the Likud, broad segments of the public continue to support
them. Reports of the dismay in Israel over the Uprising and the
repression of it have given way to those of the increasing support
for the Likud line. Should this be seen as moral insensitivity, a
result of the demagoguery that has vulgarized political thinking?
Is it an expression of blind loyalty, or is the failure to demand that
leaders take responsibility for their deeds symptomatic of widespread cynicism. Whatever the reason, many of those who voted
for the Likud are reluctant to blame it for the ensuing disasters.

In the past, the masses greeted Begin as "king of Israel"; now
they have seen the extent to which he lacked the mettle of authority. But admitting that he was unfit for his office means confessing
that they were deceived, that they failed to discern his true nature.
Thus, changing their political affiliation forces them to revise their
mindset, which naturally arouses psychological resistance. The
recognition that Begin and the Likud are to blame for the Lebanon

War is likely to cause bereaved families and friends great pain, as if it were their votes that killed their sons. People are reluctant to accept this, so paradoxically they continue to support the leaders whose decisions led to this disaster. The leaders themselves, having brought this catastrophe upon Israel, astonishingly continue their demagogic appeals and, denying any responsibility for it, press their claim to be entrusted with the reins of government.

The way of thought that guided the Likud government must be abandoned so that Israel can follow policies that do not lead to disaster. This will occur only if it is understood that the failures of recent years have a common cause in the Jabotinsky-Begin ethos. The thrust of criticism must be directed against the way of thought rather than against individuals, and particularly not directed against those who merely followed rather than molded the ethos. To call attention to the continuing and disastrous influence of Revisionist ideology and the Jabotinsky-Begin ethos is an effective weapon in the struggle against them. Despite Begin's assertion that his policies are faithfully derived from the teachings of his master, Herut members do not like to be reminded of their ideological genealogy. They esteem Jabotinsky for his literary skills, but they feel a certain discomfort over history's judgment of his path and ideas.

It is worth noting that Jabotinsky's attitude toward Begin appeared to have been quite equivocal. For example, in a famous incident during the final Revisionist Convention in 1939, Jabotinsky took issue with Begin's speech as so much "chattering," particularly his protégé's plan to liberate Eretz Yisrael in much the same way that Garibaldi had liberated Italy (Book of Betar). And it was Begin who was "the father of the Revolt," though he attributed his program of terrorism to Jabotinsky's inspiration.

It is true that Jabotinsky sensed in the 1930s that the days of Eastern European Jewry were numbered, and called for mass evacuations to Palestine. The idea itself was a good one; its flaw was that it could not be realized, for four reasons: 1. The Jews were not about to pack their bags and leave their homes. 2. The implacable opposition of the British. 3. Enormous logistical difficulties. 4. The likelihood that coping with several million immigrants would have brought the Zionist enterprise tumbling down and led to a mass exodus of Jews from Palestine. Of course these can be dismissed as merely practical problems; one can say that the idea was brilliant and blame the Jewish Agency for the failure to implement it. The fact is that not even Jabotinsky's supporters organized themselves to leave Europe. And when the evacuation of the Holocaust survivors became possible after World War II, the Revisionists played only a minuscule part in it.

Ben Gurion's evaluation of Jabotinsky is to be found in a short volume, *The Wordsmith versus the Pioneers of Action,* written in 1964, at a time when he was terrified by the expectation that Begin and Herut would come to power. Since he was a bitter political antagonist of Jabotinsky, we must take his evaluation with a measure of reserve; but we ought not to dismiss it.

Ben-Gurion summarized the difference between his own and Jabotinsky's school of thought as follows:

> Opposed to this Zionism [of the Labor Movement] stood the demonstrative Zionism of Jabotinsky (and after that of Revisionism that he created), which sees the center of gravity in an external governmental force, in the attitude of governments, in the position of the Mandatory government—something external to the Jewish people. This is an "easy" Zionism that requires only an appropriate and convenient political regime on the part of the British for everything to work out of itself; and for this reason, its demands are directed outwards, at others. . . . In every deed and event . . . the basic difference between these two conceptions of Zionism manifests itself. The pioneering Labor movement saw and sees the center of gravity in internal forces and the historical will of the people; Jabotinsky and Revisionism saw the Archimedean point somewhere outside, in a foreign rule, in an external governmental power.

There are those who admired Jabotinsky in their youth for his eloquence and his common touch, but have changed their mind today. Interesting and perhaps symbolic is the testimony of Boaz Evron (*Yedioth Ahronoth,* July 28, 1983), who once esteemed him greatly and today recognizes that Jabotinsky's words were so much glittering tinsel. Evron finds a contradiction in the fact that Jabotinsky championed *Realpolitik,* based on the perception that in international relations might has the deciding voice and countries conduct themselves exclusively in accord with their own self-interest, while at the same time he believed that he could persuade Britain to support Zionism, even to quarrel with the Arabs for its sake.

That is, on a basis of powerlessness he tried to make a gesture of strength; but ultimately this is derisory and arouses much more pity than simple weakness. This, without doubt, is among the basic reasons for the empty posturing that characterized Revisionism from the outset—and also a main reason why one cannot relate to Revisionism and Jabotinsky's thought as a systematic political doctrine.

Evron esteems Jabotinsky's courage and charisma. What he criticizes is his political intelligence. He continues describing the impact Jabotinsky made on him when, as a young boy, he first read his writings:

For a lad of 14, Jabotinsky was truly an intellectual revolution. But anyone who has taken the trouble to study genuine political thinking knows that it isn't serious. It's fine for 14-year-olds. When you observe people who have sworn faith to his memory and his teachings you realize that in terms of their political understanding they have to a large extent remained 14-year-olds. And in view of what his chief disciple in our generation brought down upon our heads—a man who is approaching 70 but has remained so "youthful" in his political ideas—one cannot but remember the ancient Biblical curse: "and a child shall lead them."

Some of his disciples still quote Jabotinsky to illuminate various problems in the present. There is a wide selection to choose from. There are passages that reflect an extreme nationalist position, but there are also those expressing a liberal and humanitarian attitude. On the one hand he gave priority to the nation, which he made into a supreme value: "In the beginning God created the nation; whatever assists its rebirth is holy, whatever disturbs it is impure, whatever hinders it is black, its faith is black, its banners are black." This is in stark contrast to an equally radical individualism: "In the beginning God created the individual; every individual is a king equal to his fellows, and each of his fellows too is a 'king'; better that an individual sin against the community than that society sin against the individual; society was created for the benefit of individuals" (Nevada, *op. cit.,* p. 358–359).

An evaluation of an important and perhaps fundamental aspect of Jabotinsky's spiritual world and teachings can be found in *Meditations on Israel* by Yisrael Eldad, who points out the strength of his aestheticism. In Jabotinsky's historical and political world view, beauty was the chief criterion. Jabotinsky rejected the Diaspora because it was "ugly"; he rejected Weizmann's diplomatic approach for similar reasons. In his teachings, as we have observed, the heroism of the event is more handsome than the heroism of the process. In his book, Eldad has noted that Jabotinsky's chosen inspirational symbols were "not *Modi'in,* the symbol of bravery that resulted in [the Maccabean] victory, but rather Jodefat, Massada and Betar, bravery that ended in destruction. . . . The unhappy endings of his literary works were not merely a matter of aesthetics. They became the reality of his personal destiny and of the destiny of the nation he loved so dearly."

In Eldad's view Jabotinsky was imbued with the sentiment that destiny, both individual and collective, is always bleak. Nevertheless, the attempt must be made—perhaps a miracle will occur. There are only two possibilities: achieving the goals in full (aestheticism), or else doom (heroic tragedy): "to die or to conquer the mountain." If it is to be catastrophe, at least let it be a glorious one. Here we see the profound difference between the two schools of Zionism discussed in Chapter 3: accomplishment through a spectacular event, maximalist demands accompanied by a heroic readiness for tragic failures—i.e., *aesthetic* values—versus more limited accomplishment as a laborious and cautious process, hedged against a tragic failure—i.e., *moral* values.

Nonetheless, it must be noted that the ascent of the Likud to power was important in molding Israel into one nation—no longer were large sectors of the nation excluded from power by the sentiment Ben-Gurion expressed in his famous dictum that he was willing to form any coalition so long as it was "without Herut and without the Communists." Many people who had previously felt alienated from the state because of their reservations about Mapai, which for so long had symbolized the state, gained a new sense of identity and national pride. It was also recompense for the Revisionists' claim that their part in establishing the state had not been recognized.

The willingness of the Labor government under Levi Eshkol to fulfill the terms of Jabotinsky's will and bring his body to Israel was taken to be a gesture of national reconciliation. Some will protest that by presenting Jabotinskyism as the source of the failures of recent years I am reopening old wounds. Moreover, they will argue that Herut itself has in many respects turned its back on Jabotinsky's teachings; that it upholds his name as an ornament rather than as a standard, and that we should not be led astray by this. The imperative of the hour is national unity to confront the difficult problems that beset Israel. I believe this is a serious argument. Nevertheless, I am convinced that unless the Jabotinskyite pattern of thought is rejected Israel cannot extricate itself from the flawed policies of recent years, and in particular cannot move toward a solution of the fateful and decisive problem—the occupied territories.

Begin's exit confounded his movement, which had always been based on authoritarian leadership and the cult of personality. The mantle of leadership had passed from Jabotinsky to Begin; it is difficult for a group accustomed to the cult of personality to accommodate itself to the absence of a charismatic leader, which Shamir is not, and even more so to develop new approaches to policy. The question is whether Herut and its leaders can rise above the Jabotinsky-Begin ethos. Although the mostly Polish leaders of Herut, and their older protégés, find it difficult to abandon the traditional thought patterns of Herut, the new generation, who are not historically linked to the Revisionist movement, may find it easier. They were not influenced by Polish romanticism or inspired by Marshal Pilsudski, and one sees this, for example, in the measured delivery that has replaced the bombastic oratory of the early leaders. These new figures are talented men. Israel will only lose if they are not allowed to make their contribution to leadership on the national level and in municipal government.

There are signs that some of Herut's sophisticated younger leaders are searching for a way to give up the dead-end position of de facto annexation, provided it does not entail acknowledgment of the party's ideological bankruptcy. This trend is already apparent in the defection of some previously staunch members of the party, such as Aryeh Naor and Moshe Amirav. It also finds expression in equivocal, off-the-record intimations, especially to foreign audiences, of a budding willingness to moderate the Likud's hard line. The riots have apparently given this slow shift an additional impetus.

But there is also reason to fear that at times of crisis the thought patterns of the old ethos will resurface and that at the moment of truth—in the contest for votes—even the new leaders will once again draw on the ideology and mentality of Herut, their unique heritage. Another impulse toward this is likely to be the need to guard their right flank against the Tehiya party and Rabbi Kahane.

Rejecting the Jabotinsky-Begin ethos and especially the way of thinking it has left behind is, as I have said, essential for national survival. I do not say this easily. But if the catastrophes that threaten the country's existence do occur, it seems to me that it will be because of the influence of Revisionism and Herut. Zionism succeeded and Israel exists today because the Revisionist movement was shunted off to the margins. Had it come to power in the period before the establishment of the state there would have been much noise and commotion, but almost certainly there would not have been a state. A state is not established by demonstrations and petitions, or by the expectation of a redemptive event. Eldad has said as much in *Ha'aretz* (August 30, 1985): "We would not have established a state. . . . Begin would not have brought to Israel a million Jews from the Oriental countries."

In my opinion, it is no coincidence that, since the time when Herut moved from the margins to the center, Israel's national survival has been endangered. The threat has been made tangible by all of the ominous developments Israel has suffered since 1977, and up to the present moment of the Shamir government.

It has been argued that the intransigent position of Shamir represents a defection from the more flexible one Begin would have adopted toward the West Bank, as he did toward the Sinai in the Camp David negotiations. To my mind, this difference is very doubtful. On the contrary, I believe that, as with much else in the Jabotinsky-Begin ethos, the mindset of the past continues to determine that of the present.

It is true that Begin was the leader of the Irgun from which Shamir, as a member of the more extreme Lehi group, seceded. It is also true that Shamir's position is one of absolute rejection of any negotiation toward a political settlement. He believes that the status quo can endure indefinitely and will even prove to be beneficial to Israel. There can be no doubt about his inflexibility, particularly after his continual dismissal of George Shultz's criticism of Israeli policy and of Shultz's initiative to bring about negotiations.

Nonetheless, Shamir's position, to my mind, remains a concrete continuation of Begin's hopes. It should be remembered that the concessions Begin offered Egypt were made mainly to obviate the need to make concessions about the West Bank, the possession of "Judea and Samaria" being much more integral to the Likud vision of a Greater Israel than was the Sinai. Begin was ready to accept a partial military withdrawal but only for the sake of continued political domination. Shamir's position is, in effect, what Begin's would have been once these hopes for recognition of Israel's hegemony were thwarted. When it became clear to Shamir that a political settlement that recognized Israel's domination of the West Bank was out of the question, he adopted the position that the next best thing was simply to sit tight. Since his retirement, Begin has not indicated any disagreement with this policy.

5
Nationalistic Judaism

Judaism and Zionism

Zionism's attachment to the Land of Israel is rooted in the Jewish religion; but Judaism itself is not Zionist, and Jews throughout the generations have not been Zionists even if year by year they uttered the fervent hope "Next year in Jerusalem!" or the admonition that "Living in Eretz Yisrael is of equal weight to all the other commandments." In doing so they were expressing their longings and desires—their grand design (the abstract will)—and not their policy (the practical will). For the most part Jews continued to live in exile. Of course there were a handful who did emigrate to the Land of Israel, but their intention in most cases was to die there rather than to build a Jewish independent state.

Zionism is not an ideal; it is the realization of an intention, a political program. One has to distinguish between a wish and an intention. An intention depends on some practical beginning. For example, to say "would that so and so were dead" is to express a wish, not necessarily an intention to murder. A wish becomes an intention by means of taking a decision and implementing it by some action that leads toward its realization; in our example, obtaining a weapon. Zionist historiography has thus erred in describing the Jews as having always been Zionist, for the distinction between love of Zion and Zionism as a political program is essential to a proper understanding of Jewish history. Zionism was born when the messianic wish, embodied in the ideal or grand design of the ingathering, became a political intention embodied in an organization to settle Jews on the land.

From the time of the Bar Kochba Revolt until the rise of Zionism, the central political idea of Judaism was expressed by the three Talmudic "oaths" that God required. They can be paraphrased as follows: there would be no mass movement of the Jews from the lands of the Diaspora to the land of Israel, no rebellion against the nations of the world, and no excessive oppression of the Jewish people by gentiles. This was an important Jewish doctrine, even though it did not arouse much discussion, since in the historic circumstances of those times it seemed obvious almost to the point of banality. The core of this idea is passivity—avoiding political action while patiently waiting for the Messiah to come, without attempting to precipitate His coming, which was strictly forbidden.

Thus Zionism was proscribed. Modern religious Zionism attempted to reinterpret and blunt the force of the oaths. It claimed, for example, that the oaths were a sort of package deal: because the nations of the world had not upheld their part of the bargain as expressed in the third oath, Jews may now immigrate collectively to their homeland. Such an interpretation makes Zionism merely conditional: were it not for the gentiles' ignoring the oath not to oppress the Jews, the Jews would have to refrain from migrating en masse to Eretz Yisrael. (We might note that the anti-Zionist Satmar Hasidim exploit the oaths to castigate Zionism and interpret them as a package deal in precisely the opposite sense; it was the Jews' violation of the oaths—by pursuing the Zionist enterprise—that led to the Holocaust.)

The oaths can be understood, then, as a decision to prevent any initiative that would undermine the Jewish way of life as it developed in the Diaspora. Jewish Orthodox circles, afraid of changes that would undermine this way of life, were strongly opposed to Zionism. They suspected that the realization of Zionism would create a new and difficult challenge for Judaism.

Judaism and Statehood

The laws of Judaism were promulgated by the Jewish sages on the basis of traditional legislation and customs. By and large this occurred at a time when there was no longer a Jewish state, so that the problem questions of how a Jewish state should function were ignored.

The major task that confronted the Jewish sages after the destruction of the Second Temple and the repression of the Bar Kochba Rebellion (132–35 c.e.) was to guarantee the survival of the Jewish people in a hostile milieu. As they saw it, in order to survive the Jews had to isolate themselves from their surroundings. They enacted this intention in the *halakha*—the body of religious laws designed to encode a unique and binding lifestyle. Jewish uniqueness, deeply rooted in the Jewish religious consciousness, now received precise external expression in all details of life, as stipulated in the Talmud, the principal repository of Jewish laws. Maimonides summarized: "[Jews] should not follow the customs of the Gentiles, nor imitate them in dress or in the way of trimming the hair, as it has been said. 'And ye shall not walk in the customs of the nations which I cast out before you' " (Leviticus 20:23). By making Jews conspicuous in their outward appearance as well as confirmed in their attitudes and beliefs, the sages made assimilation by degrees extremely difficult; it had to take place as a total change of life. In short, Jewish religious law was of maximum effectiveness in preserving the Jewish people in the Diaspora. This remained the situation until the Enlightenment, when wide breaches were forged in the barriers the rabbis had created.

Not having a country of their own, the Jews had to live under the rule of foreign governments. Relations with the sovereign power were conducted according to the Talmudic principle enunciated in the third century. "The law of the kingdom is the law"—that is, the ordinances of the civil authorities are binding. For the Jews, the two normative systems existed side by side: halakha, the divine law regulating the lives of Jews mainly among themselves; and the statutes of the country in which they lived, which regulated their contacts with their non-Jewish surroundings. However, the Jews never felt the same sense of identification with the laws of the land as they did toward their own religious legal system. This is expressed in such Talmudic precepts as "Do not seek to become intimate with the authorities," and "Be cautious with the ruling authorities."

For some, this duality has been carried over to the secular Jewish state as well, its government being seen as the successor to the alien authorities. Such a tendency appears in particularly emphatic fashion among those for whom halakha is a vital force that directs every hour of their lives and is expressed in a sense of alienation from civil legislation. With this legacy, educating these Israelis in citizenship is not an easy task.

The idea of renewing Jewish statehood is certainly central to Judaism. Maimonides saw the Jewish kingdom as a framework that would make it possible to attain the spiritual perfection of the individual. However, the task of achieving statehood—the Redemption—was assigned to divine providence and to the Messiah, as an event that would occur not through historical processes but at the end of history. Perhaps a sense of the difficulties that might be anticipated in applying halakha in a Jewish state was another factor restraining an indigenous effort to restore Jewish sovereignty. Precisely those regulations intended to preserve the Jews as a community made the realization of Jewish statehood problematic: the focal point of a nation-state is independence, which is incompatible with dependence on the services of others. The Jews cannot exist without gentiles, stressed Chief Rabbi Kook, because they are needed to perform necessary functions that Jews must avoid. The Sabbath is a conspicuous example of this dependence, but it is not the only one.

The establishment of the Jewish state made this quite clear. A community can avoid profaning the Sabbath, but a modern state cannot close down one day a week. Services such as electricity and water need to be supplied every day. The responsibilities of government office also created halakhic problems. For example, police work involves public desecration of the Sabbath, as do the Saturday-afternoon football matches, and radio and television transmissions. Yet all these activities have at times been under the jurisdiction of government ministers who were Orthodox Jews, who thereby contravened the religious law. Perhaps they told themselves that their jobs permitted them to safeguard the sanctity of religion, so that their overall contribution as ministers was positive. But the problem remained nonetheless.

Furthermore, a Jewish state is expected by religious Jews to implement halakha as the law of the state. A host of laws that apply only to Jews living in Israel now became effective, while religionists exerted pressures, which secularists resisted, to enact halakhic observances such as Sabbath ones and regulations of such matters as its definition of Jewish identity as laws of the state. Thus the establishment of Israel gave rise to tensions and dilemmas. The problems are twofold: the problems the Jewish religion produced for the Jewish state and culture; the problems the Jewish state produced for the Jewish religion.

American readers may need to be made aware that in Israel Judaism essentially means Orthodoxy. Conservative and Reform, the other two main branches of Judaism in many countries, still lead a relatively marginal life in the Jewish state. Hence, in the following pages, my references to Judaism and religion should be taken as referring principally to the Orthodox.

The Place of Religion in Zionism

Despite the hope that God would overcome the impediments to Redemption and the difficulties of implementing halakha in a future Jewish commonwealth, Judaism always expected that man would be a partner with God in this task. This was exploited by some rabbis in order to endow the Zionist idea with a religious content—Zionism preparing the path to Redemption. The founders of political Zionism, however, were secular Jews. Their dream was not to renew the ancient order but to establish a modern state, in the spirit of the then-fashionable idea of nationalism. Zionism was in fact fostered by the great change that occurred in Europe with the decline of religion and the rise of a secular world view.

The religious motivation for Zionism played only a marginal role in political Zionism—except for the attachment to the Land of Israel, whose origin is unquestionably religious. Religious ideas of Redemption and Messianism were irrelevant. The secular fathers of Zionism saw the land of Israel as a refuge for the Jews from their distress in foreign lands—a secular and national redemption. They did not intend the Jewish state to be based on halakha, or to pave the way for the kingdom of heaven on earth. Religious Zionism followed in the footsteps of secular Zionism and endeavored to find positive aspects to it, but did not attempt to guide the Zionist enterprise in a particular direction. At best, religious circles consoled themselves that a Jewish state might implement halakha as time went on and even be the setting for the coming of the Messiah, though it would not be a precondition or reason for that.

Until 1967, in fact, religious Zionism was moderate both in its domestic policies—its demand to implement halakha within the laws and ordinances of the country—as well as in foreign affairs. Despite the Zionist enterprise, religious Zionism continued the Jewish tradition of caution and moderation with regard to non-Jews and the nations of the world, in accordance with the Biblical precept "Do not provoke them" (Deuteronomy 2:5). Thus the ultra-Orthodox Agudat Yisrael party tended to moderation in its foreign-policy positions.

Throughout this period, religious Zionism was linked politically to Mainstream Zionism, so much so that this link was regarded as a historical alliance. This situation was to change radically after the tumultuous events of 1967, which eventually led to changes of such magnitude in religious Zionism that it eventually switched camps and formed a coalition with the adherents of the Jabotinsky-Begin ethos.

The Awakening of Nationalistic Religious Extremism

The awakening of a nationalistic Judaism was a slow, evolving process, following the victory in the Six Day War, which was interpreted as a manifestation of God's intervention. For religious Jews, the conquest of parts of the historic land of Israel in this war cast a brilliant light on the Zionist enterprise. Taken together with the victory of 1967, the achievements of Zionism were now seen as the harbinger of a new age of great religious and national eminence. Significant sectors of Israeli Judaism adopted Herut's position of entitlement to the occupied lands, which were now referred to by their Biblical names, Judea and Samaria. The religious Gush Emunim movement assumed the principal role in pioneering settlement activities in the occupied territories. The bond between religious Judaism and the state was changing. Whereas in its old borders the state had been merely a secular refuge, for many religious circles its new boundaries, which included the holy places in Jerusalem, Hebron, and elsewhere, endowed it with a theological significance. The Yom Kippur War and withdrawal from territory on the Egyptian and Syrian borders did not controvert the notion that a new age had begun—the "beginning of the Redemption."

Thus, within the Jewish state, Orthodox Judaism has changed its stance in recent years: instead of being content to be a follower it has demanded a role of leadership, insisting that both domestic and foreign policy be derived from religious law. Whereas Herut opposes conceding and withdrawing from the West Bank for nationalist reasons (with security considerations a secondary factor), many religious circles offer religious arguments against withdrawal. For them, the security problems associated with withdrawal are secondary to the religious behests: because of the achievements of the Six Day War in recovering holy places, militant Jewish nationalism has become a significant factor in bringing closer the ultimate expression of Judaism—Redemption. The relationship between religion and policy has become more intimate;

religion in the service of national policy, and national policy as the implementation of religious commandments.

I am not a scholar of Jewish religion. In what follows I shall merely be drawing attention to the actions and mindset of the religious camp I designate "nationalistic religious extremists." (I should point out that where I quote traditional sources, the sources are ones that the nationalist religious extremists use to support their arguments.) My emphasis on these manifestations is not meant to assert that they are widely dominant. Nevertheless, the nationalistic religious extremists are by no means a lunatic fringe; many are respected men whose words are widely heeded. Their demand that halakha direct policy is shared with different emphases by many religious circles.

The designation "nationalistic religious extremists" is of course very general, and includes various groups who are at loggerheads with one another. When I call them "extremists" I am not assessing them according to a religious standard, but from the perspective of the policies they believe that Israel should adopt, especially in foreign relations. Theirs is religious extremism in political terms.

Many in the religious camp find justification for the annexation of the occupied territories, or at least a prohibition against withdrawal, in Nachmanides's (1194–1270) commentary on Maimonides's (1135–1204) *Book of Commandments:* "We are commanded to inherit the land that God gave to Abraham, Isaac, and Jacob, and must not leave it in the hands of any other nation. . . . We must not leave the Land in the hands of the [seven Canaanite nations] or of any other people in any generation." Rabbi Zvi Yehudah Kook, the mentor of Gush Emunim, commented as follows: "These are explicit words of halakha. . . . The main thrust of the commandment is conquest by the state, Jewish national rule in this holy territory."

Nachmanides's words, then, are the starting point for the politico-religious conceptions of a broad stratum of Orthodox Jews. For them, halakha is binding, except in rare cases where life is threatened. Religious ordinances have absolute validity; historical circumstances cannot contradict the Creator of the Universe. The very existence of such a law is a guarantee that reality will not contravene it, and so there is no need to trouble oneself with calculations of feasibility. Thus halakha serves as a means to prevent a separation between the grand design of the Zionist dream and the policy entailed by historical circumstances.

Rabbi Zvi Yehudah Kook declared in a public meeting:

I tell you explicitly that the Torah forbids us to
surrender even one inch of our liberated land. There are
no conquests here and we are not occupying foreign
lands; we are returning to our home, to the inheritance
of our ancestors. There is no Arab land here, only the
inheritance of our God—and the more the world gets
used to this thought the better it will be for them and
for all of us (*Year by Year*, 1968).

In this view, violating the prohibition against withdrawal will hurt
not only the Jews but the whole world.

In generations past, the fundamental concept of being the Chosen People served the Jews as a shield against persecution and a
consolation in distress. Since 1967 it has taken on an aggressive
significance as a license to act in contradiction to accepted political
norms. The idea of being "a people that dwells apart, not reckoned
among the nations" (Numbers 23:9) has become sanction for devi-
ant behavior in the international arena. International law, public
opinion, the United Nations, the superpowers—for the religious
extremists none of these matter. In the world at large, religion
cannot provide legal title to a territory. But for those religious
extremists who believe it does, the Biblical promise of the Land of
Israel for the people of Israel is transformed from a religious and
spiritual matter into a necessity that requires immediate implementation. True, it was in the name of the Biblical promise that
the idea of the historical right to the land was raised as a fundamental trend of Zionism, but this concept was accompanied by acceptance of the limitation posed by the Arabs already residing there.
The founders of secular Zionism promised that they would take
account of these residents and not discriminate against them. In
the world view of the religious extremists, this is unnecessary: as
they see it, the Arabs lived in the land throughout the centuries in
contravention of the Law, and their assertion of a right of residence is no better than that of a squatter.

Rabbi Shlomo Aviner, the former rabbi of Bet El (the Jewish
settlement established in Samaria on a site of religious significance) and today the rabbi of the Ateret Kohanim Yeshiva, explained this as follows:

Let me draw you an analogy. It's as if a man goes into
his neighbor's house without permission and stays there
for many years. When the original owner returns, the

invader claims: "It's my house, I've been living here for years!" All of these years he's been nothing but a thief! Now he should make himself scarce and pay rent on top of it. Some people might say that there's a difference between living in a place for thirty years and living in a place for 2,000 years. Let us ask them: Is there a statute of limitations that gives a thief the right to his plunder? . . . Everyone who settled here knew very well that he was living in a land that belongs to the people of Israel, so the ethnic group that settled in this place has no title to the land. Perhaps an Arab who was born here doesn't know this, but nevertheless the fact that a man settles on land does not make it his. Under the law, possession serves only as proof of a claim of ownership; it does not create ownership. The Arabs' possession of the land is therefore a possession that asserts no rights. It is the possession of territory when it is absolutely clear that they are not its legal owners, and this possession has no juridical or moral validity (*Artzi,* p. 10).

For Rabbi Aviner and his followers, then, the first Arabs to settle in the Holy Land were thieves, and the crime has been bequeathed from father to son down to the present generation. Perhaps he is referring to collective ownership of the land and not to the ownership by each individual Arab of his own small plot. But he says that all the title deeds for land recorded in government registers have no "juridical and moral" force.

Is there a court anywhere in the world that would endorse such an argument?

Rabbi Zvi Yehudah Kook, who was in fact the inspiration for Rabbi Aviner's ideas, has written in a similar vein in *Arzi*:

We find ourselves here by virtue of the legacy of our ancestors, the basis of the Bible and history, and no one can change this fact. What does it resemble? A man left his house and others came and invaded it. This is exactly what happened to us. Some argue that there are Arab lands here. It is all a lie and a fraud! There are absolutely no Arab lands here.

Rabbi Yisrael Ariel has argued that Rabbi A. I. Kook (Israel's first Ashkenazi chief rabbi and the father of Rabbi Z. Y. Kook) was also of this view, believing that the Jewish National Fund was under no obligation to pay for the lands it had purchased; rather, its payments went beyond the strict letter of the law, from a desire for "relations of justice and uprightness with every nation and people."

I once expressed the fear that the Arabs might interpret the Jews' idea of the historical right as requiring their expulsion. At that time I wrote:

> Israelis must understand that Zionism's assertion of an historic right to the land is apt to imply to the Arabs that their residence in the land was morally flawed, as if their possession was merely exploiting the temporary absence of the legal property owner. This view, with the conclusion it entails that they must evacuate the place in favor of the legal owner, must seem to them a fraud and radical presumption.

I never imagined then that Israelis would so interpret the concept of the historical right.

From Expulsion to Annihilation

If Jews see the Arabs' residence in the land of Israel as making them criminals, the conclusion that they should be expelled is quick to follow. Knesset member Rabbi Meir Kahane has given widespread publicity to this idea, but he did not invent it. It is based on ancient sources, and first and foremost the Biblical verse "You shall dispossess all the inhabitants of the land" (Numbers 33:53) and the interpretations of it given by classical commentators. The eleventh-century scholar Rashi, for example, explained: "You shall drive out the land and you shall dispossess it of its inhabitants, and *then you will dwell in it,* i.e., you will be able to remain in it [if you dispossess it of its inhabitants], but if not, you will not be able to remain in it." Thus the Biblical verse was interpreted not as a commandment directed to the Jews in the past, when they came out of Egypt, but as a standing order binding for the future.

Rabbi Yisrael Ariel explicitly demands expulsion of the Arabs as entailed by Jewish religious law:

> On the one hand there is a commandment to settle
> Eretz Yisrael, defined by our sages also as the

commandment of "inheritance and residence"—a
commandment mentioned many times in the Torah.
Even the new student understands that "inheritance and
residence" means conquering and settling the land. The
Torah repeats the commandment—"You shall dispossess
all the inhabitants of the land"—many times, and Rashi
explains that this means to expel them. The Torah itself
uses the term expulsion a number of times. . . . The
substance of this commandment is to expel the
inhabitants of the land whoever they may be. . . . This is
also how Rashi understands the commandment. In the
Talmudic passage that mentions the commandment to
settle the land Rashi explains: "Because of the
commandment to settle Eretz Yisrael—to expel idol
worshippers and settle Jews there." Thus according to
Rashi the commandment to settle the land means to
expel the non-Jew from Eretz Yisrael and settle it with
Jews (Zeffiyya).

Note the association of idol worshippers and non-Jews. This identification has a basis in Jewish tradition.

In Rabbi Kahane's version, expulsion of the Arabs would fulfill
two functions: the first is political, preventing the Arabs from
becoming the majority and thereby undermining Israel from
within; and second is religious—it would provide a proven means
to hasten the Redemption and the coming of the Messiah:

The Arabs of Israel are a desecration of God's name.
Their non-acceptance of Jewish sovereignty over the
Land of Israel is a rejection of the sovereignty of the
God of Israel and of his kingdom. Removing them from
the land is therefore more than a political matter. It is a
religious matter, a religious obligation to wipe out the
desecration of God's name. Instead of worrying about
the reactions of the Gentiles if we act, we should
tremble at the thought of God's wrath if we do not act.
Tragedy will befall us if we do not remove the Arabs
from the land, since redemption can come at once in its
full glory if we do, as God commands us. . . . Let us
remove the Arabs from Israel and hasten the
Redemption (Thorns in Your Eyes, pp. 244–245).

Rabbi S. D. Wolpe, presenting himself as an exponent of the
ideas of Menachem Mendele Schnayerson, the Lubavitcher Rebbe,

stresses that not even a "resident alien" (i.e., a non-Jew who has accepted the seven Noachide commandments—see pages 151–154 below) can live in Jerusalem, and how much less so Muslims and Christians who are not included in this category:

> According to *halakha* it is forbidden for a non-Jew to live in Jerusalem, and in accordance with the ruling by Maimonides it is forbidden to permit even a resident alien in Jerusalem. . . . True, this applies when Israel has the upper hand, but today too, although it is not possible to expel them by force, this does not mean that we have to encourage them to live there!

Rabbi Kahane actually submitted to the Knesset a draft bill that would make the halakha ban on the residence of a "resident alien" in Jerusalem the law of the state, but it was disqualified by the Knesset praesidium on December 3, 1984.

Rabbi Eliezer Waldenberg, winner of the 1976 Israel Prize (given for outstanding achievement), has said:

> It is forbidden for gentiles to live in Jerusalem. I, for example, favor upholding the halakhic prohibition on a gentile's living in Jerusalem. If we would uphold this *halakha* as we should, we would have to expel all non-Jews from Jerusalem and purify it absolutely (Cited in *The Zionist Dream Revisited,* p. 117).

Implicit in this view is that failure to expel them is a transgression of religious law.

Some nationalistic religious extremists frequently identify the Arabs with Amalek, whom the Jews are commanded to annihilate totally (Deuteronomy 25:17–19). As children, we were taught that this was a relic of a bygone and primitive era, a commandment that had lapsed because Sennacherib the Assyrian king had mixed up all the nations so it was no longer possible to know who comes of the seed of Amalek. Yet some rabbis insist on injecting a contemporary significance into the commandment to blot out Amalek.

Rabbi Yisrael Hess, formerly the campus rabbi of Bar-Ilan University, published an article in the student newspaper, *Bat Koll* (February 26, 1988), entitled "The Commandment of Genocide in the Torah," which ended as follows: "The day will yet come when we will all be called to fulfill the commandment of the divinely ordained war to destroy Amalek." Knesset member Amnon Rubinstein, citing this article, adds: "Rabbi Hess explains the commandment to blot out the memory of Amalek and says that there is no mercy in this commandment: the commandment is to kill and destroy even children and infants. Amalek is whoever declares war against the people of God." In the same article quoted by Rubinstein, Hess writes:

> Against this holy war God declares a counter *jihad*. . . .
> In order to emphasize that this is the background for
> the annihilation and that this is what the war is all
> about, that it is not merely a conflict between two
> peoples . . . God does not rest content that we destroy
> Amalek—"blot out the memory of Amalek"—he also
> mobilizes personally for this war . . . because, as has
> been said, he has a personal interest in the matter, it is a
> prime goal for us as well.

Hess implies that those who have a quarrel with the Jews instantly become Amalek and ought to be destroyed, children and all. Amalek is identified with the Arabs: the use of the term *jihad* (holy war) is but one allusion to this meaning. Amalek is not an ancient extinct tribe but a generic enemy that each generation may identify for itself.

Rabbi Yisrael Ariel, in a collection of articles intended to justify the religious terrorist Underground that emerged in Israel in the mid-1980s, explained that the killing of a non-Jew is not considered murder:

> Anyone who looks through the code of Maimonides,
> which is the pillar of *halakha* in the Jewish world, and
> searches for the concept "thou shalt not murder" or the
> concept "holy blood" with regard to the killing of a
> non-Jew will search in vain, because he will not find it.
> . . . It follows from Maimonides' words that a Jew who
> killed a non-Jew was exempt from human judgment, and
> has not violated the prohibition on murder. As
> Maimonides writes in the Laws of Murderers: "A Jew
> who killed a resident alien is not sentenced to death by
> a court of law" (*Zeffiyya*).

But let us note that Maimonides also said: "Everyone who kills another human being is transgressing a negative commandment, as it was said, 'Thou shalt not murder.' "

The Status of Non-Jews under Israeli Rule: "Resident Alien"

Alongside precepts requiring decent and humane conduct toward the "stranger" (or gentile) and asserting that he must not be treated worse than a fellow Jew "because you were strangers in the land of Egypt," the Jewish heritage also has very severe regulations directed against the stranger. In the past no one alluded to these with regard to the Arabs who live in Israel. Rabbi Yehudah Leib Fishman, the leader of the Mizrachi party, had a hand in drafting Israel's Declaration of Independence, which states explicitly: "The State of Israel . . . will ensure complete equality of social and political rights to all of its inhabitants irrespective of religion, race, or sex." Rabbi Yitzhak Meir Levin of Agudat Yisrael, Rabbi Kalman Kahane, and Rabbi Ze've Gold also signed this document; it never occurred to them that Arabs who had been "conquered" had to accept the status of "resident alien." The laws that grant equal rights to all citizens of Israel were passed by the Knesset with no opposition.

Today, in contrast, the demand is voiced that all non-Jewish residents of the Jewish state be dealt with according to halakhic regulations—which, not incidentally, support the nationalist aim of decreasing the number of Arabs living in the country by making their lives difficult. Supporters of this view willfully ignore international norms having to do with racial nondiscrimination and with civil, economic, and social rights as formulated in international conventions, even where Israel has formally ratified them.

It should be noted that Rabbi Yitzhak ha-Levi Herzog, Israel's late chief rabbi, stated that the halakhic category "resident alien" has lapsed: "[The concept of] a resident alien is not accepted except when the regulations of the Jubilee Year are in force; obviously resident aliens cannot be accepted in this day and age. . . . Muslims are no longer in the category of idolators but have not obtained the category of resident aliens." Christians, too, as we shall see below, are also not considered to be idolators. It is therefore halakhically permissible for Muslims and Christians to live in the land of Israel. But not all religious circles accept his conclusions.

Rabbi Meir Kahane, for example, asserts that: "A non-Jew who wants to live in the Land of Israel can obtain only the status of 'resident alien' (*Ha'aretz,* August 13, 1983). Citizenship, political status . . . the right to vote and hold office, all of these are reserved exclusively for Jews." Again, these ideas are not without foundation in traditional sources. Maimonides himself is a major source on the treatment of non-Jews who have been conquered and have come under Jewish rule, a category that is clearly applicable to the Arabs of Israel proper, Judea, Samaria, and the Gaza Strip:

> If the inhabitants make peace and accept the Seven Commandments enjoined upon the descendants of Noah, none of them is slain, but they become tributary, as it is said: "They shall become tributary unto thee, and shall serve thee" (Deut. 20:11). If they agree to pay the tribute levied on them but refuse to submit to servitude, or if they yield to servitude but refuse to pay the tribute levied on them, their overtures are rejected. They must accept both terms of peace. The servitude imposed on them is that they are given an inferior status, that they lift not up their heads in Israel but be subjected to them, but they be not appointed to any office that will put them in charge of Israel. The terms of the levy are that they be prepared to serve the king with their body and their money (*Hilkhot Melakhim,* ch. 6:1).

That is, a non-Jew may reside in a Jewish state under the following conditions: (a) accepting the seven Noachide commandments, such as acknowledging God, refraining from murder, theft, and adultery; (b) paying tribute; and (c) servitude. In line with Maimonides's general approach toward the commandments, which applies to Jew and non-Jew alike, the individual's acceptance of the seven Noachide commandments must not be a "reasoned conclusion" based on his conscience, but must derive from a recognition that these are divine commandments that must be obeyed, whether they seem reasonable to him or not.

Maimonides defines a "resident alien" as one who accepts the seven Noachide commandments: "If he undertakes to observe the seven precepts, he becomes a [resident alien]; we only accept a [resident alien] at the time when the law of Jubilee is in force. But at the period when the law of Jubilee is in abeyance, only a proselyte of righteousness is accepted" (*Hilkhot Avoda Zara* 10:6). Observance of the Jubilee Year had already lapsed at the time of the Second Temple. Two possible conclusions can be drawn from the link between the acceptance of resident aliens and the Jubilee Year: either the validity of the regulations concerning resident aliens has lapsed, as Rabbi Herzog held; or the regulations are still in force, and resident aliens cannot be accepted. Moreover, acquiring the status of resident alien is not an automatic process; it depends on the individuals' acceptance by the Jews. Thus, some contend, it is impossible for the Arabs to be accepted as resident aliens because they are at war with the Jews.

A reasoned analysis of the status of non-Jews in a Jewish state can be found in an article entitled "A New Approach to Israeli-Arab Peace" published in *Kivvunim* 24 (August 1984), an official publication of the World Zionist Organization. The author is Mordechai Nisan, a lecturer on the Middle East at Hebrew University in Jerusalem. According to Dr. Nisan, Jews are permitted to discriminate against foreigners in a way that Jews would angrily denounce were it done to them. What is permissible to us is forbidden to others:

> While it is true that the Jews are a particular people, they nonetheless are designated as a "light unto the nations." This function is imposed on the Jews who strive to be a living aristocracy among the nations, a nation that has deeper historical roots, greater spiritual obligations, higher moral standards, and more powerful intellectual capacities than others. This vision, which diverges from the widely accepted egalitarian approach, is not at all based on an arbitrary hostility towards non-Jews, but rather on a fundamental existential understanding of the quality of Jewish peoplehood.

Thus the concept of the "Chosen People" as an aristocracy provides sanction for the unequal and discriminatory treatment of non-Jews, who are inferior. Nisan does not consider the possibility that other nations might also claim aristocratic status for themselves.

Nisan continues in a passage that must be presented in its entirety to register the tribalism of this mindset:

> The Land was the special divinely granted territorial promise to Abraham and his seed. . . . Non-Jews, without a role on the highest plane of religious endeavor, are thus without a role on the plane of public activity. The linkage of politics and religion in the Jewish experience is supported by the equally tight connection between kinship and politics. Those of "the tribe" are

the sole bearers of authority to determine national
affairs in the Land of Israel. . . .

The category of *ben-noah* [son of Noah] defines the
non-Jew who has accepted the seven Noachide laws. In
return for being permitted to live in the country of
sacred history and religious purpose, the *ben-noah* must
accept to pay a tax and to suffer the humiliation of
servitude (see Deut. 20:11). Maimonides, in his legal
code on the Laws of Kings, states explicitly that he be
"held down and not raise his head against Jews."
Non-Jews must not be appointed to any office or
position of power over Jews. If they refuse to live a life
of inferiority, then this will signal rebellion and the
unavoidable necessity of Jewish warfare against their
very presence in the Land of Israel. . . . However Jewish
law, *halakha,* recognizes another category for a non-Jew
which signifies a higher human status: he is known as
the *ger toshav* (resident alien). In comparison with the
ben-noah, the *ger toshav,* while remaining a non-Jew, goes
through a kind of religious conversion and accepts the
authority of *Torah* even though he still does not commit
himself to observe all its precepts. . . . Unlike the
ben-noah who suffers the disability of servitude, the *ger
toshav* is able to be a part of Jewish society, though he
remains outside of the Jewish national fold and
community.

Nisan is not presenting merely a theoretical analysis; he offers
practical suggestions as well. A non-Jew must not be appointed to
any public post in Israel. With regard to the "autonomy" concept
of letting the Arabs have self-rule only under Israeli supervision,
he writes: "This political solution is thus in the spirit of the traditional Jewish approach, both with regard to the Land of Israel and
with regard to non-Jewish minorities within it."

If Canada, of which he was formerly a citizen, treated Dr. Nisan
as a *ben-noah,* a member of the servant class with restricted rights,
he would have protested it as deplorable discrimination, but he
sees no contradiction in the Jews, as the chosen people, having a
license to treat non-Jews in just this way. This is tribal morality
given theological justification. I do not know how many Jews share
his belief, but the publication of the article in a leading Zionist
periodical is cause for grave concern.

In an addendum found in the English text Nisan criticizes the former deputy foreign minister, Dr. Yehudah Ben-Meir of the National Religious party, for telling the *Jerusalem Post* (December 3, 1982) that "to annex [Judea and Samaria] and absorb the people, and then turn them into second-class citizens, would be anti-Jewish." Nisan counters that even granting autonomy while denying sovereignty is "in itself a diminution of full rights. Yet this . . . is not anti-Jewish but rather the application of Jewish principles." Nisan also strongly criticizes David Glass, a former representative of the relatively moderate National Religious party, for claiming that Judaism demands one law for Jews and Arabs alike. Glass is in error, he claims, because the demand for equal treatment applies not to aliens but to converts. Maimonides stated: "Love of the proselyte who has come to shelter beneath the divine presence"— that is, an alien who has accepted the commandments of the Jewish religion. Meir Kahane, in *Thorns in Your Eyes,* wrote in a similar vein: "We should remember that in the Torah the word *ger* does not mean the non-Jewish stranger, but one who has converted to Judaism" (p. 241).

Nisan finds a correspondence between the discriminatory treatment of minorities, *dhimmis,* in Islamic countries, and the Jewish treatment of Noachides and resident aliens. For him, inequality is a Middle Eastern norm and therefore a fair basis for peace. He seems unaware that he is legitimizing the historical discrimination against Jews in Islamic countries; or perhaps this legitimation is a worthwhile price in order to institute discriminatory regulations against all Arabs under Israeli rule. But this ostensible symmetry is not in fact symmetrical. The Muslims accepted every Jew and Christian as a *dhimmi,* whereas, according to Nisan, for an Arab to acquire the status of resident alien requires his partial Judaization. If he refuses to undergo this "religious conversion"—essentially abjuring Islam or Christianity—he must leave. No wonder Nisan assumes that even with annexation there would be only a small number of "resident aliens."

Meir Kahane, too, is of the opinion that "a small percentage will agree to the conditions imposed on a resident alien who does not have the status of a citizen. These will be principally old people. They will remain." In this view, applying the resident-alien regulations is an elegant alternative to expelling the Arabs; the decision is transferred to them, and they will remove themselves.

Maimonides's attitude toward non-Jews was undoubtedly influenced by the condition of his age. His father's family had been forced to feign conversion to Islam, and even when he lived under more tolerant regimes he suffered from Muslim ordinances against *dhimmis.*

One can sympathize with our forefathers, who, in their suffering of all kinds of persecutions and discriminations, found solace in specifying the measures that would be imposed on non-Jews once there was a Jewish state. In many cases they simply copied the discriminations to which they were subjected themselves. Such expressions of hostility may have had for them the cathartic effect of indulging in writing what they could not practice—the vengeance of the helpless. They envisaged the reestablishment of a Jewish state only after the coming of the Messiah. Furthermore, they did not worry how such doctrines might affect Jews in the Diaspora, as they considered that the ingathering of the Jews of the Diaspora into the Jewish state would be total. Thus, all those enactments against gentiles were utopian, meant to be carried out, not in historical circumstances, but in an extrahistorical era. Nonetheless, the religious extremists use Maimonides literally to support their bigotry. For instance, the chairman of the Great Synagogue in Tel Aviv in a letter to the editor of *Ha'aretz* (October 30, 1986) invoked Maimonides as an authority to oppose the appointment of an Arab as a deputy minister of education.

Idolators

The focus of Judaism is service to God and obedience to his commandments; idolatry is the grossest contradiction thereof. This is the origin of Judaism's stern position with regard to idolators. They must be destroyed lest they seduce Jews to follow in their footsteps and sin.

Maimonides wrote:

An affirmative precept is enjoined for the destruction of idolatry and its worshippers, and everything made for its sake. . . . In the Land of Israel, it is a duty actively to chase out idolatry until we have exterminated it from the whole of our country. Outside of the holy land, however, we are not so commanded; but only that whenever we acquire any territory by conquest, we should destroy all the idolatry found there (*Hilkhot Avodah Zara,* ch. 7:1).

E. E. Urbach has explained that "the term idolatry *(Avoda Zara)* was coined by our Sages and includes everything connected with a god other than the God of Israel . . . in practice the laws dealing with idolatry cover all relations between Jews and non-Jews." Thus in many contexts "non-Jews" may be synonymous with "idolator" (*Encyclopedia Hebraica,* 26, p. 618). Another definition of the term is that everyone who has not accepted the seven Noachide commandments is considered to be an idolator. The broadening of the term "idolators" to refer to non-Jews in general raises difficult problems with the Israeli laws regulating relations between Jews and non-Jews.

Maimonides summarized the laws on the treatment of idolators as follows:

> It is forbidden to show them mercy, as it was said, "nor show mercy unto them" (Deut. 7:2). Hence, if one sees one of them who worships idols perishing or drowning, one is not to save him. . . . Hence you learn that it is forbidden to heal idolators even for a fee. But if one is afraid of them or apprehends that refusal might cause ill will, medical treatment may be given for a fee but not gratuitously. . . . The foregoing rules apply to the time when the people of Israel live exiled among the nations, or when the Gentiles' power is predominant. But when Israel is predominant over the nations of the world, we are forbidden to permit a gentile who is an idolator to dwell among us. He must not enter our land, even as a temporary resident; or even as a traveler, journeying with merchandise from place to place, until he has undertaken to keep the seven precepts which the Noachides were commanded to observe (*Hilkhot Avodah Zara,* ch. 10:8).

Maimonides exempted the Muslims from the category of idolators, but the Christians, by contrast, were explicitly included. His unfavorable view of Christians was influenced by his view of the Trinity as incompatible with strict monotheism, and perhaps also by the historical circumstances of his age. He lived in Muslim countries and apparently had little direct contact with Christians. Still, he was familiar with the consequences of the Crusades, of which there were three in his lifetime, and the terrors they held for the Jews. His scorn for Christians was possibly also influenced by his Muslim milieu, especially after the loss of Jerusalem to Saladin during his lifetime. Nevertheless, Maimonides thought that the condition of Jews in Muslim countries was worse than that in Christian countries. He wrote in his Epistle to Yemen: "The Arabs . . . passed painful and discriminatory legislation against us. . . . Never did a nation molest, degrade, debase, and hate us as much as they."

Maimonides wanted to uproot idolatry from all territory that came under Jewish rule and to destroy those who refused. Yet he did not call, as Islam did, for launching holy wars to conquer territory and force the inhabitants to abandon idolatry.

Despite Maimonides's stand on Christianity, many later sages have exonerated Christians from the ignominy of idolatry. The most far-reaching among them was Rabbi Menachem HaMeiri (1249–1316). HaMeiri exempted them not on pragmatic but on moral grounds. Many other important rabbis have since cleared Christianity of the stigma of idolatry, on the principle that "the non-Jews of this age are not idolators." Yet some in our own generation would turn back the clock in this regard. Such a view can be inferred even from the writings of former Chief Rabbi Ovadiah Yosef, who is considered to be a political moderate. He points out, in an article in the publication *Oz Le-Shalmon* (3, 1980), that not only is there no possibility of displacing "non-Jews who are idolators" who "live among us," but

> quite the contrary, the Israeli government, by virtue of international law, must defend and protect the Christian holy places and churches in Eretz Yisrael, even though they are houses of idolatry and reserved for their worship, and even though it is a Torah commandment to destroy idolatry and those who serve it and to uproot it until it has totally vanished from our land and from every place that we conquer (see Maimonides, ch. 7 of *Hilkhot Avoda Zara*, Halakha 1). And certainly from the halakhic perspective this weakens the force of the conquest by soldiers of the Israeli Defense Force.

Evidently Rabbi Yosef has returned to the position of Maimonides, namely, that only the Muslims are not idolators. His assertion that the inability to expel idolators weakens the force of the conquest is also interesting. The explanation for this is found earlier in the same essay: "According to all opinions, in the present age, when Israel is not stronger than the nations and cannot expel non-Jews from the Land of Israel because of fear of the nations, this law is certainly not applicable."

The editor of the publication in question concludes: "According to most [of the medieval sages] the prohibition 'They shall not live in your land' does not apply to Muslims because they are not idolators." He does not extend this to include Christians, and the omission may not be accidental.

The classification of Christians as idolators has apparently become widespread and accepted in religious literature. This is not merely a theoretical matter, since practical conclusions flow from it. For example, in 1979 Rabbi Yosef issued a ruling that copies of the New Testament should be torn out of any edition of a Bible owned by a Jew and destroyed (*Ha'aretz*, October 23, 1979). This ruling did not remain a dead letter. An item in the newspaper *Ma'ariv* (June 14, 1985) reported the burning of a copy of the New Testament found in the library at the base of a chief educational officer of the Israeli army.

These manifestations of hostility—the designation of Christians as idolators, the demand to invoke "resident alien" ordinances, and the burning of the New Testament—are distressing. Outside the Land of Israel Jews never dared behave in this fashion. Has independence made the Jews take leave of their senses?

"When Israel Is Stronger than the Nations"

Cultures, like religions, are composed of various beliefs of which one or another may prevail at a particular period in their history. The question is why particular beliefs receive emphasis at a certain time.

The Jewish culture and religion comprise many different strains. There are uplifting manifestations of a gracious attitude toward foreigners and of humanity, even toward the enemy. On the other hand, there are also manifestations of hostility and scorn toward non-Jews. As I have noted, this is hardly a surprising reaction from a people that suffered such grievous persecution, especially as verbal expression was generally the only form of retaliation possible.

Unfortunately, in recent years, the xenophobia has increased in intensity and extended to new areas. For some it is now not merely an attitude but also the basis for deriving general principles of conduct—including proposals for laws against non-Jews and against their residence among Jews. As we have seen, Arabs were not called Amalek in the first years of Israel's statehood, nor were Catholics designated idolators. It never even occurred to rabbis that the halakhic restrictions applicable to resident aliens and Noachides be imposed on the Arabs living in the twentieth-century Jewish state. Neither did the idea of expelling the Arabs appear.

Religion is influenced by external factors such as the political climate of opinion. During the long period when pragmatic realistic political attitudes of Weizmann, Ben-Gurion, and the Labor party prevailed, religion kept the hostile component submerged. That was the achievement of the religious moderates like those in the Mizrachi party. Once the climate of opinion changed during 1967–1977, the hostile elements in religion surfaced with their political implications on the issues of the West Bank and annexation. Thus a wide segment of the Israeli population, because of its traditionalist inclinations, could be enlisted to support the policy of annexation, and though unversed in the Revisionists' ideology, it adopted some of their core values. Jews with collective memory of oppression, especially from backward countries, could be swayed by the idea of ethnocentric power, once they felt they could afford it. Unfortunately, the political leadership did not rise to restrain such a tendency and counsel reasonableness. On the contrary, the leaders of Herut exploited these militant, proprietary attitudes to get into power.

The victory of 1967 led certain extremists to the belief that the age had in fact come when Israel was stronger than the nations of the world, or nearly so. Maimonides explained that the restrictions on idolators (identified with non-Jews in general) are applicable only in such a period: "The foregoing rules applied to the time when the people of Israel lived reviled among the nations, or when the gentiles' power is predominant. But when Israel is predominant over the nations of the world, we are forbidden to permit a gentile who is an idolator to dwell among us" (*Avoda Zara,* 10:6). Thus Maimonides distinguished between two periods: when "the nations of the world are stronger than Israel," and their wrath is to be feared, and when "Israel is stronger than the nations of the world," and may treat them in a high-handed manner.

Thus the alteration in the theological climate derives from the change in the political climate, whose most conspicuous expression is the endorsement of power-politics in the spirit of the Jabotinsky-Begin ethos, and thus the judgment that the political and military situation permits a policy aimed at annexing the territories occupied in 1967. The adoption of a provocative attitude toward non-Jews is also consonant with this ethos. Thus, nationalistic religious Jews have an interest in seeing the supporters of the Jabotinsky-Begin ethos amass political power and hold the reins of government. The claim that they support the Likud because of the subventions they receive is only part of the truth; there are strong ideological affinities as well. Thus religious extremism is not an indigenous theological growth engendered by religious developments: it is a product of historical and political factors.

The common adoration of power links extremist nationalist religion and the Jabotinsky-Begin ethos. Conservative religious circles which are opposed to this movement rightly feel that it is based on an exaggerated view of Israel's military capacity. They cite the Biblical admonition: "Beware lest your heart grow haughty and you forget the Lord your God . . . and you say to yourselves, 'My own power and the might of my own hand have won this wealth for me' " (Deuteronomy 8:14–17).

For the extremists, Israel's might is a guarantee that no harm will befall them. According to Rabbi Z. Y. Kook, the IDF is "holy" and even its weapons are "holy" (for all that some of them are manufactured abroad by non-Jews and "idolators"). Generals who openly violate religious precepts are venerated like saintly rabbis. A phenomenon which is perhaps related is the creeping militarization of religious language, and perhaps even of religious thought. Maimonides would be dumbfounded to hear a rabbi like Rabbi Hess speak of the "personal interest" of a God who "mobilizes" himself.

The faith in Israel's military capacity becomes a functional, psychological, and cognitive need, because without this faith the entire theological structure, including the idea that we are living at the beginning of the Redemption, would collapse. Little wonder that this faith is in full flower. Israel is stronger than all the forces in the Middle East, they believe, and not even the Soviets dare raise a finger. In this view, setbacks are caused not by intrinsic limitations of Israeli might, but by a leadership that is too timorous to exploit the means at its disposal.

Such a faith is a vital part of the world view of the extremists who have settled in the occupied territories because it seems to offer an insurance policy against the collapse of their entire enterprise. Every sign of Arab resistance, every stone hurled at a passing vehicle, is explained as stemming from a single source—the feebleness of Israeli will power, government impotence or negligence—but never from any intrinsic or circumstantial limits. The failures disclosed by the Lebanon War were likewise due to domestic and foreign criticism. Were it not for this, Israel would literally have put the fear of God into the Syrians and the Shi'ites and commanded their instant submission. The same analysis has returned to explain away the Uprising.

Proponents of this view hold that Israel need have no fear of future wars, and can even provoke them at will. Rabbi Shlomo Aviner has written: "We must live in this land even at the price of war. Moreover, even if there is peace, we must instigate wars of liberation in order to conquer it" (*Arzí,* p. 11). He does not specify what additional territory should be conquered, but his words are clearly based on the assumption that everything is possible and all is permitted. It does not occur to him that going to war is a dangerous gamble.

One can understand why soldiers and other young Israelis like Meir Kahane's thesis that Israel is indeed a mighty power but its leadership is too hesitant to make proper use of its forces to solve all Israel's problems with one blow, eliminating terrorism and expelling the Arabs. All of this comes close to the spirit of the Jabotinsky-Begin ethos—the solution in a single energetic event.

Gush Emunim leaders proclaim their discomfort with Kahane and his positions, but do not seem to be aware of how close to him they are. Meir Kahane merely takes one additional step and concludes that, if Israel can found settlements despite the opposition of the Arabs and the world community, it can also succeed in expelling the Arabs. Kahane is merely more conclusive in his positions than Gush Emunim and Herut. His recurrent declaration, "I'm saying what you're thinking" (Ha'aretz, March 31, 1985), is not an empty boast. Nor is it a coincidence that Kahane calls his movement Kach, perhaps an allusion to the old slogan of the Irgun, *Rak Kach* ("only thus"). In his youth Kahane belonged to the Revisionist youth movement, Betar.

Extremist religious circles, including Kahane, frequently repeat the simplistic view that immediately after the victory in 1967 it would have been possible to expel the Arabs, that Israel squandered a golden opportunity because of a weakness of will. Rabbi Wolpe sweetens the bitter pill by saying that the Arabs should have been bribed to leave:

> During the war the Arabs were sure we would kill them all and not leave a single Arab alive; that, at least, is what the Arabs thought, because they imagined that what they would, Heaven forbid, do to the Jews is what we would do to them. Thus if when we conquered Jerusalem and the territories we had announced that we would spare the lives of the inhabitants and even give them monetary compensation, provided they crossed over to Trans-Jordan, they would be thanking us for it till the present day and remembering our mercy to them. . . . But what did the leaders do? They left the Arabs where they were and spent millions of dollars on their welfare (*The Opinion of the Torah*, p. 145).

He sees no impediment to his view—neither international law with regard to occupied territory, nor the United Nations, nor the great powers.

Since the religious perceptions are based on erroneous perceptions in the secular realm we may assume that their decline will come about not as the result of refutation in a religious discourse, but with the downfall of the Jabotinsky-Begin ethos. Let us not forget that the two ideologies also share a profound belief in radical nationalism grounded in the idea of being a Chosen People. This concept has nurtured two major historical currents in the Jewish religion:

1. *Noblesse oblige.* For Jews to be worthy of being a Chosen People they must excel in their deeds. God's choice is conditional; the Jews themselves must prove that they are worthy of that choice. It is not a fact, but a goal. Because conduct is the determining factor, others—that is to say, non-Jews—can also merit status by their deeds. The difference between Jew and non-Jew is not essential or ontological. The sages said, "The righteous of the nations have a share in the world to come"; a "non-Jew who observes the Torah is equal to the High Priest"; "man is dear because he was created in the image of God"; "everyone who preserves a single soul is considered to have preserved the entire world." In this view, the attitude toward the non-Jew is open. The greatness expressed by election stems from one's own exertions and accomplishments.

2. *Nobility is a license.* The Jews, as the Chosen People, are superior in their essence to all other human beings. Their divine

election is a fact, an absolute fact. The difference between Jews and non-Jews is thus part of the very nature of things. "[God] separated between the profane and the holy, between the light and the darkness, between Israel and the nations." The sages have provided us with passages in this spirit too: "Israel is dear, having been called sons of the holy one"; "anyone who preserves a single life of Israel is considered to have preserved an entire world"; "all Israel has a share in the world to come" (not only as a reward for fulfilling the commandments); "no non-Jew has a share in the world to come." In this view, Jews and non-Jews were molded from different matter. True, a non-Jew can convert to Judaism, but by doing so he changes his essence. The attitude toward the non-Jew is closed, and the emphasis is on strict segregation. The greatness expressed by chosenness is embodied in the Jewish collective essence.

In the first approach, the uniqueness of the Jew stems from obligations and is conditional on their being fulfilled; hence, there is an element of tension and self-criticism in this concept, which was embodied in mainstream Zionism. In the second approach, the uniqueness is derived from privileges and is unconditional; it is a source of tranquillity and self-satisfaction. Herein resides its appeal to populism and is embodied in Revisionist Zionism.

The second approach, which distinguishes the Jews from other human beings in their very substance, is essentialist: it explains historical and cultural manifestations as engendered by fundamental qualities that do not vary over time. It is a reasonable assumption that those who take this attitude toward the Jews will also be essentialists with regard to the Arabs and present them as having fixed character traits. This is likely to lead to the development of stereotypes and an insensitivity to the changes that take place in all human societies. It is a stumbling block to understanding.

The second approach merges with the radicalism that attributes supreme value to the concept of the nation or race. Its natural extension is the idea that "the whole world is against us." In its most extreme forms it presents nonsegregation and openness toward strangers as "treason" against Judaism, as Kahane repeatedly says. This view of a unique essence also breeds the belief that the Jews are allowed what is forbidden to others.

On the political level, the idea that the greatness of the Jews stems from their essence is translated into self-righteousness: Israel is not responsible for untoward developments in the Arab-Israeli conflict, and indeed cannot be. It is no accident that Begin promoted this attitude, and found immediate support for it and himself among religious circles. At first sight this link between the Likud ethos and religious Jews is positive, encouraging high morale. But it has a very important negative aspect, in that it prevents Israelis from comprehending their true situation, from understanding the adversary and his motives. It thus stands in the way of Israel's doing its part to resolve the conflict.

Judaism has been radicalized in two ways: politically, in supporting extreme nationalism and annexation of the West Bank; socially, in fostering hostility to gentiles in general and Arabs in particular. We find ourselves in a grave predicament. True, expressions of hostility and discriminatory enactments existed earlier, but until now they were moot. Since 1967, they are no longer so and the possibility has been breathed into them by the demand that such laws should be applied here and now. Thus, they have been actualized and made plausible. We can no longer shrug our shoulders at the hostile material on the pretext that it is a very minor as well as extinct part of the Judaic tradition. Indeed, I suspect that the new developments in the Jewish religion constitute transmutation of great significance. As these changes occur before our eyes we may fail to appreciate how revolutionary they are. What has surfaced cannot again be routinely submerged.

Messianism

One belief in the religious outlook goes far beyond the evaluation of the Jabotinsky ethos that reality permits the Jews to behave as they wish: the belief that the Messiah's arrival is imminent. If the Messiah is on his way there is nothing to fear; he will bail us out of all misfortunes and grant Israel the final victory. The Messianic idea serves as a sort of insurance policy against all complications, countering all fears that reality might be a stumbling block on the road to desired goals. To many religious Jews, the successes of Zionism are signs that the Redemption has begun. On the other hand, a state with a tottering economy, which failed in the Lebanon War, which released over one thousand terrorists under shameful conditions, hardly seems to be on the threshold of Redemption. These religious Jews explain the disasters as the "birth pangs of the Messiah." In this way both successes and failures are evidence of the Messiah's approach. The idea is immune to refutation.

Even many Jews fail to grasp the strength of the faith in the imminent arrival of the Messiah among some religious extremists, including members of Gush Emunim. Most Israelis are simply unaware that these circles deny any possibility that the Messiah might yet be long in coming, may even not come, and the extent to which this faith supports them through hardships, prepares them for catastrophes, and encourages their adventures. They scorn all who doubt that the Messiah is coming soon and see tangible signs of his coming in every Zionist success and military victory.

This faith also has a functional significance. Without it there is little sense to the settlement movement. In addition, the more circumstances contradict their political ideas—the more it becomes evident that the territories cannot be held, that the Arabs are multiplying and will attain a majority, that the Arabs cannot be expelled and are rebelling—the more tenacious their belief that the Messiah's coming is imminent.

Placing the ideas of Redemption and Messianism at the center radically changes the Zionist ideology and the goal of the establishment of the Jewish state. The goal of Zionism ceases to be the solution for the historical vulnerability of the Jews and becomes the establishment of a state that will serve as a means to bring on the Redemption.

The Messianic idea has always had an important role in religious thought, promising that the suffering of this world and its injustices are not ultimate, that a better and just age is yet to come. History is then not merely a mass of disasters, but has a purposive direction. For the Jews the Messianic idea has also mediated between the concept of election as a chosen people and the distresses of the exile that contradicted this concept. Nevertheless, whenever signs of the Messiah's arrival have been discerned—whenever Messianism has taken on a more tangible imminence—the consequences have proved dire.

The Jewish sages, aware of this danger, censured and cursed all those who would attempt to bring the Messiah before his time. This never completely stopped the Jews from calculating the date of the Messiah's coming, but preoccupation with such calculations was widely considered harmful. In practice, then, the Jews evolved a way of life based on applying halakha as a self-sufficient regimen that had no need of Messianism in day-to-day life. They held fast to the Messianic idea as a way of making exile endurable, while at the same time placing his arrival in the indefinite future.

The Messianic idea takes many forms. Messianism as symboliz-ing an ideal, a wish, a distant dream differs from Messianism as a means and sanction for action in the present, as a situation that has immediate political implications. In such a situation Messianism is transformed from a religious belief into a political ideology: Mes-sianism as a program and movement. One must be especially wary of Messianism seen as a way to change political circumstances, to transform them into a desired reality that cannot be achieved ex-cept by the coming of the Messiah. In such a guise the Messiah then becomes a *deus ex machina,* a guarantee that the unrealistic will nevertheless be realized. Thus Messianism deteriorates to a sort of cosmic hocus-pocus: no need to worry, the miraculous event will occur.

It should be noted that in this respect Jewish activist religious radicalism is in a category all by itself among the religions of the Middle East. Although the Messianic idea is to be found in Shi'ite and Sunni Islam, it lacks the urgent significance of Jewish Messian-ism. Muslim policies and conduct are not based on any presump-tion of the coming of the Messiah, and his failure to come is irrelevant to their present situation and positions. The Second Coming is likewise not central to Christianity.

The traditional Jewish view expects the Messiah to arrive every day; in that case all of history is the beginning of the Redemption. The explicit assertion that a certain period is the beginning of the Redemption arouses a hope that can only be destructive. Paradoxi-cally, no idea poses a greater menace to the survival of the State of Israel than that which links Zionism with Redemption and Mes-sianism. The attempt to do so undermines the State of Israel, since any Zionism that does not bring on the Redemption thereby loses its point.

So, in effect, does religion. The religious radicals who anticipate that Zionist successes indicate the beginning of Redemption see this as leading to a spiritual uplifting and the advancement of religious thinking. On the contrary, association with political power has generally debased rather than elevated theological thought.

The present Messianism is a sign of impatience and lack of understanding. The pretension of being able to disclose the hid-den secrets of the Creator and decipher the divine plan are totally contrary to Isaiah's truly religious attitude—as when God says to him, "As the heavens are high above the earth, so are my ways high above your ways and my plans above your plans" (Isaiah 55:9). It is true that Jewish tradition includes recurrent boasts and even systems of precise knowledge about the deeds and will of God; what is strange about the present claims is the use of events in the real world as signs of the Creator's intentions. Rabbis claim to have seen such signs in Zionism and its realization. (But with the same force, and perhaps with even greater confidence, Muslim theologians can assert that the presence of so vital a natural resource as petroleum in the Arab countries is evidence that the Muslims are the elect of God.) In the interim, the successes that were seen as heralding imminent Redemption have been accompanied by events such as the evacuation of Yamit and the settlements in the Sinai—which the prophets of the imminent Redemption had loudly proclaimed would not occur because divine Providence would intervene—and the Lebanon War. But the believers remain undeterred by negative developments in the real world.

The Jewish sages offered many contradictory ideas as to when the Messiah will come, what set of portents will indicate the Redemption is beginning. In our time, Rabbi A. I. Kook and even more so his son, Rabbi Z. Y. Kook, have stressed that it is denial of the fact that we live at the beginning of Redemption that is deferring full Redemption. At the other end of the spectrum, Rabbi S. D. Wolpe, representing the position of the Lubavitcher Rebbe, asserts that "those who call our age the beginning of the Redemption are deferring the Redemption" (p. 35); repentance must precede the Messiah's coming. But Rabbi Meir Kahane offers an easier remedy: "We have it in our power to bring the Messiah" (*Ha'aretz*, August 8, 1984). The desires of the Almighty are merely a technical detail; the decisive factor is the Jews' own will. If the Jews' own will can bring the Messiah, who can stand against them? The Arabs? The Americans? The Russians?

Only those with an unshakable faith in the imminent arrival of the Messiah could have begun to plot the demolition of the mosques on the Temple Mount, as the members of the so-called "Jewish Underground" did, without worrying about the consequences of such an act. How else could they ignore the strong possibility that some or all of the forty Muslim states, from Indonesia and Pakistan to Morocco and Mauritania, would retaliate by declaring a holy war against Israel, that the superpowers would intervene to prevent a general conflagration, and might even demand that Jerusalem be placed under international rule? Perhaps those who planned this deed hoped that God, confronted by the danger to Israel's existence from a Muslim *jihad,* would be "compelled" to send the Messiah in order to prevent the destruction of the "Third Temple."

The fact that there were Jews who plotted to blow up the Dome of the Rock should be a source of grave concern. It cannot be assumed that those who were brought to trial were alone. Might a group opposed to eventual negotiations for resolving the Arab-Israeli conflict plant a bomb in the mosques as a means to derail them? Given the psychosis prevalent in some circles in the country, the chance that something like this will happen is not negligible. In this context we cannot dismiss the significance of the widely disseminated aerial photograph of the Old City in which the mosques were airbrushed out of existence and replaced by a model of the Second Temple. Such a picture is apt to inspire yearnings for its realization. Jewish extremists call the mosques an abomination, and this designation itself seemingly requires action to remove them. In a yeshiva adjacent to the Temple Mount, garments for the Temple priests are already being woven in anticipation that they will be needed in the near future. In other yeshivot, the detailed laws of animal sacrifices have become a popular topic of study, as if they will soon have contemporary relevance. Before the Messiah was a hope; now he has become a necessity.

The ideas of Redemption and Messianism are a portent of disaster in two respects. In the short term, the Messianic idea is a distraction from the need to consider reality and encourages unrealistic and rash policies. What is the benefit of a Messianism whose practical result is that through the annexation of territories Israel becomes an Arab country or nearly so? Some would defend the new Messianism by presenting Zionism as a manifestation of a natural, historical Redemption. But what is the benefit of a Messianism without a Messiah? The disappointment caused by disasters not mitigated by heavenly salvation can have serious consequences. A widespread obsession with Messianism is liable to end in grief.

Meir Kahane is certain that disaster is not on the cards: "The State of Israel is not a political creature; it is a religious creature. No power in the world could have prevented its establishment, and no force can destroy it" (p. 244). For him, "History is not a sequence of detached and chance events. There is a plan for history; the Jew is coming home for the third and final time. . . . 'The first redemption was the redemption from Egypt; the second was that of Ezra; and the third redemption has no end.' " The verses from *Midrash* are guarantee enough for him.

The very suspicion that political processes might compel Israel to part with locales that are deeply connected with historical and religious memories, with all the pain this entails, disposes one to grasp solutions that are not natural and historical. In the throes of religious and nationalist fervor, human beings are able to follow suicidal courses of action, both as individuals and as groups. The risk of death is no obstacle. Thousands of Japanese pilots volunteered for kamikaze raids, and close to thirteen hundred actually killed themselves crashing their planes into the decks of American ships. Religious ecstasy is infectious. Hundreds of Americans took poison under the influence of the mad preacher Jim Jones. People are apt to follow a risky course when they accept the idea that the most they can lose is their lives, and all the more so when they believe that death is not final and they will be rewarded by their Creator, whose will they are fulfilling.

If resolution of the Arab-Israeli conflict would involve withdrawal from parts of the God-bequeathed heritage, and if the absence of a political settlement is liable to lead to further wars and catastrophes, only one solution remains: the Messiah. Moreover, the contradictions besetting the situation of religion in the modern age foster throughout the world, West as well as East, extremist religious positions that are quite irrational, in part because men who have gone astray are loath to acknowledge their error. The view that the only solution available to the State of Israel is to achieve the goal in full, while any other course leads to oblivion, is likely in itself to lead to greater extremism and a readiness for mindless risks and gambles.

There are in fact two opposed positions with regard to the relationship between the State of Israel and Messianism and Redemption. Ultra-Orthodox circles such as the Natorei Karta and Satmar Hasidim see Zionism and the establishment of the State of Israel as tantamount to rebelling against the divine command to wait patiently. For the disciples of the Rabbis Kook, father and son, by contrast, the State of Israel is the beginning of the Redemption. The first view has a long life expectancy, since every disaster can be interpreted as punishment for the Zionist idea and the establishment of the state. The second view is vulnerable to the vicissitudes of time. As the years pass and the anticipated event does not occur—and, quite to the contrary, the situation gets worse—it will tend to refute itself.

A third and intermediate position, which should be encouraged, ascribes some religious significance to the vision of Jewish political independence, but does not trespass on God's province and pretend to decipher his plans or chart his course for him. Here Messianism remains a goal, not a fact, and certainly not a boast of certainty that the Messiah has only a short road left to travel before he arrives.

The Impact of Nationalistic Judaism on Israel and the Jews

The growth of radical fundamentalism is common to all three of the monotheistic religions. In Christianity, however, the traditional separation between church and state and a tendency to focus on matters of faith and conduct direct most of its branches away from direct political involvement. It is true that Christian fundamentalism takes positions on political questions, both domestic and foreign, but it is more or less the exception that tests the rule.

The common denominator of Judaism and Islam is that both are based on religious law and do not recognize a separation between church and state, and therefore seek to dictate all details of life. Thus we can compare the new trends in the two of them.

Religious fundamentalism has appeared in the Islamic countries. However, as Emanuel Sivan explains in his *Radical Islam,* Sunni fundamentalism, especially in Egypt, directs the brunt of its attack inward, against manifestations of Westernization and deviations from Islam. It gives less attention to the area of foreign policy, since it is considered to be merely an outgrowth of domestic corruption; consequently, the Arab-Israeli conflict has low priority. The problems of foreign affairs will be resolved as a by-product of the resolution of domestic problems—religious reform and a return to Islam in lifestyles and politics. These changes will strengthen the Islamic states and give them the capacity to overthrow their external enemies, including Israel. Sunni Egyptian fundamentalists are thus not tolerant toward Israel, but see it as a minor annoyance that will disappear when the state becomes truly Islamic. Sivan emphasizes the pessimism and despair that have gripped Islamic fundamentalism because of the penetration of Western modernism and secularism into every corner of Arab society. It should be noted that Sunni fundamentalism elsewhere, particularly in Syria, is much more militant toward Israel.

In Khomeini's Shi'ite revolution, foreign affairs play a much more important role because Khomeini aspired to unify the Islamic world and to this end endeavored to blur the distinctions between Shi'ism and Sunnism. The practice of applying Islamic religious law in all realms is fundamental to Khomeini's teachings: he dictates political matters as well as legal ones and has the authority to determine which elements of religious law will be applied and which not. In Judaism and Sunni Islam, religious law is above religious leaders; in Khomeini's brand of Shi'ism religious leaders are superior to religious law.

In Israel religious extremism has two poles: conservative (Natorei Karta) and revolutionary (Gush Emunim and Kahane). The conservative stream is not active in the political realm, since it envisions Redemption only by means of divine intervention. It views life in the State of Israel as no different from life in the Diaspora in a non-Jewish state, and perhaps as even worse, because Israel is a state of nominal Jews who have cast off the yoke of Torah. The religious radicals are distinguished from the conservative stream by their stress on foreign affairs, their hostility to non-Jews, and their tolerance and even sympathetic attitude toward secular Jews, so long as they play a positive role in their view of the national endeavor.

A conventional explanation for the rise of an extremist Judaism in Israel is that Zionism failed because it had no spiritual content other than the idea of Jewish sovereignty; once this was realized it lost its appeal. It seems to me that the failure of Judaism to cope with the problems posed by modern life is no less conspicuous. The nationalistic turn in Orthodox circles and the hostility toward the stranger that has become so central to it result from forgetting the moral and spiritual role of religion. The rise of radical religion has meant not a deepening of religious thought but the establishment of a cult of the sanctified state and army.

When Judaism enters the arena of foreign affairs, the success or failure of foreign policy influences the standing of religion. If it sanctions a particular political line, such as settlement activity and annexation, and this line ends disastrously, there are likely to be repercussions on the status of the religion that courted the disaster. That is why it is so dangerous to make religion the underwriter of a particular political course. God must not serve as collateral for annexing the occupied territories. It would be a political and religious disaster if the fate of Judaism in Israel were discredited by the political outcome of the West Bank and the Gaza Strip.

Throughout the generations, Jewish sages have been aware of

this problem and have been careful not to make history into the proving ground of theology. The persecutions of the Exile were deliberately not given a religious meaning so that the Jewish people could endure despite the contradiction between their faith in their election and their misery. Not so with Islam, in which history has been mobilized to prove theology; Cantwell Smith explained the difficulties Islam encounters by virtue of seeing political success as a proof of religious truth, especially in the modern age. Perhaps Jewish extremism will travel the full circle, and return to the traditional distinction between history and theology and the belief that the failure of Messianic hopes is a sign that the generation is not worthy of Redemption. The revolutionary pole of extremism will then find refuge in the conservative pole, sinking deep into theology and a forgetfulness of history and divorcing itself from political life. There are already signs of this trend. The knitted skullcaps of the religious extremists are already being exchanged for the black ones of the conservatives, the militant green windbreakers for the traditional long, black coats.

We must not expect religious leaders to be free of human weaknesses and impulses. They too are only human beings. But to the extent that they perform religious tasks, or represent a political party whose entire justification is that it is religious, the public will view them with a critical eye and judge the influence of religion for good or evil according to them. It is indeed difficult to separate religion from its upholders and representatives. The licentious behavior of popes and clergy played a large part in causing the Reformation. The growth of religion in Israel has led to increasing materialism, aggressiveness, intolerance, excommunicatory bans, religious hooliganism, and vandalism.

The behavior of religious leaders in Israel is frequently no recommendation for religion. The press is full of critical articles on the goings-on in the rabbinical courts; their verdicts that discriminate against women particularly disaffect the public. The application of public funds to favored religious institutions by members of the Knesset has become scandalous. Religious groups wrangle among themselves unceasingly. The ultra-Orthodox communities may seem to be united, but those who leave the fold tell of unpleasant strife "within the wall." The dishonesty expressed by denying the legitimacy of the State of Israel while being happy to enjoy its money will inevitably redound on these groups.

Religion in Israel is now a big business. The religious establishment has become immense. A vast number of people make their living from religion: rabbis, religious court judges, teachers, well-supported yeshiva students, organizers of weddings and other ceremonies, kashrut supervisors, ritual circumcisers, workers in ritual baths, ritual slaughterers, sextons, morticians, and many more. The system is self-perpetuating. Religion is not only a way of life, but social security as well, a way to find employment in one of the functions reserved exclusively for the religiously observant. It is difficult to arrive at the number of those who make their living from religion in Israel, but it must bear comparison, on a proportional basis, to the number of priests, monks, nuns, and religious functionaries of various sorts in the Catholic countries at the height of religious domination in the Middle Ages. This is a significant burden on the economy of the state.

On the one hand, this phenomenon strengthens religion, because it becomes the personal interest and source of livelihood for many; but on the other hand it is a corrupting factor. To the extent that this apparatus is swollen disproportionately it will be harmed when economic straits make it increasingly difficult to allocate the requisite funds from the state budget. As government supervision of expenditures becomes tighter, the freedom enjoyed by the henchmen of religion to distribute benefits and supports will be limited, and dissatisfaction will grow. An ugly war for survival may yet break out among the religious circles themselves.

The problem of the relationship between religion and state is much more severe in Israel than in other nations, and in orthodox Judaism than in other religions. In Christianity the sundering of the religious and secular authorities has theological grounding in the principle that God created two realms, which work in tandem to fulfill vital roles respectively in human life. Each is an emissary of God, and each represents him. This doctrine did not prevent the prelates of the church from seeing themselves as superior to the lay rulers, and the consequent struggle lasted for centuries. The separation became historically secure only after the popes gave up their attempt to impose their authority on secular princes. But the nature of Christianity as a religion of faith, restricted for the most part to matters of personal conduct and belief, made the separation easier.

Such a division is very difficult in religions based on laws, such as Islam and Judaism. But Islam did not lay down the details of daily life to the same extent that Judaism did. Islam, according to popular Arabic, is a lenient religion. It has no need to segregate

the congregation of believers from their non-Islamic surroundings. Originally the caliph was a religious authority who was also
entrusted with political power. Over the course of time the relationship was inverted, and the caliph became a political potentate
who was also head of the believers, not by virtue of his piety but
because of his political eminence. Furthermore, over the generations the Islamic world was subject to secular rulers whose authority was accepted by the scholars of religious law. The pattern of the
relations between ruler and religious law was established in a climate of religious domination. Nevertheless, religious law made its
peace with the authorities and its scholars generally supported
them. This gave the pattern a permanent validity. The religious
establishment was weak, and this weakness was institutionalized in
history. Religious scholars demanded obedience even to a tyranni-
cal ruler, out of fear of domestic strife that could wreak more harm
than the most corrupt of rulers could. The authorities also maintained a system of civil jurisdiction. In Islamic countries Islam was
defined as the source of all legislation, but this was never truly the
case. Thus Islam made its peace with civilian rule.

In Judaism the situation is quite different. There was no Jewish
civil state for nearly two thousand years. Jews were subject to the
rule of foreigners, whose laws they had to obey. The law with
which they identified was always the halakha. Rabbis were mostly
the leaders of the community, and its judges. Jews followed the
discipline of halakha and its interpreters, and this became institutionalized historically.

For the Orthodox extremists, a Jewish state that is not founded
by the Messiah and that does not make halakha the law of the land
lacks any legitimacy. The problem of the relationship between the
divine law and rule of halakha, on the one hand, and civil law, on
the other, is by no means resolved. This is an area with great
potential for problems. The assertion that halakha is superior to
civil law, and that basic decisions with regard to the national lifestyle must accord with the halakha, which need only be interpreted
to meet the particular exigency, rather than by the political and
parliamentary process, is fraught with peril. The problem becomes
more severe when the claim is made that external policy must also
follow the dictates of halakha. Moderate religious groups have
tried to find some sort of modus vivendi on these questions, even
if only as a pragmatic compromise. But such a compromise is alien
to the spirit of religious extremists.

This is an important problem that should be considered further.

States have always had policies. The innovation made by the Greeks was public debate—politics—aimed at shaping policies. Politics is born when policy decisions are liberated from subordination to a king or a religion. The modern democratic state demands an open political life that enjoys freedom in molding policies. In the Jewish religion, by contrast, halakha demarcates boundaries that political deeds and decisions cannot transgress. This conflict complicates daily life in Israel.

Christianity solved this problem by separating church and state. In Israel this was harder to achieve: first because of the halakhic dictation of all phases of life; second because the dominant political parties have wooed the religious ones to form coalition governments, which has magnified their influence. Nevertheless, it would seem that Israel cannot escape a similar separation of powers, to be effected by expanding the role of the state in legislation and policy and restricting the realm of religion.

This separation will not, however, come as a single event, as a principled decision, but as a painful process—the accumulation of compromises and patchwork solutions. This, it seems to me, is how the contradiction will be resolved between religion's demands that all actions accord with halakha and the civil state's need to proceed in accordance with calculations of political interest. This slow resolution may be unsatisfactory, but it is the only one possible. The contradictions between the demands of halakha and those of a sovereign democratic state are not necessarily sufficient to trigger an explosion, as is sometimes predicted. Societies typically have manifold contradictions, but usually find ways to get around or overcome or control them.

All societies consist of secular people and religious people, and there are other places in the world where there are serious disagreements among them; but the deployment into two rival camps seems nowhere as pronounced as in Israel. Anticlericalism reached fierce heights in many Catholic countries, but ultimately a modus vivendi was created that expresses the people's attachment to religion alongside their identification with secular values. Again the basic separation of the two realms helped this along. Islam has its month of Ramadan, and public violation of its restrictions is a criminal offense in most Muslim countries. But Islam does not have a Sabbath, whereas the Jewish Sabbath spurs fights among Israelis at regular seven-day intervals. The Sabbath may have preserved the Jews over the generations, but today it severely complicates the relations among them and divides them into warring factions.

Certainly Israel should have a Jewish character, but this is a point on which full consistency is not possible. The State of Israel can perhaps be the state of the Jewish people, as proclaimed by a Knesset resolution of July, 1985, but Israel cannot be the state of Jewish religion. There are elements of halakha that are not applicable in practice. The sages said, "Custom nullifies halakha," and "we do not pass decrees that the public cannot endure." A significant portion of the Israeli public is of the opinion that many decrees and elements of halakha are unendurable. The true challenge facing Israel's religious leaders should be that of adapting halakha to modern life and to the new phenomenon of Jews having a state of their own.

As the self-confidence of religious circles in Israel has grown, so have their demands: this tends to intensify the tension between the religious and the secular. The secular Jews are in the majority, and there is no sign that this is likely to change; when their tolerance gives out they are apt to react forcefully. Many religious circles in Israel display an extreme sensitivity to Christian missionaries but seem oblivious of the threat that their conduct and attitudes pose to the continued adherence of Jews to Judaism.

Negative religious manifestations in Israel are also likely to influence the attitude of Jews in the Diaspora toward Israel and the Jewish religion. It would be tragic if the status of Judaism was to decline because of the emergence of fanatical tendencies that cause Jews to disassociate themselves from their religion on the grounds that in the final analysis Judaism must be judged by its constituents and their conduct. This response is likely to impact upon the State of Israel as well. Religious domination of Israeli society may perhaps attract religious Jews to the country; but by the same token it will deter the immigration of secular Jews, who constitute the majority. Yes, there are groups among American Jewry who tend to nationalist religious extremism, but the fact that they function in a pluralist environment and are directly opposed by the leaders of the great majority of moderate Jews tends to muffle their influence there.

Still, one should not discount the financial as well as inspirational impact of American religious extremists on their counterparts in Israel. Moreover, considerable support for the religious extremists comes from wealthy American Jews who think their donations are used only for purely religious education.

Jewish religious extremism has been associated with a startling deterioration in the quality of theological thought. Its leaders usurp God's role and decide what his position should be, claiming to know the secrets of his mind. Rabbis have confidently asserted that the disaster of the Lebanon War resulted from the immoral behavior of women soldiers, that the fatal collision between a train and a school bus was punishment for nonobservance of the Sabbath in Petah Tikvah. They "know" that God has signed up to back the Israel cause, is angry with gentiles, can no longer restrain his wrath, and is about to explode against them. Meir Kahane has explained that the establishment of the State of Israel was "the beginning of God's wrath, his vengeance on the gentiles who ignored his existence" (p. 244).

These manifestations are distressing. In contrast to the present situation, when the second-century sage Rabbi Yosi b. Kisma expressed concern at the risks that Rabbi Hananniah b. Teradyon was taking in contravening the Roman decree by teaching Torah publicly, and Rabbi Hananniah tried to comfort him by saying, "Heaven will have mercy," Rabbi Yosi replied, "I'm telling you something sensible and you answer that Heaven will have mercy?" (*Avodah Zara*, 18A.) The confident assertion that Heaven will have mercy is not a sensible remark. This applies to every assertion that God will intervene in the political and military process.

The pattern of thinking implied by Rabbi Zvi Yehudah Kook's statement that the entire world will have to get accustomed to the idea that Israel will not yield a single inch of the occupied territories, and it will be better for them when they do so, is also distressing. The statement implies a threat that if the world does not accept annexation it will be punished. If "Heaven will have mercy" is accounted folly, what would the ancient sages have said of the assertion that "Heaven will punish?"

There is a trend toward populist and primitive religion. One example is the sermons of a propagandist for the return to religion, Rabbi Amnon Yitzhak, which are distributed on cassettes. He promises that those who wear the *tallit katan* (fringed undergarment) will be rewarded with material treasures and benefits, including "2,800 slaves" (*Emdah*, 2, 1985, p. 11). Where will such versions of Judaism lead? They are not so marginal as one might think; the cult of flesh-and-blood "saints" who sell holy water and amulets and claim to have a direct line to God—a familiar phenomenon in contemporary Israel—is not so far from this.

Some rejoice at the difficulties that are besetting Western culture, as if it has foundered into bankruptcy. Self-examination would reveal that our own situation as Jews is no better. We must be sober not only in our dealings with others, but also with ourselves, which is much more difficult.

Substantial benefits are likely to stem from a critical attitude to religious extremism. It will become clear that not everything said in the name of Judaism is the word of God. Judaism consists not only of a divine message but also of interpretations and regulations added over the generations by religious leaders who have woven a splendid fabric of religion, belief, and law. This is undoubtedly a glorious enterprise, but, in the manner of human beings, such leaders are not immune to error. The sages of old, recognizing the relativity of their words, dared to disagree with one another. Seeing the tradition in a relative perspective is a condition for all spiritual and religious renewal. Renewal and innovation stem from the recognition of failure and limits.

Reducing the idealization of Judaism will benefit religious and secular Jews alike. The establishment of the State of Israel confronted the Jewish religion with problems it had not had to cope with previously. This led to conflict and even crisis. But this can have positive results if religious leaders are able to rise to the occasion and deal with the new situation with insight and humility. A moderate and tolerant approach stems from a profound religious awareness, whereas fanaticism is a symptom of spiritual arrogance and narrowness. The sages said: "The splendor of wisdom is humility."

External Influences

Religions have a great internal validity that endows them with the capacity to overcome their own contradictions. The congregation of the faithful explains these sources of doubt and perplexity—for example, the problem of evil—in such a way as to soften their thrust, to restrain and contain their influence. The collective commitment to religion emerges victorious. But the problems aroused by religious extremism in Israel are different. It is not enough to overcome them internally because they also have external repercussions. The rise of extremist Judaism and the dissemination of its political positions inevitably affects world public opinion toward the State of Israel, Judaism, and the Jewish people.

The elements of the Jewish heritage that are hostile to non-Jews have long been known to the world, and anti-Semitic writings quote them at length. Until recently few would have seriously asserted that these passages reflect the opinions of Jews in our own generation. But, when religious extremists inject a contemporary relevance into these passages, such as Maimonides on the treatment of resident aliens, they acquire a new and dangerous significance. They provide ammunition for anti-Semites, who can assert that the true Jewish character is revealed not when Jews are subjugated in Christian or Muslim society but precisely when they are free. It is in their natural environment, not in subjugation, that they dare disclose their true face, and the nations of the world must redefine their attitude in view of the strong Jews rather than the impotent Jews. Jewish religious extremists are quite unaware that they are providing retroactive justification for anti-Semitic atrocities. Anti-Semitism does not exist because of the utterances of religious extremists, nor are they mainly responsible for its increase in recent years; but they do assist and encourage it.

When Jews see themselves as superior to all other human beings, an "aristocracy" in Mordechai Nisan's term, they are claiming license to do what is forbidden to others. The Catholic church has made worthy efforts to expunge from its liturgy expressions of abuse toward Jews and to exculpate them from collective deicide. This initiative has been far from easy, because it dealt with matters that have long been the foundations of the Christian religion. When Jews describe the Christian religion as idolatry they are in fact employing language they loathed when it was used against them. Centuries after great rabbis ruled that Christianity is *not* idolatry, why are Jews now returning to the old positions?

It is naturally difficult for the adherents of one religion to recognize the validity of another, since each religion claims a monopoly on the truth. But, if Jews begin to draw upon traditional texts that call for the expulsion of Christians and their institutions from Jerusalem, why should the Vatican accept Israeli rule in Jerusalem and not reassert its old demand for the internationalization of Jerusalem? Likewise, many Christian institutions and churches were built in the latter part of the twelve hundred years in which Muslims ruled Jerusalem, whereas there was fierce opposition in Israel recently to the construction of a building for a Mormon university. Should Israel cause the Christians to long for Muslim rule in Jerusalem? If Israel bans Christian academic institutions, Christians will ask why they should allow Jewish schools to operate in their lands. Is Israel behaving sanely if it permits intolerance that undermines Jews' moral and political position?

In Rishon Lezion two young men exhumed the body of a Chris-

NATIONALISTIC JUDAISM 181

tian woman who had not converted to Judaism from her grave in a Jewish cemetery, even though she had lived for many years as a member of the secular Jewish community, and her son had served in the Israeli army and regarded himself as a Jew. The two were tried and convicted, but, as was reported in the press, the local religious court and the Israeli Chief Rabbinate in Jerusalem expressed support for their deed, asserting that religious law forbade the burial of a Christian in a Jewish cemetery. It was also argued that, in cases of conflict between civil and religious law, "divine law is above human law." Outside Israel Jews never dared make such claims, and held fast to the sages' principle that "the law of the kingdom is the law." Religious Jews seem unaware how much explosive material is latent in the assertion that halakha takes precedence over the law of the land.

If, as Meir Kahane and many others assert, Jews have the right to expel Arabs and aliens from the Land of Israel, why do the nations of the world have to allow Jews to live in their countries? The same reasoning applies to Rabbi Yosef's ruling that the New Testament should be burned and the unfortunate case of the actual burning of a copy thereof: it provides retroactive legitimacy to the burning of Jewish holy books by Christians.

The most revolting manifestation of this trend—even if it involves only a tiny minority in Israel—is the revival of the command to blot out the memory of Amalek and the identification of Amalek with the Arabs. How can a rabbi's assertion that the killing of a non-Jew is not murder be justified? Christians might say that killing Jews isn't murder, thereby providing sanction for all the pogroms of history. How can Jews hold up their heads when they hear such claims and not actively combat them?

The world has accepted the view that, despite the fact that a state is sovereign and ostensibly permitted to act as it likes in its domestic affairs, and no outside agency has the right to intervene, a country nevertheless bears responsibility for its domestic policies toward humankind as a whole. This is the principle on which the Universal Bill of Human Rights is based. Jewish leaders, including important rabbis, have made frequent public promises that Israel would treat its non-Jewish minorities decently and fairly. Similar phrasing appears in Israel's Declaration of Independence. No rabbis ever so much as hinted that Israel would regress to the regulations of resident alien and Noachides, and that only under such conditions could non-Jews live in the Jewish state. How can thinking Jews accept the anachronistic concept of resident alien?

Meir Kahane does not mince words. "There is an absolute and irresoluble contradiction between the State of Israel . . . and the modern nation-state that sees all of its citizens as possessing equal rights. . . . There is a potential confrontation . . . between the Zionist Jewish state . . . and modern ideas of democracy and citizenship" (p. 109). Can we as Jews confront the world with such an assertion? Certainly there is much discrimination and repression in the world, but few openly proclaim the right to treat others as inferior and laud themselves for doing so. The claim can now be made that Khomeinism has appeared among us.

A case can be made against me that by revealing these tendencies of the Jews and Israel I am providing ammunition to enemies. I find myself in a painful conflict. There is no escape from it, though there is comfort in knowing that I am not alone and am not divulging any secrets. Much of what I have written here has been aired elsewhere, including the problem of the identification of Amalek with the Arabs. Amnon Rubinstein's book, from which I have taken a number of citations, has appeared in English (though we should not pretend that non-Jews do not read Hebrew and follow what is published in the Israeli press). The article by Rabbi Yisrael Hess, "The Commandment of Genocide in the Torah," received widespread publicity and was even discussed in an English-language publication of the University of Cape Town. The burning of the New Testament was discussed in the Foreign Affairs Committee of the Knesset (*Ma'ariv,* July 5, 1985) and debated on Israeli television. Meir Kahane publishes his views in English. A conspiracy of silence about these beliefs and this use of the tradition allows them to go unchallenged and encourages those who propagate them. There can be no remedy without first identifying the problem. By hiding our shame from outsiders we hide it from ourselves as well. The Torah says many times, "You shall sweep out the evil from your midst." At the very least we must cry out against it.

The apologists who claim that non-Jews understand that Jews, like every human society, have lunatic fringes who should not be taken seriously are being irresponsible. Kahane won election to the Knesset, and support for his position in Israel has been rising. The same applies to other religious extremists; they are not a negligible element. Perhaps memories of the past and the bad conscience that many Christians have because of centuries of persecution of the Jews restrain them from responding in word and

deed. But it is foolishly shortsighted to assume that these sentiments will stem hostile reactions indefinitely.

The absence of a strong opposition to religious extremism by
recognized Jewish religious and lay leaders abroad and by the chief
rabbis and the political leadership in Israeli is apt to be considered
a tacit tolerance of its views. So far the reaction of moderate religious circles has been weak. Stronger reactions will come only if
the matter becomes urgent, if public debate embarrasses the religious and lay leadership. It will not move of its own accord, because of the roots that the extremist positions have in the tradition.
It is not the call for a discussion of the problem that is damaging
but rather the reluctance to grapple with it.

Let us remember that what is at stake is not some secondary
question, or a problem that will go away if it is ignored. The
struggle is for the soul of Judaism and its status in the world, and
for the moral and political status of the State of Israel.

The Impact on the Arab-Israeli Conflict

Jewish religious circles also promote the expansionist tendencies
of the State of Israel. An item in *Ha'aretz* (August 24, 1985) reported on the distribution of information sheets for school excur-
sions to sixty principals. The author of the document explained:

> We're talking about the most convenient method for
> expansion. . . . From the political perspective, we have
> to reach the Tigris and Euphrates. It's written in the
> *halakha.* There's no argument about this, the only
> argument is over applying it in practice—whether it
> needs to be done by force or not. As for the boundaries
> of the Land of Israel, there are no arguments; they are
> clear axioms.

It didn't occur to this educator that the Arabs are a factor as well.
For him, it is enough that the borders of the Land of Israel are
defined by tradition. The Arabs can conclude from such opinions
that, even if they make peace with Israel, the state itself under the
pressure of certain groups within it—whose size they are likely to
exaggerate—will still strive to expand.

A more pointed example of the harmful political use of religion
is found in Mordechai Nisan's *The Jewish State and the Arab Problem*
in which he attempts "to show the relevance of the halakhic mate-

rial to the present circumstances between Jews and Arabs in Eretz Yisrael." He exemplifies this relevance by laws such as these: There is no need for compensation in case an ox owned by a Jew gores an ox owned by a gentile, whereas there is need for compensation in the opposite case (*Hilkhot Nizkei Mammon,* ch. 8:5). An article lost by a Jew should be returned but not one lost by a gentile (*Hilkhot Gzeilah VeAvedah,* ch. 11). Dr. Nisan justifies these discriminations on the grounds of "cultural differences" *(ibid.).* These discriminatory laws can now be transposed from the private to the political domain. Thus, Israeli Jewish claims to Eretz Yisrael are superior, and the Palestinian claims can be summarily rejected, thus there is no need for a compromise with them. The West Bank should be annexed by Israel forthwith, and the ensuing demographic problem be solved by a "transfer" of the Arabs to other countries (p. 124).

The conflict rests on competition and mutual imitation. It is true that religious radicalism in Israel is not the cause of religious radicalism on the Arab side, and vice versa. Nevertheless, the greater the role of religious extremists in shaping Israeli political positions, the more Islamic ones will influence the Arab side. An emphasis on the religious aspects of the conflict also pushes Israeli Arabs to see themselves as a sector of the pan-Arab and pan-Islamic battlefront.

The conflict has the potential to turn into a war of religions, a development that is not in the Israeli interest. It is not true that religion necessarily propounds extreme positions in the Arab-Israeli conflict—witness the moderate political stance of Natorei Karta and of Mizrachi during the Mandate. Just as some religious leaders now reinforce the injunction not to withdraw from the territories and, relying on military opinions, claim that such a withdrawal would risk lives, other religious leaders can invoke this same basic halakhic principle in the name of requiring withdrawal despite other halakhic principles.

Religion can lead to moderation, on the grounds, for example, of the Talmudic comment, "It is not for you to complete the task." Religious leaders can adopt a moderate and patient policy while holding fast to the grand design embodied in the divine promise to Abraham to give the land to his descendants.

Judaism can serve as a countervailing force against its own political extremism, as the religious peace groups such as Oz Ve-Shalom and Netivot Shalom repeatedly demonstrate. Radical positions in the Arab-Israeli conflict are engendered not by religious influence but by the combination of expansionist nationalism and religion. This combination is common in many religious circles today, including non-Zionist groups like Agudat Yisrael and Habad. Paradoxically, such groups, which were historically never advocates of the Zionist state, have now become vocal in their demand that Israel not concede an inch. While continuing to oppose nationalism (which is a fundamentally secular idea), they have become the key figures of nationalist extremism.

We must bear in mind that the Arab-Israeli conflict was an important factor in the rise of nationalistic religious extremism. If the conflict is not resolved it will be very difficult to prevent the further growth and expansion of that extremism.

Coping with Religious Extremism

After Rabbi Meir Kahane's election to the Knesset, many religious Jews began to describe him as an anomaly, an aberrant weed that had grown in the garden of Judaism. It seems to me that this explanation is simplistic and evasive. First, Kahane is not alone in holding these views. Focusing exclusively on him distorts the true picture: significant parts of his platform are shared by many others, including important rabbis and heads of yeshivas. The Kahanist phenomenon extends far beyond the narrow confines of his declared supporters, even if most religious Jews have grave doubts about many of his positions. Second, Kahane and other religious extremists certainly do not represent all of Judaism (who does?) but they do represent certain elements found within it. They mark the extreme of traditional Jewish concepts. As has been said, their stand is based on texts drawn from the greatest sages of our tradition. Citing "good" texts for humane attitudes toward "the stranger" does not refute or erase the "bad" texts.

Kahane's use of the tradition hinders the religious moderates' campaign against the extremists, for fear that opposition to him will be taken as an attack on the great sages upon whom he relies, which would disqualify the moderates in the eyes of the religious public. If Kahane is twisting and distorting the texts and the meaning of halakha, the rabbis ought to prove it. The assertion that Kahane and his ilk are perverting the spirit of Judaism is rather far-fetched. It is hard to say what the true spirit of Judaism is; ultimately this is a matter of subjective impressions. By what criterion should it be judged? By the frequency of texts in a certain vein, or by the authority of those who said or wrote them? Traditional arbiters of the first rank are quoted by Kahane in support of his position.

Some argue that the best course is to ignore the extremist stand since reacting to it makes it more important than it is. There is some truth to this; but it seems to me that such an approach will in the long run prove dangerous. These groups have become too important in the Israeli context and elsewhere to be ignored. Moreover, the traditional sources they cite will not go away. It might have been possible to ignore them before the religious extremists gave these texts a contemporary relevance, but now they must be dealt with.

Many Israelis, religious and secular alike, recognize the need to fight religious extremism in its nationalistic version, and perhaps even ponder how to do so. The following seem to be the less and the more possible ways.

1. *Ad hominem attacks.* Resorting to personal attacks on Kahane and his cohorts is larely ineffective: the message frequently emerges unscathed. Moreover, an attack on Kahane the man does not diminish the currents of thought represented by his doctrine and does not impinge upon Kahanism. What is needed is not attacks on the person who quotes but coming to grips with his quotations from the most-venerated sources.

2. *Calls to oppose racism.* Injunctions against racism can also be no more than partially effective. They apply only to calls to discriminate against Arabs. A ban on racism is of no avail when there are passages in the traditional literature that embody a discriminatory attitude toward non-Jews: quoting them can hardly be made into an indictable offense. Focusing on legislation in the Knesset against racism is apt to have a negative outcome if people think that by passing such laws they have fulfilled their obligations to the matter. Moreover, Meir Kahane is not a racist in the fundamental sense of this term. He does not view racial origin as an insurmountable obstacle, since he recognizes the possibility of conversion to Judaism. Accusing him of racism is likely to backfire. Moreover, to the extent that Kahane relies on halakhic sources, the charge of racism will pass from him to them. Are the halakhic regulations concerning a resident alien not racist from the perspective of our generation? It is not accidental that almost all religious groups adamantly opposed anti-racialist legislation in the Knesset.

Accusations of racism will also allow Kahane to assert that the

State of Israel, which defines itself as a Jewish state, is itself racist, and his call to expel the Arabs is merely a logical extension of the Law of Return.

3. *Highlighting and ignoring.* This approach holds that Jews opposed to the extremist stand should emphasize and reiterate passages from the traditional sources that prescribe a just and humane attitude toward the non-Jew or otherwise call for moderation and ethical conduct. Jewish religious literature can supply a wide and varied choice of these; there is much of which Jews can be proud. When wider publicity is given to the positive expressions, the negative ones, which are in fact significantly fewer, will perhaps be forgotten.

The techniques of consigning ideas to oblivion are not new. Rabbis have always made halakhic rulings that contradicted the plain meaning of earlier halakhic literature. At times they have chosen to ignore certain texts, and their rulings were accepted. The problem is that bypassing discriminatory passages is effective only so long as no one calls the new ideas into question. The rabbis who signed Israel's Declaration of Independence, which advocates equal treatment of Arabs, were circumventing the religious laws concerning resident aliens, but they could not abrogate them. They remained on the books and have now been resuscitated.

4. *New interpretations.* Because the existing texts cannot be erased, there is a need to devise new interpretations for the negative content on which the religious extremists base their case. This method, it is argued, is preferable to a frontal assault on the sources. The sages, for example, interpreted the Biblical "an eye for an eye" to mean monetary compensation, thus leaving behind a primitive justice based on vengeance and forging a practical solution to the problem. It is quite true that new interpretations are possible, and in the past the rabbis have worked wonders in this way. Such new interpretations express the creative potential and dynamism of halakhic thought. But this method has serious limitations, namely, that some will attack the new interpretations, and the authority of those who propose them, accusing them of distorting the texts—a plausible charge, since the plain sense of the texts will be at variance with the new interpretations. We can marvel at the brilliance of new interpretations of the past, but we rarely know what opposition they encountered and how long it took for them to be accepted.

In short, if new interpretations make it possible to clean doctrinal dirty linen, the method is desirable; but I suspect that it leaves many stains. In the past, before the civil emancipation of the Jews, rabbis were more inclined to innovation and change than in the more recent generations, when their position has hardened in reaction to the trends promoting secularism and reform; the path of new interpretations has also become more restricted.

5. *Direct confrontation.* It seems to me that there is no alternative, despite the unpleasantness involved, to coming out strongly against the texts I have cited as being used in support of extremist ideas and denying that they possess any necessary validity. A powerful means to do this is the assertion of *historical relativism.* There are important precedents—for example, when Rabbi Menachem HaMeiri excluded Christians from the category of idolators despite Maimonides's authoritative position on the matter. Meiri relied on a principle that recurred a number of times in his argument: "All of these things were said in their own age." That is, regulations that were appropriate for previous circumstances may no longer be so.

Other rabbis whose influence was far greater than Meiri's also explained, time and again, that circumstances had changed and so had customs. This course has the advantage of being cogent and not at all apologetic. In past centuries a hostile attitude toward foreigners was a natural and understandable reaction to the gentiles' persecution of the Jews. But times have changed. I do not imagine that this would be a smooth path for religious leaders to follow, but it is essential. As has been said, HaMeiri was unique in that he removed Christianity from the category of idolatry for ethical reasons, and not only pragmatic ones; this is the line that must be followed today. If HaMeiri had little influence while his works were lost, now that his writings and his ideas have been rediscovered his approach must be placed at the forefront of the moderate position.

One last example will suffice. Rabbi Herzog, before the establishment of the state, expressed the opinion that Muslims, Christians, and pagans should be allowed to live in a Jewish state and the regulation regarding resident aliens be ignored, because in his view they had lapsed. He relied on a twofold argument to support his position: one utilitarian, the other based on historical relativism. The establishment of the Jewish state, he explained, was a sort of partnership between Israel and the nations of the world, from which Jews have benefited both as a people and as a religion.

Therefore, the condition of allowing non-Jews to live with us should be accepted. Moreover, the restrictions on the residence of non-Jews originated in a different set of historical circumstances, and therefore are no longer applicable.

It is true that relying on a utilitarian standard, examining a halakhic regulation according to its results, opens a wide breach for halakhic changes and innovations. Rabbi Herzog asserted that no rabbi in Israel endowed with intelligence and common sense would attack his stand, but unfortunately such rabbis have been found. It is not enough to give a halakhic ruling; one must confront the arguments of its opponents. Thus, Rabbi Herzog, though quite aware that Maimonides had a different view on these questions, chose to refrain from mentioning him; he did not see himself bound by Maimonides's opinion. The problem is that just as he went around Maimonides, others ignore him today.

Still, the issue is fundamental. For religious extremists, both the utilitarian and the historical-relativity arguments are likely to seem invalid. The former will be condemned as commercializing the Torah. The religious extremists rest their case on citations from the Bible, Talmud, and the rabbinical arbiters. It is true that halakhic thinking has advanced in the interim, among other reasons in order to make it possible for Jews to live together with non-Jews, and the rulings of rabbis in more recent generations are a sort of new oral tradition. But the religious extremists ignore these additions. Who will come to the defense of religious innovators, such as Rabbi Herzog, who are ignored by the religious extremists? The religious extremists are apt to argue that Maimonides's authority is greater than Rabbi Herzog's. There is no choice but to wrestle directly with them and their texts.

There are issues on which Jews who oppose the emerging fundamentalist direction must take a stand and act vigorously—such as repudiating those who designate Christianity, particularly Catholicism, as idolatry. One method might be to modify the meaning of the term, to make it less derogatory. But even then the need would remain to deal with the excessively strict interpretations of how to behave toward idolators. The demand not to treat them as human beings, and even to destroy them, even if only within the boundaries of the land of Israel, is simply intolerable. It is easy to deal with the identification of the Arabs as Amalek, since this is absurd. But, again, we must fight against it. Even the traditional contention that the Messiah will identify Amalek and only then will the Jews be called upon to destroy Amalek is unacceptable, as it still implies

the principle that there is a human group that deserves total annihilation. Genocide, even apocalyptical, should not be part of Judaism. It is also possible to deal with the new Messianism; great
rabbis have censured and condemned this movement, and they
have strong support in traditional Jewish positions.

The distinction between two standards of conduct—one applicable when Israel is stronger than the other nations, one when it is
weaker—must also be confronted head-on. This distinction is perhaps understandable, but its inherent immorality is reprehensible.
The same consideration applies to a whole series of passages that
require a coldheartedness toward non-Jews—not helping them,
not returning lost property to them, not giving them medical treatment, and the like—which are sometimes accompanied by the ca-
veat that gentiles should be treated well, even though the law
strictly speaking does not require it, "for the sake of peaceful
relations." Here the demand for humane and fair treatment is
presented, not in the name of morality (because the non-Jew is also
a human being created in the image of God), but because of expe-
diency. The ethical nature of Judaism must be maintained. Judaism
must not become a religion whose adherents are waiting impa-
tiently to be stronger than other nations in order to humiliate
them. Even asserting that decrees against non-Jews were intended
to have effect only after the coming of the Messiah does not solve
the ethical problem. Do we wish the Messiah to inaugurate an age
of bigotry?

The battle against religious extremism must also decry the
denial that a problem exists—for example, asserting that Judaism
is a religion that loves the stranger and abounds with selfless
humanism while concealing anything that contradicts this argument. We cannot build on such a foundation. Evading the problem
by means of self-deception will only make it worse. Likewise our
fight must not ignore the politicization of religion and the clericali-
zation of politics. The successes of Zionism are not heralds of the
great light of Redemption in the religious sense.

The religious peace movement Oz le-Shalom should be con-
gratulated for coming out against these extremist positions. But
the summary of its position states: "All agree that in this age, when
Israel is not stronger than the nations and thereby able to expel
non-Jews from the Land of Israel, the prohibition against their
living in the Land is not in force" (*Publishers of Oz Ve-Shalom*, No.
3). From this it might be inferred that the argument is not over the
morality of expelling non-Jews, but only about the timing of this

expulsion. If this is the approach, or even likely to be taken as such, the argument is lost from the outset!

Let us remember that every problem is an opportunity. Meir Kahane holds up a mirror in which we see our own disfigurations, which until now we have managed to ignore and impels us to correct them. One of the worst things our enemies have done to us by their outrages, is to habituate many Jews to blame others for our problems and spare ourselves the need to examine and criticize our thoughts and conduct.

My fear is that the xenophobia that has been allowed to penetrate Judaism, if not purged, will ultimately lead to the estrangement of many Jews from their heritage, and will come to represent Judaism to the outside world. Moderate religious leaders are caught in a web of embarrassment and despair. They reject and fear that the extremists' maniacal and bigoted fundamentalism will boomerang against us. But their hands are tied, lest they be considered to have cast off the bonds of the Torah and to have violated the principle that, in Maimonides's words, "nothing must be added to or subtracted from the Torah and its statutes."

Expressions of hostility toward gentiles and the religious extreme positions on Israel's foreign affairs calling for annexation stem from the same body of religious doctrines. They are basically two facets of the same disposition: one, on the social level, in the attitudes toward gentiles, and the other, on the political level, in the relations between Israel and its neighboring Arabs. Actually, the hostility on the social level is more basic and reinforces the newly contrived political positions.

The stand of politically moderate religious groups, which do their best to propound religious arguments for a dovish position, will founder so long as they do not concomitantly challenge the more basic religious positions on the social level of hostility toward gentiles. They are caught in an inconsistency. Their opposition to the use of religion as underpinning for political radicalization regarding the occupied territories and the Palestinians is vitiated by their failure to deal with the religious elements of hostility and discrimination against gentiles. Many simply prefer to ignore these elements. In order to be more effective in the political domain, they should also confront energetically those components in our heritage of hostility to non-Jews in general.

In short, the struggle against religious extremism must be waged on two fronts: one of religious, halakhic, and ethical principles, and one that is pragmatic and political. Moral arguments will not

impress those who see their conduct as sanctioned by the suffer-
ings of the past and view the international arena as untouched by
ethical considerations. Similarly, so long as religious circles hold
back from tackling the problem on a religious and halakhic level,
the pragmatic approach, whose success depends on the struggle to
refute the political positions that underlie religious extremism,
increases in importance.

We are burdened with an onerous heritage of mixed baggage.
It is only natural that sediments of a negative nature have accumulated in Judaism owing to the circumstances of our tragic
history. We must discard these embarrassing remnants. For many
Jews, the disclosure of our hostile doctrines may come as a shock,
sufficiently so as to subvert their allegiance to the Jewish religion
and people. Let us now take steps to forestall such a possibility.
Reform begins at home. We have to set our house in order, not
only because of external criticism but for our own sake.

I am not saying that Judaism has to be modernized to suit the
contemporary world, and thus reformed. This line of attack is not
convincing. Modernity means greater compatibility with present-
day fashions. Who says that they are good? Why should Judaism,
at whose center is the idea of God rather than man, not make
painful demands? Weeding out growths that have accumulated
and have deformed and disfigured the religion is a much better
cause.

Ultimately, only rabbis can counter the religious extremists in
the arena of Torah and halakha and deal with the texts they cite.
The factional infighting among the rabbis, their mutual differences
and recriminations, are a major impediment to this function. But
the Jewish people as a whole have the right and obligation to ask
them to do so. I ask forgiveness for pretending to be the spokes-
man of the Jewish people as a whole, but it is almost certain that
the rabbis will not lift a finger unless public pressure, from religious and secular circles alike, forces them to do so. Thus my
intention is to awaken Jewish people to the seriousness of the
problem. Let no one be deluded that the task is a simple one. But
we must always bear in mind the impending disaster if nothing is
done. This new championing of ideas that provide retroactive
justification for the massacre of Jews, for their expulsion from
country after country, for persecution and discrimination, the
burning of their holy books—is this not a betrayal of all of Jewish
history? How can we remain silent?

Only by such changes in our religion can a modus vivendi be

achieved between Orthodoxy and the other currents in contemporary Judaism, and between the religious and the secular sectors in Israel. Only then will religion become a unifying rather than a divisive force among the Jewish people. In so doing we can avert a crisis in Judaism, without relying on the coming of the Messiah, and alleviate the blow to the Jewish religion when the political position of annexation of Judea and Samaria supported by religion comes to grief. More generally, by assuming a critical stance we can identify ourselves with the totality of Jewish history, with all the currents and undercurrents in Judaism, with its history and counterhistory. We can best remain Jews by self-criticism; blinkers can benefit only the narrow-minded.

The changes that are required are ultimately a matter of national cultural and religious survival. The struggle is for the soul of Jewish religion, our inner life and our image in the outside world. Furthermore, the fight is for our survival as a sovereign state, and perhaps even as a people. The need to behave in accordance with international norms—in Rabbi Herzog's words, our partnership with the nations of the world—which he defined as a condition for the establishment of the state, has now become a condition for the survival of both the state and its people.

6
What Is There to Do?

STATES MAY HAVE AMBITIONS TO INCREASE THEIR STRENGTH, amass wealth, and expand their territory, but the statesman's first duty is to take reality into account. Not everything is possible, much less achievable, and the statesman must consider where the demarcation lies between necessity and freedom and between what can and cannot be done to improve the lot of his country. When nations are attracted to a path that is too presumptuous, it is not self-persuasion and understanding that compel them to mend their ways, but the historical retribution that besets them. This is what happened to Germany, Japan, and Italy. These countries have since totally remade their political thinking, to the point that when their citizens look back they are unable to comprehend how they could have gone so far astray.

Yet these states were lucky, for there was a way back from their mistaken policies. The unique feature of Israel's situation is that Israelis cannot permit themselves the luxury of learning through adversity. Israel cannot afford to annex the occupied territories and try to cope as a Jewish state with an Arab majority or near-majority, nor can it court the risk of recurrent wars with the neighboring countries or a pan-Islamic holy war. Israel's margin of error is thin.

Israel must be particularly careful not to reach a point from which there is no return. Toward the end of the siege of Jerusalem in 70 C.E., the Zealots may have realized the error of their revolt and the catastrophe it had brought upon the people, as the moderates had warned them. The radicals may then have asked the moderates that they assume the leadership of the people in order to save them; but the way back from revolt was no longer open. The tragic situation was that recognition of the error of the radicals' way came at a time when there was no longer any alternative to following it. Perhaps the radicals saw this as proof that their path had been the only way possible. But this was a mistake; there had been an alternative, but it had been missed. The same applies to the tragic possibility that in the Arab-Israeli conflict Israel might find itself at the juncture where it must continue on the path laid out by its extremists, because the more favorable options have all been closed.

It is almost impossible for Israel to remedy its mistakes through the political process—that is, by means of party rivalry. Statesmen may advocate new policies, but if the old policies were engendered by a basic mindset and some of the fundamental values of many of the people, they will find it difficult to change course. They can make the change only by first altering the climate of political opinion.

Statesmen are called upon not merely to make policy but to teach their people. It is not always easy to persuade the people that the change of direction is warranted and that the new paths are in fact the right ones. Happy are those statesmen who are assisted in this task by the educators, the media, and the intelligentsia.

The Abdication of the Intelligentsia

A distressing recent phenomenon in Israel is the abdication of the intelligentsia from its traditional role of influencing the public at large. No doubt there are many reasons for this. People have written provocative books and articles and discovered that their words had no impact; they began to ask themselves why they were doing it. I must confess that I ask myself this question frequently. It seems that everything has already been said, criticism and thought have ceased to impress or influence. In recent years television, the chief conduit of the mass media, has tended to put itself at the service of politicians; only occasionally are academics invited as experts to give their opinions on the sensitive issues. The gravity of the decisions and the possibility of bleak results also deter academics.

Intellectuals are in the habit of expressing themselves in moderate and detached explanations, but the severity of the present situation is such as to require strong words. The populist mentality that the Likud brought with it made the intelligentsia uncomfortable. It is not their way to compete with demagogues. Yet gentle and circumspect responses are not appropriate to a time of national emergency. Intellectuals want to explain, but the political arena requires an unremitting struggle to advocate one's opinions. It is also difficult for the social scientists and humanists to find a common language with ordinary people.

Nor have intellectuals been as brave and outspoken as they need to be. I have been distressed to see friends decide it would be more prudent to refrain from expressing their opinions publicly. The problem is not what a man can afford to say, but what he *must* say. I do not think I am slandering anyone if I say that many intellectuals have failed in their duty to stand in the breach against developments they firmly believe to be catastrophic.

Intellectuals and academics, like other men and women, suffer from vanity, but theirs takes a highly individualistic form. If, for example, they appear on a panel and have more or less the same point of view—say, on the peace process—each tries mainly to underline the differences between his or her position and those of the others. Ultimately all lose. In order for the intelligentsia to have influence, they must begin to form groups that share a position and speak out on behalf of it.

Thus the intelligentsia cannot disclaim all responsibility for its reduced public influence. Having recognized the deteriorating political climate it should have tried to intervene. The intelligentsia is sometimes taunted that its electoral strength is less than that of a small village, but its strength is formidable when it comes to instilling and shaping ideas. One of its most significant failures has been in the schools. Many teachers express their fear for the extremist tendencies of the youth, but from whom will students learn if not from their teachers?

The most prominent moderate activist organization is Peace Now, but it is itself symptomatic of the political malaise of the Israeli intellectuals. There is no question that its demonstrations have been important in highlighting the opposition to the war in Lebanon and the advocacy of a negotiated settlement in the West Bank. However, demonstrations cannot address the essential task—that is, improving the political climate by changing public opinion. To affect these changes, Peace Now must transcend the "event" mentality of sporadic demonstrations (which attract smaller and smaller crowds). Instead, they must be prepared to conduct an extensive and persistent campaign of political education. The first prerequisite is a coherent and cogent position. The second is to communicate it as widely as possible through speeches, debates, and pamphlets.

Until the present, Peace Now has been a coalition of diverse positions and personalities which inevitably encountered difficulties in developing such a position. Instead it has settled for the lowest common demoninator of agreement, typically expressed in negative terms: "Stop the War in Lebanon" and "No settlements." Peace Now has also evaded issues about which the public is sensitive, such as negotiating with the PLO. Hence the message of Peace Now has been vacuous and will remain so until it addresses the thorny problems of a settlement and provides an analysis of the changes in the Arabs' positions that make peace possible. It is imperative to contradict the Likud claim that there is no partner for negotiations. But to do so, Peace Now must advocate negotiations with the PLO and not merely with "the Palestinians."

It is precisely because of Israel's critical situation and the possibility that the Jewish heritage will distort its perceptions of reality that the intellectuals have an important role to fill. Politicians are busy solving and creating the problems of the day and are hard pressed to find time to think about basic national questions. This is the task of the intellectuals.

History is full of examples of the influence of intellectuals in society. Thinkers and writers have shaped ideologies that have transformed the world. Philosophers put together the system of ideas that led to the French Revolution. Thinkers like Marx have changed regimes and countries. Zionism itself, along with socialism, formed the agenda of enlightened Jewish secularism of the past century and the State of Israel was as much a product of Jewish intellect as it was of its labor. The intelligentsia has again the opportunity to play an important role in Israel. As a result of the political failures, the public is more open to proposals for changing the national policies than ever before. Intellectuals ought not to try to grapple directly with details of policy, but should endeavor to influence the attitudes from which policies derive. Public attitudes are the soft underbelly of hardened policies. The changes required in Israel, which amount to a total alteration of the climate of opinion, must begin with the beliefs and attitudes that mold opinion. Dealing with attitudes is thus a way of outflanking the policies to which individuals and groups feel committed. For example, instead of attacking annexation, the demographic danger should be explained and dramatized. The whole problem of peace negotiations with Jordan, the Palestinians, and the PLO changes its character if one understands the urgency of an accord for Israel, or if one at least is roused to comprehend that deferring an agreement is increasingly self-defeating.

Changing Minds

There are two fundamental approaches to the problem of altering Israeli attitudes and policies:

1. *Identity.* Israel can annex the occupied areas and overcome and suppress Palestinian resistance only at the price of losing its democratic character; ruling over a foreign people is corrupting. The struggle is about Israel's identity, and the argument is a moral one.

2. *Existence.* A change of policy is imperative to ensure Israel's survival. Current attitudes must be changed because they undermine the country's existence: annexation has demographic and military dangers, not only moral ones; an Israel that follows the path of the nationalist and religious extremists cannot endure.

It seems to me that the second approach is preferable, given the psychology of a people who have suffered greatly and see their suffering as a license for political obduracy, and even for domination. Arguments based on morality and the need to avoid "ugliness" are likely to miss their mark. They will even be condemned as weakness, as the sanctimonious preaching of the soft-hearted and soft-headed. It will be said that positions of high morality are a luxury that Israel cannot afford. Better that Israel be broad in area, dominant in power, and strong in arms, even if preachers of morality find its record sullied.

One might also merge the two arguments—that is to say, the ugliness of our policies threatens our existence. Personally I believe this argument, but fear that such reasoning is too sophisticated. It is better to emphasize that, if Israel is to survive, a change in policy is essential.

Events should be exploited to direct public attention to the need for a change in attitudes. The Lebanon War can serve to provoke second thoughts about the limits of Israeli power and the recourse to force. It should also lead to a reconsideration of the wisdom of the leaders who dragged Israel into the morass. The lessons of the Lebanon War may stimulate the thought that other proposals for the "decisive event" such as formal annexation or expelling the Arabs, will also wind up disastrously for Israel.

The economic crisis has given the public a more realistic under-standing of the limits of Israel's economic capacity. This can serve as the starting point for understanding the limits of military and political power and the constraints within which Israel must act. Finally, the Uprising can be used as a trenchant proof, to be ham-mered in, that retaining the occupied territories is nasty, exorbi-tant, and ultimately impossible.

Maximalist policies are to no avail unless backed by overwhelm-ing power. In religious thought maximalist demands rest on the assumption of heavenly and Messianic intervention. But Israel should by now have discovered that it is not omnipotent and can-not impose its will on the entire Middle East, and that it must limit its demands and follow the path of compromise.

Many Israelis are suspicious of Arab intentions. There is wide acceptance of the notion that the Arabs still want to annihilate Israel and will not be diverted from their goal even after a peace agreement is concluded. It is therefore important to make the public understand by harping endlessly on the difference between grand design and policy, and the process by which once an agree-ment stabilizes it becomes likely that the grand design will pass into oblivion. Also Israelis should be regularly reminded that many Arabs also know that they will suffer greatly if the conflict contin-ues.

The role of religion in the state and the problem of increasing extremism as a result of political developments is another subject to be debated and analyzed. Open discussions in Israeli schools would help to check its growing influence. There should be discus-sion of the dangers that religious extremism pose to the state, to the status of the Jewish people in the world, and to Judaism. The dangers of Messianism must be presented candidly, with full expo-sure of the catastrophes produced by false messiahs in the past.

All these lessons can be summed up as the pressing need for self-criticism. Certainly Israel is not guilty of everything that has gone wrong in the occupied lands. But self-criticism is imperative in order to counterbalance the tendencies to self-righteousness and self-pity that stem from basic Jewish attitudes, from the histori-cal experience of persecution, and from the ethos fostered by Menachem Begin. No factor endangers Israel's future more than self-righteousness, which blinds us to reality, prevents a complex understanding of the situation, and legitimizes extreme behavior. Self-criticism can stem the tendency to explain Israel's shortcom-ings as the result of unfortunate historical circumstances and the shortcomings of Israel's enemies as the result of vicious natures and bad wills.

The principal mission of the teachers of this generation is to inculcate a critical attitude, particularly in matters that concern the state. Israel's future depends more on this than on any other factor. Without self-criticism there can be no improvement. The sages said, "Jerusalem was destroyed only because they did not reprove one another." Intellectual life has always been man's struggle with his blind spots.

Some have spoken of an ideological vacuum in Israel. But an ideology cannot be delivered on demand. The outcry that the Zionist ideology must be renovated will not bring it about. But collective self-criticism can fill part of the ideological vacuum; self-criticism is the message, or at least an important part of it. It seems to me that Israel's future depends less on ideology and more on the mentality that dominates it.

The problem facing Israel is difficult because it requires that certain patterns of thought, some of them planted long ago as part of the early Zionist ethos, must be uprooted or cut back:

- The belief that developments will prove to be more favorable than foreseen, which is based on remembering precedents in which optimism proved to have been justified, and forgetting those in which it proved unfounded.
- The glorification of the will, as if that is sufficient to achieve a goal; also the refusal to accept the givens of the situation and to understand that the enemy too has a will that must be taken into account.
- Deriving policy abstractly from the demands of Zionism, whether Labor or Revisionist, as though we live in a vacuum, ignoring other nations and their demands.
- A lack of interactive thinking between ourselves and the Other. It is enough that we present an iron determination, as if it is our trick alone and the enemy is incapable of acting as we do. Ethnocentric beliefs—such as that we are the only people in the Middle East who have legitimate national aspirations.
- Inconclusive thinking—such as recognizing the damage of the ongoing conflict without recognizing the urgency of the need for a settlement; or recognition that the Palestinians must be a party to the settlement while at the same time disqualifying the PLO from participation, although the Palestinians insist

that they are represented only by the PLO. Also a lack of circumspect thinking—a failure to compare what the various options available to us entail—such as limiting consideration to the deleterious consequences of withdrawal, or to the establishment of a Palestinian state, without comparing those consequences to what is likely to occur if we do not withdraw.

- The evaluation of leaders and events by intentions not by consequences—such as judging the Lebanon War favorably on the basis of its intentions.

- The preference for short-term benefits while ignoring the long-term damage, such as that resulting from annexation.

- Attaching importance to unity as though it were another sufficient condition for success, and hence any criticism or divergent opinion is breaking ranks and betrayal. This is probably the hardest habit of Israeli thought to break, but also the most dangerous. Today, unity means unanimous backing for a mistaken policy and marching together to calamity, whereas remedy and salvation are dependent on diversity and criticism. The world will not be overcome by fear at the sight of our unity and let us do as we please.

International Relations

It is vitally important to provide the Israeli public with a better knowledge and understanding of political realities, particularly in the realm of Middle Eastern and international relations. The Jewish people have had little practical experience in handling power. Independent and united Jewish states have existed only briefly: under David and Solomon, and under the Hasmoneans. The sages taught for the most part at a time when an independent Jewish state no longer existed. Consequently, traditional Jewish wisdom, so rich in its treatment of individual human existence and communal life, has little to say about the relations between states and the exercise of power.

International relations in the modern sense depend on a conception of a plurality of nations. Jewish thought divides the world into two: the Jewish people versus the gentiles. The British certainly do not perceive the whole world as being against them; they distinguish between the French, the Irish, and so on. Furthermore, the Jewish state is a unique entity, whereas Islam and Christianity have been and are divided into many states. Consequently Christians and Muslims had to cope with the problem of the relations among these states, and between them and countries affiliated with other religions.

Israeli misgivings about the rest of the world are reinforced by its country's political difficulties and its bitter experiences in the international arena, as in the U.N. True, reality constrains the Jewish state to comply with the accepted world order, but we must be aware of the problematic nature of this compliance in light of basic Jewish and Israeli experience.

The citizen must become more aware of the problems of exercising power in the international area. International relations should be taught in Israeli high schools, considering such issues as what a state can and cannot accomplish in the present world; how states conduct themselves toward one another; how they succeed, and, even more, how they fail; the constraints that the international order imposes on how a state shapes its foreign and domestic policies.

The great dangers looming over humankind are more in the field of international relations than within countries, however serious some of these domestic problems may be. As President John F. Kennedy put it, internal failures may defeat us, but external failures will kill us. For Israel, too, the major problems involve foreign affairs, especially relations with the Arabs. Although the country has serious domestic challenges, these cannot be separated from foreign issues. For example, providing badly needed allocations for welfare and education hinges on cutting the defense budget.

In the past, diplomacy and foreign affairs were the preserve of the aristocracy, which, as an educated élite, could allow itself to ignore public opinion, which hardly existed. In modern democratic regimes, however, popular positions constitute a constraint on a government's freedom of action in designing its foreign policy. Policy has thus come to depend on the quality of public thinking; a democracy will succeed only if it is blessed with a sophisticated public opinion. An island of political wisdom surrounded by a sea of boorishness and folly will soon be drowned by the waves. The teaching of international relations is a national priority, especially in a democracy.

The rudiments of an understanding of international relations can help refute the notion implicit in the Jabotinsky-Begin ethos that such relations are motivated solely by crass calculations of the national interest. This idea, known as *Realpolitik* or power politics, stood at the center of a philosophy of international relations that arose as a reaction to the idealistic view that states bow to international law and morality. Jabotinsky affirmed this idea in his essay "The Human Wolf." The idea has since been found lacking because it ignores the frequent instances of cooperation and even altruism in the relations among states. Actions in the international sphere are not ruled by morality, but neither do they ignore it. The *Realpolitik* approach is partly correct—for example, we must recognize that the quest for security is the prime motive in the conduct of states.

Realpolitik assumes that a country will be friendly to Israel only if Israel constitutes a strategic asset for it. But basing the relations between Israel and the United States on the assumption that Israel is a strategic asset for America is to place these relations on an unsteady footing. From strategic considerations, the United States ought to maintain good relations with Arab countries rather than with Israel (as George Marshall believed many years ago). Israel cannot help the United States meet a Soviet challenge to an invasion of the Middle East; hence the United States refuses to station forces in Israel.

Realizing that proclaiming Israel to be a strategic asset gratifies certain Israelis, sympathetic American leaders are willing to do so. They do feel that its regime, spirit, and accomplishments constitute an asset to the West in its confrontation with the Communist world. Which is to say that the American attachment to Israel is mainly ideological, based on the fact that both countries are democracies and share common values. This is a much more enduring link than one based on strategic benefits, but the proponents of *Realpolitik* cannot perceive this. The commitment to Israel as an asset is based on its mere existence, whereas the ideological bond is based on Israeli achievements. It is no wonder that those who subscribe to the Jabotinsky-Begin ethos, whose outlook focuses on existence rather than accomplishments, are disposed to the asset line. But, since American hearts and minds are really won by Israeli achievements, we must strive to continue to excel—and not only in the military arena.

Qualifying the power-politics approach can help dissipate the Israelis' excessive suspicion of the nations of the world. It can help engender an understanding that foreigners' criticism of Israel stems not only from opportunism, hatred, and anti-Semitism, but also from what they may see as fair and moral considerations.

The refutation of *Realpolitik* is significant in the context of the

Arab-Israeli conflict as well. Thus Israelis will understand that Arab positions and complaints against Israel are motivated not only by revenge but also by a historical and moral outlook. Your enemy is not a criminal merely because he is an enemy.

A better understanding of international relations would teach us that states are part of a system, and that when Country A acts against Country B it is likely to forget that Country C is also involved and may react, at times in a most forceful manner. A gunshot in Sarajevo and the consequent Austro-Hungarian ultimatum to Serbia led to the German declaration of war against France. This nexus of international alliances and interests is likely to lead to the intervention of third parties who had been ignored, and thus to results other than those intended.

A similar case of expanding consequences occurred in the Lebanon War, although mercifully without leading to a wider conflagration. Israel attacked the Palestinians; the position of the Christians improved as the Palestinians' position weakened; concomitantly, the position of the Christians' rivals the Druse worsened. Israel had had no intention of harming the Druse but failed to consider that in Lebanon any improvement in the status of the Christians entailed a decline in that of the Druse. The Druse, for all their distaste for the Syrians, found that they had no choice but to look for Syrian assistance to redress the balance. Israel's military planners were oblivious of these linkages, which were to affect the outcome of the war significantly.

The international arena is an interactive system in which actions are not linear and unidirectional but reciprocal and dialectical. Each side endeavors to frustrate the intentions and achievements of the other side. It is not enough to calculate what we will do to our enemies; we must also consider what they will do to us.

The tendency to ignore the interactive nature of the international arena stems from an excess of self-importance—egocentricity in the individual, ethnocentricity in the group. Ethnocentricity has been the source of serious errors in conceptions of national security and has colored political attitudes as well. It can cloud our view of what is being done around us; it is a sort of national autism. Awareness of the pitfalls of ethnocentricity is important for a people like the Jews whose self-image is apt to distort their view of the relations between themselves and the rest of the world. The study of international relations could well correct that tendency.

Nations must live with one another. The Jewish sages were very aware of the fact that individuals must live with one another: in many respects they gave primacy to relations between man and man over relations between man and God. Rabbi Hillel's principle, which he believed summed up all of the Torah—"What is hurtful to you do not do to your fellow"—must be raised to the international level, and applied to relations between states and to non-state players on international fields. We must not treat others as we would not have them treat us.

With regard to individuals, the sages said: "He who is pleasing to his fellow men is pleasing also to God; and he who is not pleasing to men is also displeasing to God." On the international level this means that we must not dismiss public opinion lightly; our success may depend on persuading the world that our cause is just. There is some basis for the belief that the party consistently supported by world public opinion will ultimately prevail. Thucydides, a sober observer, explained that Athens's scorn for Greek public opinion worked to its disadvantage in the Peloponnesian War and contributed to its defeat by Sparta.

A widely held but erroneous belief is that Ben-Gurion's view of world opinion is contained in his remark "It doesn't matter what the *goyim* say; it matters what the Jews do." The truth is Ben-Gurion was acutely aware of and sensitive to the reactions of the United Nations, the major powers, and world public opinion, even as he recognized that it is not always possible to please them. He believed that a positive international attitude toward Israel was a precondition for Israeli security. Addressing the Knesset on October 31, 1960, he said: "Without sympathy among the nations the army by itself cannot guarantee the peace of Israel."

The study of international relations will lead to an understanding that analysis of the Arab-Israeli conflict as a closed system—as if it were merely a struggle between Israel and the Arabs of the territories, in which Israel is the stronger side, or between Israel and the Arab states, in which Israel has defeated their armies—is not enough. The capacity to achieve goals depends not only on the strength of the local forces that have to be overcome, but also on the support for these goals in the world community, and, even more than this, on the strength of the forces throughout the world that are opposed to these goals. Learning this will rescue Israel from its provincial and local perspective and teach it to take into consideration world trends that may decide political developments, including those in the Middle East. Should the gap between Israel and the countries of the world, especially the United States, widen, Arab hopes that they can defeat Israel will grow, and Arab extremism will be greatly encouraged.

History can provide cases in which a strong arm and ostensibly bold policy culminated in disaster, and thus correct the tendency to think in terms of "big bang" solutions. As Liddell Hart concluded, the more one contemplates historical experience, the more one realizes how weak are the solutions that were achieved by force, and how one must even suspect those cases in which the use of force apparently was efficacious.

The study of international relations teaches that in negotiations the distance between success and failure can be very small, and depends not only on the gaps between the positions but also on the behavior and skills of the negotiators. In the military sphere as well, the difference between victory and defeat may stem from the fact that one side reaches its breaking point just a little bit later than its adversary. It is not true that the results of negotiations are influenced only by the objective distance between the positions of the two sides. Subjective factors, such as diplomatic ability and the ability to inspire trust and good will, are also decisive.

Nor is it true that the enemy, because he is the enemy, will do everything to hurt his opponent, limited only by his capacity to do so. This applies in personal relations as well. Your enemy may want to harm you, but this does not mean he will ambush you at the street corner in order to stick a knife into your stomach. Of course, if you provoke him to excess, he may do just that.

When the Arabs' goal was to destroy Israel at whatever cost, no Israeli actions could possibly influence their position. It is true today that Arab positions are not always in response to Israeli deeds and positions. The contention that concessions to the Arabs are of no avail because of their essential hostility toward Israel, that nothing can divert the Arabs from their evil intentions, is false, as the example of Egypt demonstrates. Let Israel not be so foolish as to believe that it can win the Arabs' unending love; but neither should it assume that Arab hostility cannot be modified by Israel's behavior.

Studying international relations will also teach us that political positions are variable rather than fixed. Europe's history is replete with conflicts and wars in which alliances changed frequently and today's enemy became tomorrow's friend. Of course there are serious conflicts that persist longer, but political phenomena must not be conceived in terms of eternity.

I have presented several examples of the insights that the study of international relations can provide. Some may be rather banal, but banal truths are too often forgotten when we need them most.

The realization that the Jews are a people with no historical legacy in international relations may also assist the necessary complication of our attitude toward our heritage, recognizing that it contains gaps. As a people we have much to learn.

Realism

We all aspire to be realistic, and believe that we are so. Political facts are not natural phenomena, but are created by human beings. We do not fashion them *ex nihilo,* however, but out of the legacy of human deeds over many generations. When we set out to change the face of reality we are limited by two main factors: the starting conditions—that is, the given circumstances; and the fact that we are not alone and cannot mold reality to our liking. Our efforts run up against the opposing ones of our adversaries and of other parties. Thus reality is the outcome of actions by many actors, each of whom attempts, as it were, to pull reality in his direction.

Being realistic means knowing how one should behave in given circumstances. There is, however, no clear formula for recognizing what is realistic, what can and cannot be achieved. The wisdom that has been amassed in this realm is more negative than positive—that is, it mainly draws our attention to those factors that prevent us from understanding reality and cloud our vision.

Many Israelis have the strange idea that Zionism and the establishment of the state were in their day unrealistic dreams, which nonetheless were realized. This ostensibly "proves" that one should not refrain from setting distant goals, even if they seem to be unattainable, for those are precisely the ones that are apt to be reached. This is a gross error that is likely to wreak havoc if it takes root, because it dismisses the need to be realistic. Realism determines the bounds of the possible; the unrealistic is not and never will be realized.

It is true that human beings confuse their subjective evaluation of what is possible with what is objectively so. The success of Zionism despite the erroneous (subjective) evaluation by those of little faith that was a pipe dream has proved that this idea was (objectively) realistic. But, by the same token, one must not infer from the case of Zionism that whatever seems to be unrealistic will ultimately prove to be realistic. Not every fantasy is a vision. A fantasy is a set of images that fulfill a need that reality denies, a vision is a set of images that anticipate and provide for a future reality. The difference is profound. The tendency to blur this distinction is characteristic of the Jabotinsky-Begin ethos. The difficulty in clearly assessing what is realistic does not absolve us of the responsibility to make an attempt and not give free rein to fantasy.

Realism does not mean that one must diminish goals and pare ideals but that one must endeavor to distinguish between what can and cannot be achieved. Realism is not servitude to what is, but it is certainly opposed to intoxication with what is desired. Realism does not require us to accept the current state of affairs as final, but to be aware of the obstacles and difficulties involved in changing it. Hence it does not ignore the need to overcome them, examines whether the means to do so are to hand, and makes the effort to prepare or acquire these means. Likewise, it does not view a political situation as a constant, but at the same time it understands that the situation is not so plastic that we can reshape it as we fancy. We are not prisoners of history, but neither are we its warders. Finally, realism does not require us to refrain from attempting what appears to be unlikely, so long as the effort does not involve an excessive risk of catastrophe and retribution.

Realism guards against vainglorious policies that exaggerate one's ability and set exaggerated goals, as well as against timid policies that underestimate one's ability, undervalue potential achievements, and miss opportunities to improve the situation. Realism is the golden means praised as such by both Maimonides and Aristotle.

Realists do not begin by defining their desires, as if the clear definition of a goal guarantees its attainment; rather, they use their critical imagination to discern what it is possible to desire. Defining a national goal as vital does not imply that it can be realized. One hears in Israel the call, "We have to define clearly what we want!" as if that is the only problem facing us.

Realism is the comprehension that important goals are generally achieved by a gradual process—what was referred to earlier as "gardening." Although it may sometimes be possible to go straight to the goal by means of the decisive act favored by the "mechanics," this possibility should not blur the great difference between the two approaches. Realism requires thinking about goals, and at the same time about the means to achieve them; in military terms, one must consider both the mission and the method. Realism understands that both are important, and does not discount planning as mere technical detail. It draws up a program of consistent and sequential stages while being prudent, to the extent possible, to avoid gaps that will require a leap, some hocus-pocus magic.

Realism relies on broad, comprehensive, systemtic, strategic thinking, and does not focus merely on one of the steps, which is tactical thinking. If there are several possible courses of action, realism compares the advantages and disadvantages of each. It is not transfixed by one possibility (the "mortal danger" of withdrawal from the West Bank) and examines the risks of the alternative path (annexation). Being realistic does not mean being moderate, but being circumspect. A realist can take drastic action if circumstances require.

Realism involves situational thinking, which examines the facts and is not carried away by nationalist rhetoric. It aspires to permanent assets and is not seduced by transitory gains. Realists keep their eyes fixed on the long-term horizon without stumbling over the first obstacle in their path.

Realism does not mean concentrating on intentions. Realists attempt to foresee short-term results as well as the longer-term consequences, all the while being aware that there may often be unforeseen side effects that require caution. Realists refrain from undertaking an initiative without first considering where it will get them.

Realists seek to improve their situation without provoking hostile forces. They are aware of the wisdom in the sages' adage "In grasping too much one grasps nothing." They avoid being dazzled by a self-righteousness that assumes that because they are right they will emerge victorious. They recognize that the other side too believes it is in the right and will fight for it with all its might. The sages said that "no man leaves this world with [even] half his desires in his hand"; so too states do not achieve everything they desire and must compromise among themselves.

A Critical Attitude Toward Recent History

A realistic attitude in the present depends on a realistic view of the past, and an unrealistic approach to the past nourishes fantasies in the present. This is true no less of the distant than of the recent past.

It is no accident that the Likud government made strenuous efforts to glorify Jabotinsky's role in the history of Zionism. An extensive effort was also made to educate the public in the magnificent contributions of the Revisionist movement to the Zionist enterprise and the centrality of the Irgun and Lehi in the establishment of the state. There would be no need to consider these claims and open old wounds were it not for the use made today of the alleged achievements of the Irgun and Lehi undergrounds to validate and justify the Herut ideology. History is enlisted as an empirical proving ground for the Jabotinsky-Begin ethos, as if the claims made for the Revisionist rebellions more than 40 years ago provide a license for Herut to govern the country today.

Here we must distinguish between the creators and disseminators of ideologies and those who follow after them. One must be stern when judging what leaders said and did, more lenient with the foot soldiers who merely carried out their orders. An individual's adherence to a party and ideology may be a matter of chance, influenced by his milieu, neighborhood, and friends. One must honor and respect the fighters of the Irgun and Lehi, but without glorifying the ideas of their leaders. This should be a guiding principle in considering all past events. In speaking of Bar Kochba, Ben-Gurion said: "Let us extend our hand to Bar Kochba's warriors." Let us extend our hand to the fighters of all the undergrounds; let us cherish the memories of those who fell; and let their sacrifice be dear in our eyes. But that does not mean that we should emulate them.

Historically, Zionism had a leadership of uncommon stature. With scant political assets, Weizmann gained significant British support. Jabotinsky declared that the British must be persuaded to the cause, but it was Weizmann who persuaded them. Ben-Gurion was a forceful leader who knew how to guide the people in a difficult hour. He was stubborn, prepared to take risks, endowed with an unflagging drive and a burning faith. He was not subservient to the British; rather, it was Jabotinsky who placed all his faith in them—until his followers in Eretz Yisrael abandoned his path in the Revolt. He is now presented as the "father" of the Revolt, though he opposed it.

The state was born not because the Revisionists seceded from the Zionist organization but despite this act. Thanks to the institutions that governed the Yishuv (the Jewish community in Palestine), the State of Israel could come into existence with relative ease in the difficult conditions of the War of Independence. Setting up the apparatus of a sovereign state was a massive task, but it was possible because there already existed institutions to which the vast majority of the Yishuv were faithful, so much so that the secession of the Revisionists did not undermine their authority.

It is true that the Yishuv and its leadership were late in realizing that war was imminent, but it was not clear to the Arabs either. The Arabs did not imagine that they would invade the country in order to prevent the establishment of a Jewish state, which is why they were so negligent in their preparations. But, even if the Yishuv did not realize that war was imminent, thanks to the realistic appraisals of the Jewish Agency and Ben-Gurion many actions were taken to anticipate war—purchasing arms, setting up a military industry, mobilization, organization, and training.

The concept of "three underground organizations" that the Revisionists try to promote distorts the picture by mixing mountains and molehills. One must distinguish the Haganah—the military and defense arm of the Zionist movement—from the two tiny underground organizations. Let us take rifles, for example, as a standard for measuring military preparedness for a war in those days: at the end of 1947 the Haganah had around 10,000 rifles; the Irgun had 180; and Lehi a few dozen. In terms of infantry units, the entire armament of the Irgun was equal to that of one and a half companies, that of Lehi to one and a half platoons. In terms of preparedness for war the relationship between the Haganah and these organizations was in the order of forty to one. In terms of heavier weapons, the ratio was even higher.

Had Israel confronted the Arabs in 1948 with the weaponry at the disposal of the Irgun and Lehi it would have been wiped out. It was Israel's good fortune that the leaders of the Yishuv and the Haganah thought beyond the weaponry required for terrorist actions against the British, which were all the underground organizations had in mind. For every street named after the Irgun, perhaps forty should be named for the Haganah.

The Zionists' problem with the British was political; their problem with the Arabs was military. The secessionist organizations merely confused the issue. Even when the war began in 1947 they thought of it as creating "disturbances" and held fast to their claim that the main front was against the British.

The importance of the underground organizations' attacks in pressuring the British to leave the country remains in dispute. As we have seen, the major factor in the British exodus was the loss of India. Countries can take a lot of punishment from terrorist attacks without giving in to terrorist demands. The British have been standing firm against the IRA for quite some time, even though Britain is no longer a major power; how much more resolute it could have been when it was still an empire! No country forgoes its objectives because two sergeants are kidnapped and hanged—or even two hundred sergeants. At the time, the British had ninety thousand soldiers and policemen in the country. With the negligible quantity of weapons at their disposal, how could the Irgun and Lehi have "expelled" so large an army?

It is true that the major strategic considerations that brought about the British departure were supplemented by a number of additional factors: the uncomfortable situation in which the conflict between the Jews and Arabs placed them, including their initial support for Zionism, which had created tension between them and the Arab states; Arab nationalism, which seemed to be a rising force; the pro-Jewish attitude of the United States; the illegal immigration of Holocaust survivors and the disrepute into which their fight against it led them; and, of course, terrorism. Their discomfort with the fight against illegal immigration and the bad press it generated had more influence than terrorist activities did. Some even assert that Irgun and Lehi operations were counter-productive, and that had it not been for them, British policy toward Zionism would have been more forthcoming and Israel would have gained political advantages that were negated by terrorism.

An adequate historical assessment must be broad and evaluate not only the practical and tangible impact of events, but also the indirect impact of psychological factors and the moral climate that prevailed in those years. One can claim that the activities of the secessionist organizations broadened the spectrum of the forms of pressure that the Yishuv could bring to bear, thus increasing its freedom of maneuver. One can even argue that these actions assisted the Yishuv leadership by allowing them to condemn the actions and thereby give greater moral and political force to the alternative policy of the Jewish Agency. By the same logic one might assert that Kahane is a blessing for Israel. But, when one part of a community rejects the negative actions of another part, the overall effect is still to diminish the effectiveness of the whole. The same applies to the political situation today. Herut's actions do not increase Israel's room for political maneuvering to resolve the Arab-Israeli conflict; quite the contrary, they shrink it.

It can also be argued that the activities of the underground

organizations provided a safety valve for the Yishuv's bitter disappointment with Britain. It is doubtful whether this is true. What
would have happened had such an outlet not been available?
Would there have been an emotional outburst? And what does this
mean in practice? It seems to me that the greatest weight should
be given to the testimony of those who manned the political helm
during that difficult period, perhaps the most difficult in the history
of the Zionist enterprise. They saw these activities as undermining
their position, as weakening rather than strengthening them.
These leaders, with Ben-Gurion at their head, made Israel's history, and should be listened to. Ben-Gurion wrote that the
secessionist organizations hindered rather than furthered the
establishment of the state. He was not alone in his opinion: on
August 30, 1985, Dr. Eldad, an ideologue of the Revisionists,
reported in *Ha'aretz* with commendable honesty:

> Our hatred for Mapai kept us from seeing that the state
> would not have been built without what was done by the
> Left and the pioneering movement. . . . We would not
> have established a state . . . Betar did not create Judaea
> and Samaria. . . . Begin would not have brought a
> million Jews from the Arab countries to Israel.

Eldad does, however, cling to the idea that "without us the British
would not have left." What else remains to him?

Today, as we have seen, Herut circles tend to give equal status
to each underground faction. The arguments of the past are forgotten. Ben-Gurion is presented as an activist and maximalist, like
Jabotinsky, as if the Herut line is a continuation of his. A tendency
to gloss over ancient quarrels and to allow old wounds to heal is
ostensibly beneficial, but in this case the result is likely to be
harmful, since Herut is using it to legitimize its current policies—as
if Herut is doing today what Ben-Gurion would do if he were still
in power. But the Revisionist movement and Ben-Gurion were at
opposite ends of the political spectrum. Ben-Gurion never ceased
to view Herut as an illegitimate and destructive factor, which is why
he was so vehement in his opposition to it. The choice must be
made: if Ben-Gurion's path is accepted, that of Herut and the
Revisionists must be rejected. Tolerance for political movements
of the past may be praiseworthy, but not at the cost of distorting
the past and the present.

In Israel's historical self-reckoning there is nothing bleaker than
Lehi's attempts to establish relations with the Nazis. At the end of

1940, seven years after Hitler had come to power and more than two years after the outbreak of the Second World War, when the anti-Semitic atrocities of the Nazis were well known, Lehi sought an alliance with Nazi Germany. The memorandum transmitted from Lehi to the Germans asserted that "according to its world view and structure [Lehi] is very close to the totalitarian movements of Europe." Not only did it claim to share with Germany "common interests for a new order in Europe and the authentic aspirations of the Jewish people," but it also claimed to be close in ideology.

This attempt to make a deal with the Nazis was no isolated incident: it continued a political line that began with attempts to make contacts with the Italian Fascist government. Words of praise to Hitler appeared in the Revisionist press, provoking a sharp rebuke from Jabotinsky himself. The Germans' response was negative but Lehi was not deterred: a few months later, it sent Nathan Yellin-Mor to the Balkans to arrange a meeting with the Germans and persuade them of the benefit to them of an alliance with the Jews against Britain.

When this affair became known, after the German diplomat von Hantig published his memoirs in 1974, Eldad and Yellin-Mor had to defend their actions. Eldad described them as a farsighted scheme to rescue the Jews of Europe, since at the time the Final Solution had yet to be adopted. Yellin-Mor reported that Avraham Stern, the leader of Lehi, had anticipated a German defeat and feared that Britain would dominate the entire Middle East. Did Stern and his colleagues truly believe that assistance from Lehi could tip the scales in favor of Germany, and that it was better for the Jews that Germany win the war?

It is doubtful whether the long history of the Jews, full as it is of oddities and cruel ironies, has ever known such an attempt to make a deal with rabid enemies—of course, ostensibly for reasons of higher political wisdom. But how could cooperation with the Nazis have furthered the establishment of the "Kingdom of Israel"? What could have induced the Nazis to cooperate with the Jews and so radically change their entire ideology to the point of intimate partnership with them?

Perhaps, for peace of mind, we ought to see this affair as an aberrant episode in Jewish history. Nevertheless, it should alert us to how far extremists may go in a time of distress, and where their manias may lead.

Most historical events are not inevitable. History could have been different. Thus our understanding of what did happen can be deepened by considering also what might have happened. In order to understand why human beings chose the path they did, we ought to consider the factors that led them to reject possible alternatives and what might have ensued had they decided otherwise. Frequently the decision was a matter of a hair's breadth. Only by considering the alternatives can we have a sense of the hesitations of those who acted in history, and realize the implications that this holds for us. Raymond Aron has said that the function of historiography is to restore to the past the uncertainty of the future.

In order to arrive at a more complete assessment of the Revisionist movement, we should ask what would have ensued if their political prescription had been accepted and become the official position of the Zionist movement. Would the British have left earlier? What would have been gained by this? Would Israel's situation during the War of Independence have been better? Could the Revisionists have offered a different strategy for that fateful war? It seems to me that answers to these and similar questions—even if they are no more than speculation—can only diminish the claims of this movement.

It is a safe guess that the progress of research into the history of the Zionist enterprise and the struggle for statehood will provide a more balanced and comprehensive picture. Future scholars will be able to analyze history free of the biases rooted in personal involvement that typify the current generation. Historical research presents movements and leaders in a more measured light and tends to cut them down to size. Every movement has skeletons in its closet; but, again, they must be compared with one another.

My guess is that historical research will uncover the ideological aberrations of the Zionist movement. The younger generation should examine them in order to understand how the tragic situation of the Jewish people led to ideological adventurism and unrealistic ways of thought. For example, how did Lehi relate to the Arab problem? How did its thinkers follow a zigzag course, from the belief that the Arabs could be mobilized to support the Zionist enterprise to calls for their expulsion? How did they go from supporting the Rome-Berlin axis to faith in the Soviet Union?

In an interview in *Ha'aretz* (August 30, 1985), Yisrael Eldad, as has already been mentioned, has candidly admitted that the Lehi ideology as formulated by Avraham Stern was detached from reality ("hovering in the sky of skies"). An ideology is meant not only to stir the heart but also to be a guide for action. True, Stern was ready to give his life for his principles, and the Jewish national pantheon should have a niche for him. Sartre said that a man is a man if he has ideals for which he is willing to give his life. That is how we demonstrate our humanity. All the same, the willingness to die for one's faith is a frequent occurrence in history, and it is not enough to defend these martyrs. Even supporters of loathsome movements have shown devotion, bravery, and martyrdom. SS soldiers fought to the death. What is scarce is not bravery, but political wisdom. That is what must be demanded of those who would lead; that is the criterion by which political movements must be judged.

One should not pat oneself on the back when surveying the errors of one's predecessors, but neither should one forgive them all their sins just because they came before. An examination of the errors of the past can engender a healthy skepticism about the promises of leaders. This must be a central topic in our educational system.

Israel's Place in the World

Israel must conduct a realistic and sober examination of its relations with the Jews of the Diaspora, taking into account their circumstances and problems. For example, it should refrain from activities such as the Pollard affair which cast a shadow on the loyalty of American Jews. It must also consider Israel's place and future both in the Middle East and in the world order. For today there are new forms of hostility toward Jews—"anti-Zionism" and "anti-Israelism." The differences between them and between them and anti-Semitism must be considered. There are degrees in all of these, not only in the intensity of the hostile emotions but in the policies they entail. Social anti-Semitism, expressed in a preference not to associate with Jews, is not at all like an anti-Semitism that calls for their murder. Criticism of the Zionist ideology or of Israeli policy in the West Bank is not at all like the anti-Zionism and anti-Israelism that preach the liquidation of the State of Israel.

There is almost certainly an anti-Semitic element in the idea that the Jews ought not to have a state; it discriminates against the Jews as compared to other peoples whose right to a state is accepted. As long as Zionism is defined as the nationalist movement of the Jews, then anti-Zionism is tantamount to seeing them as inferior to other human groups. Even so, criticism of Zionist ideology or of Israeli political actions is not necessarily anti-Semitism. Anti-Zionism may stem not from a discriminatory attitude but from the factual point that the land of Israel was not a vacant territory open for settlement. This position may not be opposed to Jewish-Zionist nationalism, but to the practical possibility of giving territorial expression to this nationalism. This is empirical rather than a priori and theoretical anti-Zionism, on de facto rather than de jure grounds. Today, since the State of Israel is an established fact, this line has lost its validity.

I believe it was a damaging error on Menachem Begin's part to insinuate that criticism of Israel is a manifestation of anti-Semitism. There is a recklessness in the grandiose assertion that "the whole world is against us." If indeed the whole world is against Israel, its future is very bleak. Only those intoxicated with their own greatness can believe that they can succeed in overcoming the entire world. But in any case it simply is not true that the entire world is against Israel.

Certainly there is a need to expose manifestations of anti-Semitism, including Arab and Islamic anti-Semitism. There is also external and domestic political benefit in doing so. For example, the exposure of such phenomena in the Arab tradition is of help in the political struggle—to refute Arab claims that they always treated the Jews well. In the past, it was also of benefit on the domestic front, alerting Israelis to the intensity of Arab antagonism to Israel. Today, however, since the Jabotinsky-Begin ethos has spread, attention must also be paid to the negative effects of publicizing anti-Semitism, namely, its reinforcement of Jewish and Israeli tendencies to self-righteousness. In my opinion, self-righteousness is a greater danger to Israel than anti-Semitism.

Once there were anti-Semites who wanted to rid their countries of Israel and supported Zionism as a way of doing so. The Arabs took just the contrary position: starting from rejection of Israel as a state based on aggression they arrived at the idea that only an aggressive people could have usurped the homeland of another people. Thus, they attributed despicable qualities to the Jews as a manifestation of their culture, as some French anti-Semites did, but not of their race, as Nazi Germany did. In keeping with this view, anti-Semitic literature in Arabic was disseminated widely and, even more significantly, at the initiative of the authorities.

The Arabs, however, were caught up in a contradiction: on the one hand they wished to undermine the status of the Jews in the world and weaken them, since Jewish support of Israel has been a major source of its strength. On the other hand, Jews are apt to immigrate to Israel if their situation in their own countries worsens. Thus it is in the Arab interest for Jews to be secure in the Diaspora. Arabs use this reasoning to prove that they have no interest in spreading anti-Semitism. Still, from the practical perspective, it was the first idea that prevailed—namely, that the Arab battlefront is not limited to Israel, but extends to the Jews throughout the world, as the natural supporters of Israel. Thus a number of Arab states became a central factor in the dissemination of anti-Semitic ideas and anti-Semitic literature in the world, and the ties between Arabs and anti-Semitic groups were strengthened.

The political and military struggle increased their antagonism. They have tended to see Zionism as the root of all evils; in fact, their revulsion from Zionism is greater than their hostility toward Israel. The demonic traits that previous anti-Semites saw in Jews were now transmitted to Zionism, including the canard that now portrays Zionism as a world-wide conspiracy.

Tactically, too, it is better that the Arabs oppose an ideology than attack a state, an action that puts them at variance with the world order that recognizes the integrity of all states. In other words, from their point of view it is preferable to reject the State of Israel by means of rejecting the ideology that it embodies. This approach underlay their initiative in proposing the "Zionism is racism" resolution in the United Nations in 1975. The idea behind this resolution was to delegitimize Israel by delegitimizing Zionism; the rejection of Zionism became an indirect way to call for the destruction of Israel.

There is an alternative point of view: although Zionism is a condemnable idea, Israel exists, and it is now too late to nullify its existence (as the rejection of Zionism in principle entails). This would mean recognizing Israel de facto, while denying de jure recognition of Zionism. Arabs claim that the accepted world order—or, as they put it, international legitimacy—does indeed require the recognition of existing states, including Israel, but does not require recognition of how states came into existence, or of their right to exist in the sense of their right to be born—in this case, recognition of Zionism. As explained in Chapter 1, this, the Arabs claim, they can never accept.

Those who adopt an anti-Israel line can argue that it is not based on a priori theoretical condemnation of Israel, but is an empirical conclusion influenced by Israeli actions. They can even claim that it reflects their disappointment with Israel—their initial attitude was favorable, but they now believe the nation has gone astray. We cannot probe the motives of those who adopt this approach, but may assume that it exists and is even widespread.

Criticism of Israel sometimes appears to be the result of the degree and kind of attention that the country receives. Israelis may well feel that they are being treated unfairly and judged according to standards from which others are exempt. For example, the measures against rock throwing in a West Bank refugee camp receive more attention in the world press than the massacre of thousands of Muslim Brothers rebelling against the Syrian regime. This sort of bias was conspicuous in the media coverage of the Lebanon War. Many Israelis tend to consider this intense scrutiny an indication of latent anti-Semitism. Some critics actually acknowledge that they apply more stringent standards to Israel, claiming that Israel should demonstrate exemplary behavior and not imitate the behavior of its former persecutors.

Israel cannot always appease world public opinion and its demands, but neither can they be ignored. Israel *should* care about what the world thinks, which also has an impact on Diaspora Jewry. In the past, a Jew remained a Jew because he had been born a Jew; the gap between the Jew and his milieu was conspicuous, and it was very hard to cross to the other side. Today this gap does not exist: Jews speak the language of the country in which they live as their first language and have adopted its culture as their own. Assimilation has become easy. Familiarity with traditional Jewish culture is often superficial. Jewish religious identification has weakened. For many Jews, Israel has become the prime focus and symbol of Jewish identity.

Jews, especially in the United States, are disposed to liberalism. When liberal public opinion is critical of Israel they experience a cognitive dissonance, and this gnaws at their Jewish identity. The future of the reputation of the Jewish people throughout the world now depends on Israel's good name and international stature. More than any other state, Israel is a hostage to world public opinion. Israelis must remember this. We Israelis must be careful lest we become not a source of pride for Jews but a distressing burden.

Moreover, Israel is the criterion according to which all Jews will tend to be judged. Israel as a Jewish state is an example of the Jewish character, which finds free and concentrated expression within it. Anti-Semitism has deep and ancient historical roots. Nevertheless, any flaw found in Israeli conduct, which initially is cited as justification of anti-Israelism, is likely to be transformed into an empirical proof of the validity of anti-Semitism. This is a general repetition of the Arab transition from anti-Israelism to anti-Semitism, which is presented as empirically justified. For this reason discrimination against Christians living in Israel threatens not only Israel but Jews throughout the world. These actions weaken the Jews' ability to defend themselves against anti-Semitism. It would be a tragic irony if the Jewish state, which was intended to solve the problem of anti-Semitism, was to become a factor in the rise of anti-Semitism. Israelis must be aware that the price of their misconduct is paid not only by them but also by Jews throughout the world. In the struggle against anti-Semitism, the front line begins in Israel.

Furthermore, Israel's standing in the world will have a great influence on Jewish immigration. In the not too distant past, Jews frequently chose to make their homes in Israel more because their milieu rejected them than because of the attraction of Zion. In the future, if there is no radical change in the situation in their countries of residence, Jews will choose to come and live in Israel only to the extent that Israel attracts them. Many Jews have an emotional identification with Israel, but this is not strong enough to overcome the interests that promote their remaining in their own countries. Sentiment and interests clash. The less the emotional identification with Israel, the easier it will be for self-interest to keep them in the Diaspora. Moreover, the less Jewish and more Arabic, in terms of population, Israel becomes, the less likely are Diaspora Jews to identify with and emigrate to Israel.

There will always be pockets of ultra-Orthodoxy outside Israel for whom the state is at best irrelevant. The birth rate of this group is high, but it is doubtful whether they can ever become a large and significant community. The modern world is gnawing away at them too, and there is no guarantee that the current "return to Judaism" movement can offset the number leaving the fold. The difficulties of intermarriage between the Orthodox and other Jews will increase the former's introversion and isolation. Another problem whose full destructive impact has yet to be grasped is that a large proportion of the Jewish people are becoming "nominal" Jews who cannot marry within the faith because of halakhic problems concerning the religious validity of their parents' marriages. This rejection is apt to drive such Jews to discard their Jewishness altogether. The danger of a devastating decrease looms over the Jewish people, and if the rabbis do not find a path of compromise they will have to bear the responsibility for part of it. If this is the price for the survival of the Orthodox minority, it is too high.

The hope that the entire Jewish people would respond to the call of Zionism and immigrate to Israel has been disappointed. Zionists have a tendency to claim that Jews in the Diaspora are living precariously because of the lurking menace of their gentile environment. But the real problem today is their survival as *Jews;* the problem is not to preserve their lives but to preserve their Jewish identity. The question cannot be avoided: what makes the contemporary Jew a Jew? What is the content of his Jewishness? Today many Jews are Jews because of no more compelling reason than that they were born to Jewish parents. There is no guarantee that their children and grandchildren will even feel this way.

Many Israeli Jews are not Jewish by religious belief; but their Jewish identity is guaranteed, even though its content may have changed, by the fact that they are living in a Jewish state where Jewishness has become the national mark of identity. In Israel the problem is not protecting Jews against assimilation, but rather preventing their Jewishness from being impoverished and safeguarding that religious extremism will not take over.

Rejection of the Diaspora is an essential part of Zionism—indeed, its justification. Nevertheless, the idea has slowly gathered force that this is impractical; most Jews will continue to live in the Diaspora. The very use of the term *Diaspora* rather than *Exile* is at least implicit recognition that it is not a temporary residence in an inferior domicile.

The relationship between Israelis and the Diaspora remains an open question. Israel can demand recognition of its centrality or primacy, but it will not sustain this recognition merely by virtue of its own declarations. Such centrality was achieved not by the fact of its existence but by its achievements. Israel's reputation is not as high in various areas of economic, social, and intellectual achievement as it was only a decade ago.

America, indeed, is becoming a second center of Judaism and of modern Jewish culture. This can help American Jews preserve their identity; for their relationship to Israel, a major source of group loyalty and pride, has become more problematic. Israel must see to it that the relationship evolving with the Diaspora is mutually supportive. Israel will gain nothing by rejecting the Diaspora. It may even be that positive innovations in Judaism and the resuscitation of halakha will take place more easily in the United States than in Israel.

The relationship between Israel and the Diaspora has changed in another sense as well. Formerly the task was to guarantee the future of the Jews as a group of individuals in the aftermath of the Holocaust. But, as has been said, today the physical existence of Diaspora Jewry seems secure; the problem today is how Israel's political future can be guaranteed. In Israel the demographic clock continues to tick.

Given that Israel's political predicament also affects Jews in the Diaspora, they too should take an active part in the debate. Israelis must allow them to do so, and listen to what they have to say. Jews abroad cannot cast their ballots for the Knesset, and therefore cannot participate in the political process that makes the ultimate decisions, but they must not be banished from the discussion, and to this end they must do their homework. They must also dare to speak their minds candidly, without being afraid to disagree with Israel. The reticence of the American Jewish leadership is not to their credit. Instead of publicly expressing their concern they act as apologists for policies and conduct of which many of them privately disapprove, abdicating their responsibilities as leaders in America and as influential advisers in Israel. Muteness is not neutrality, but an endorsement of current Likud policies. Israel alone will not safeguard the future of the Jewish people, and the Jewish people must participate in the endeavor to guarantee the future of Israel.

A Fighting and Creative Nation

Even if Israel's relations with its neighbors improve and peace reigns in the Middle East, military preparedness will remain a necessity for the foreseeable future. Furthermore, there is no guarantee that a peace will be concluded, and meanwhile Israel must strengthen its military capacity and improve its strategic thought, which the Lebanon War revealed to be sadly lacking. The army must continue to train for daring actions and vigorous combat, while preventing its willingness to take risks from turning into a national rashness. A policy that is willing to gamble the collective security is likely to detract from the individual's readiness to take risks, because the only justification for risking the individual is to protect the group. Conversely, an individual who goes on a dangerous mission must assume that his sacrifice is necessary, and that the commanders who send him know what they are doing. This faith was impaired in the Lebanon War, both by the very fact that it was launched and by the long deferral of a withdrawal. It has required much effort to repair the damage to the army and the national morale.

Despite my assessment that peace is possible, and that Israel should endeavor to achieve it and make concessions to this end, peace may not come—whether the responsibility lies with Israel or Arab extremists, or more likely both. Israel will then face a long and difficult struggle, for which it must plan with wisdom and prudence. A moderate policy and a willingness to make concessions will still be of prime importance, for two reasons. First, such a policy will make it clear to the Arabs, and especially the moderates among them, that continuing the struggle, as the radicals wish, is not imperative. Moderation on Israel's part refutes the extremists' claim that the Arabs have only one path to follow, namely, war to the bitter end. Israeli extremism pushes the Arabs into the arms of their extremists. Second, the longer the conflict lasts, the greater is the importance of showing the international community that Israel is not to blame for the lack of a settlement. Third, Israel's perseverance in the conflict depends on the conviction that the absence of a settlement and the continuation of the conflict must be a situation of no choice, and not the outcome of policies pretending that there is an alternative, such as that which demands annexation of the West Bank and Gaza Strip.

Israel must shed the remnants of the thought patterns bequeathed by the Jabotinsky-Begin ethos, not only for the sake of a peace agreement but also so that it can endure a continued conflict. The political ideas that have weakened and harmed Israeli life will not give it the strength needed to stand steadfast in the conflict, despite all the nationalistic orations. Continued struggle for many years is a distressing vision. I am convinced that it is not at all necessary, but Israel must be prepared for this contingency as well.

It can be argued that deferring a resolution of the conflict is to Israel's benefit; or that the idea that time is working in favor of the Arabs damages Israeli morale and weakens the resolve required to endure a protracted conflict; or that unbounded faith in one's rightness and the future are major ingredients of endurance. But these are precisely the habits of mind that block the road to peace. Moreover, they are likely to lead Israel to further errors that will ultimately undermine the national determination too. Steadfastness cannot be based on the false idea that deferring a solution favors Israel, on ignoring the truth. Israeli steadfastness will increase proportionally to the recognition that Israel has done everything in its power to put an end to the conflict, including an expressed readiness to make concessions. Steadfastness depends on being convinced that the lack of peace is due to one's adversaries' positions and not to one's own.

To endure a protracted struggle Israel needs to measure the relative significance of the acts and threats made against it. Israelis must learn not to see every provocation and incitement as a national humiliation, and must not allow popular emotion to determine its political response. This is the only way Israel can effectively demonstrate that it is impervious to the attacks of terrorists and their spokesmen.

Complementing the awareness that attacks are relative is the understanding that solutions, too, are never final and complete. From this recognition stems a willingness to make concessions in order to reach an agreement, even one that presents its own problems and perils. The road to peace cannot pass through the "iron wall" that recognizes only Israel's demands and rejects any demands by the other side. There must be a realistic and humane understanding that the conflict is a tragedy for both sides, and that while Israel's adversaries are indeed enemies, they are also allies in the struggle to end the conflict.

By an irony of history, war between nations may become increasingly rare—not because the human race has become more refined, but because of the ultimate horrors of modern warfare. True, this hope has been disappointed many times in the past, but that does not mean that it will not be realized. The deterrent against renewed international conflict will grow. We have already seen a beginning of the trend in Europe, as well as in Africa, where present borders, for all that they were drawn by the colonial powers, are seen as sacrosanct. This situation is apt to spread to the Middle East as well, despite those who may oppose it. The desire of the various Arab states to maintain their independence, which depends on confirming the political structure of the Middle East, may well aid the development of territorial stability in this part of the world.

On the other hand, violent domestic conflicts are likely to become more frequent, indeed to serve as a surrogate for traditional warfare. A country will strike at its rival, not directly but by supporting subversion within its borders. The decreased frequency of wars between states will not diminish the danger of civil wars and ethnic struggles.

Israel must recognize and adjust to a transformation of the world political climate. We are on the threshold of a post-heroic world. Previously a country could decide to acquire a certain territory and then look for the most feasible way to acquire it. The dense world in which we live makes this a good deal less possible. What we can achieve is not what we desire, but what will be tolerated. We should draw lessons from the recent agreement between Reagan and Gorbachev. Previously Reagan claimed that the Soviets were not trustworthy and would cheat and thus no agreement could be achieved with them. Recently, both superpowers have accepted the view that the dangers inherent in opposition—the nuclear arms race, its burdens and possible disasters—are greater than the dangers involved in a settlement. Perhaps only dubious or unsatisfactory agreements are the only ones that are possible between them. This unforeseen development is relevant to the relationship between Israel, the Palestines, and the Arab nations. It shows that a weak settlement is better than no settlement. By its very existence a settlement can give rise to developments that diminish the enmity and strengthen the trust.

Israel needs broad, coherent, and historically oriented national thinking, which comprehends all the options and risks rather than focusing on one set of them; which stares at the short term without losing sight of the long term as well. This is a type of thought inspired by the vision of the process rather than the fantasy of the event; which rises to levels of "strategizing" national thinking, rather than falling into the pit of the "tacticization" of strategy, which was so visible and so costly in the Lebanon War.

Certainly there are advantages to being a large country, but lately modern technology places a premium on the creativity and flexibility of the national productivity and not on its size. Israel's glory will not be its size, but its quality—a Zionism of quality and not of acreage. There are excellent foundations in the country and among the Jewish people for developing quality: talented persons, great inventiveness, dedication, resourcefulness, and ideas. The national effort must be directed toward developing quality as it did so remarkably in the first twenty-five years of the state. Again, our existence depends upon it. For this reason too Israel must put behind it an ethos inclined toward populism and a reduction of the demands of citizenship and of standards of civic and individual performance. Israel's basically difficult situation can again be made into a powerful modality for achieving excellence.

Israel faces a moment of truth, a fateful hour. My main message is this: let us think about our situation seriously. In Israel and in the Diaspora we need debate on the issues I have raised. I do not come to impose a line but only to propose one for consideration.

Appendix A

Security Council Resolution 242, November 22, 1967

The Security Council,
Expressing its continuing concern with the grave situation in the Middle East,
Emphasizing the inadmissibility of the acquisition of territory by war and the need to work for a just and lasting peace in which every State in the area can live in security,
Emphasizing further that all Member States in their acceptance of the Charter of the United Nations have undertaken a commitment to act in accordance with Article 2 of the Charter,
1. *Affirms* that the fulfillment of Charter principles requires the establishment of a just and lasting peace in the Middle East which should include the application of both the following principles:
  (i) Withdrawal of Israel armed forces from territories occupied in the recent conflict;
  (ii) Termination of all claims or states of belligerency and respect for and acknowledgement of the sovereignty, territorial integrity and political independence of every State in the area and their right to live in peace within secure and recognized boundaries free from threats or acts of force;
2. *Affirms further* the necessity
  (a) For guaranteeing freedom of navigation through international waterways in the area;
  (b) For achieving a just settlement of the refugee problem;
  (c) For guaranteeing the territorial inviolability and political independence of every State in the area, through measures including the establishment of demilitarized zones;
3. *Requests* the Secretary-General to designate a Special Representative to proceed to the Middle East to establish and maintain

contacts with the States concerned in order to promote agreement and assist efforts to achieve a peaceful and accepted settlement in accordance with the provisions and principles in this resolution;

4. *Requests* the Secretary-General to report to the Security Council on the progress of the efforts of the Special Representative as soon as possible.

Security Council Resolution 338, October 22, 1973

The Security Council

1. *Calls upon* all parties to the present fighting to cease all firing and terminate all military activity immediately, no later than 12 hours after the moment of the adoption of this decision, in the positions they now occupy;

2. *Calls upon* the parties concerned to start immediately after the cease-fire the implementation of Security Council resolution 242 (1967) in all of its parts;

3. *Decides* that, immediately and concurrently with the cease-fire, negotiations shall start between the parties concerned under appropriate auspices aimed at establishing a just and durable peace in the Middle East.

Appendix B

Arab League Summit Conference Declaration, Fez, Morocco, September 9, 1982

The 12th Arab Summit was held in Fez on the 27th Moharrem 1402, corresponding to the 25th November 1981.

After suspending its work, it resumed from the 17th to the 20th Doualkiada 1402, corresponding to the 6th to 9th September 1982, under the chairmanship of His Majesty King Hassan II, King of the Kingdom of Morocco. All Arab countries took part in the work of the summit with the exception of the Libyan Arab Jamahirya.

In view of the grave and delicate circumstances through which the Arab nation is passing and of the feeling of historic national responsibility, their majesties and their excellencies, the kings, presidents and emirs of the Arabs, examined the important questions submitted to the summit and took the following decisions:

I. The Israeli-Arab Conflict

The summit paid homage to the resistance of the forces of the Palestine revolution, the Lebanese and Palestinian peoples and the Syrian Arab armed forces, and reaffirmed its support to the Palestinian people in the struggle to recover its inalienable national rights.

The summit, convinced of the power of the Arab nation to achieve its legitimate objectives and put an end to the aggression on the basis of the fundamental principles laid down by the Arab summits and in view of the desire of the Arab countries to pursue action by every means for the achievement of a just peace in the Middle East, taking account of the plan of His Excellency President

Habib Bourguiba which considers international legality to be the basis for the solution of the Palestinian question, and of the plan of His Majesty King Fahd Ibn Abdelaziz concerning peace in the Middle East, and in the light of discussions and observations made by their majesties, excellencies and highnesses, the kings, presidents and emirs, the summit adopted the following principles:

[1] The withdrawal of Israel from all Arab territories occupied in 1967 including Arab Al Quds (Jerusalem).

[2] The dismantling of settlements established by Israel on the Arab territories after 1967.

[3] The guarantee of freedom of worship and practice of religious rites for all religions in the holy shrines.

[4] The reaffirmation of the Palestinian people's right to self-determination and the exercise of its imprescriptible and inalienable national rights under the leadership of the Palestine Liberation Organization, its sole and legitimate representative, and the indemnification of all those who do not desire to return.

[5] Placing the West Bank and Gaza Strip under the control of the United Nations for a transitory period not exceeding a few months.

[6] The establishment of an independent Palestinian state with Al Quds as its capital.

[7] The Security Council guarantees peace among all states of the region, including the independent Palestinian state.

[8] The Security Council guarantees the respect of these principles.

Appendix C

Excerpts from Camp David Frameworks for Peace, September 17, 1978

Preamble

The search for peace in the Middle East must be guided by the following:

—The agreed basis for a peaceful settlement of the conflict between Israel and its neighbors is United Nations Security Council Resolution 242, in all its parts.

—After four wars during thirty years, despite intensive human efforts, the Middle East, which is the cradle of civilization and the birthplace of three great religions, does not yet enjoy the blessings of peace. The people of the Middle East yearn for peace so that the vast human and natural resources of the region can be turned to the pursuits of peace and so that this area can become a model for coexistence and cooperation among nations.

—The historic initiative of President Sadat in visiting Jerusalem and the reception accorded to him by the Parliament, government and people of Israel, and the reciprocal visit of Prime Minister Begin to Ismailia, the peace proposals made by both leaders, as well as the warm reception of these missions by the people of both countries, have created an unprecedented opportunity for peace which must not be lost if this generation and future generations are to be spared the tragedies of war.

—The provisions of the Charter of the United Nations and the other accepted norms of international law and legitimacy now provide accepted standards for the conduct of relations among the states.

—To achieve a relationship of peace, in the spirit of Article 2 of the United Nations Charter, future negotiations between Israel and any neighbor prepared to negotiate peace and security with it, are necessary for the purpose of carrying out all the provisions and principles of Resolutions 242 and 338.

—Peace requires respect for the sovereignty, territorial integrity, and political independence of every state in the area and their right to live in peace within secure and recognized boundaries free from threats or acts of force. Progress toward that goal can accelerate movement toward a new era of reconciliation in the Middle East marked by cooperation in promoting economic development, in maintaining stability, and in assuring security.

—Security is enhanced by a relationship of peace and by cooperation between nations which enjoy normal relations. In addition, under the terms of peace treaties, the parties can, on the basis of reciprocity, agree to special security arrangements such as demilitarized zones, limited armaments areas, early warning stations, the presence of international forces, liaison, agreed measures for monitoring, and other arrangements that they agree are useful.

Framework

Taking these factors into account, the parties are determined to reach a just, comprehensive, and durable settlement of the Middle East conflict through the inclusion of peace treaties based on Security Council Resolutions 242 and 338 in all their parts. Their purpose is to achieve peace and good neighborly relations. They recognize that, for peace to endure, it must involve all those who have been most deeply affected by the conflict. They therefore agree that this framework as appropriate is intended by them to constitute a basis for peace not only between Egypt and Israel, but also between Israel and each of its other neighbors which is prepared to negotiate peace with Israel on this basis. With that objective in mind, they have agreed to proceed as follows:

A. West Bank and Gaza

1. Egypt, Israel, Jordan, and the representatives of the Palestinian people should participate in negotiations on the resolution of the Palestinian problem in all its aspects. To achieve that objective, negotiations relating to the West Bank and Gaza should proceed in three stages:

(a) Egypt and Israel agree that, in order to ensure a peaceful and orderly transfer of authority, and taking into account the security concerns of all the parties, there should be transitional arrangements for the West Bank and Gaza for a period not exceeding five years. In order to provide full autonomy to the inhabitants, under these arrangements the Israeli military government and its civilian administration will be withdrawn as soon as a self-governing authority has been freely elected by the inhabitants of these areas to replace the existing military government. To negotiate the details of a transitional arrangement, the Government of Jordan will be invited to join the negotiations on the basis of this framework. These new arrangements should give due consideration both to the principle of self-government by the inhabitants of these territories and to the legitimate security concerns of the parties involved.

(b) Egypt, Israel, and Jordan will agree on the modalities for establishing the elected self-governing authority in the West Bank and Gaza. The delegations of Egypt and Jordan may include Palestinians from the West Bank and Gaza or other Palestinians as mutually agreed. The parties will negotiate an agreement which will define the powers and responsibilities of the self-governing authority to be exercised in the West Bank and Gaza. A withdrawal of Israeli armed forces will take place and there will be a redeployment of the remaining Israeli forces into specified security locations. The agreement will also include arrangements for assuring internal and external security and public order. A strong local police force will be established, which may include Jordanian citizens. In addition, Israeli and Jordanian forces will participate in joint patrols and in the manning of control posts to assure the security of the borders.

(c) When the self-governing authority (administrative council) in the West Bank and Gaza is established and inaugurated, the transitional period of five years will begin. As soon as possible, but not later than the third year after the beginning of the transitional period, negotiations will take place to determine the final status of the West Bank and Gaza and its relationship with its neighbors, and to conclude a peace treaty between Israel and Jordan by the end of the transitional period. These negotiations will be conducted among Egypt, Israel, Jordan, and the elected representatives of the inhabitants of the West Bank and Gaza. Two separate but related committees will be convened, one committee, consisting of representatives of the four parties which will negotiate and agree on the final status of the West Bank and Gaza, and its relationship with its neighbors, and the second committee, consisting of representatives of Israel and representatives of Jordan to be joined by the elected representatives of the inhabitants of the West Bank and Gaza, to negotiate the peace treaty between Israel and Jordan, taking into account the agreement reached on the final status of the West Bank and Gaza. The negotiations shall be based on all the provisions and principles of UN Security Council Resolution 242. The negotiations will resolve, among other matters, the location of the boundaries and the nature of the security arrangements. The solution from the negotiations must also recognize the legitimate rights of the Palestinian people and their just requirements. In this way, the Palestinians will participate in the determination of their own future through:

1) The negotiations among Egypt, Israel, Jordan, and the representatives of the inhabitants of the West Bank and Gaza to agree on the final status of the West Bank and Gaza and other outstanding issues by the end of the transitional period.

2) Submitting their agreement to a vote by the elected representatives of the inhabitants of the West Bank and Gaza.

3) Providing for the elected representatives of the inhabitants of the West Bank and Gaza to decide how they shall govern themselves consistent with the provisions of their agreement.

4) Participating as stated above in the work of the committee negotiating the peace treaty between Israel and Jordan.

All necessary measures will be taken and provisions made to assure the security of Israel and its neighbors during the transitional period and beyond. To assist in providing such security, a strong local police force will be constituted by the self-governing authority. It will be composed of inhabitants of the West Bank and Gaza. The police will maintain continuing liaison on internal security matters with the designated Israeli, Jordanian, and Egyptian officers.

During the transitional period, representatives of Egypt, Israel, Jordan, and the self-governing authority will constitute a continuing committee to decide by agreement on the modalities of admission of persons displaced from the West Bank and Gaza in 1967, together with necessary measures to prevent disruption and disorder. Other matters of common concern may also be dealt with by this committee.

Egypt and Israel will work with each other and with other interested parties to establish agreed procedures for a prompt, just, and permanent implementation of the resolution of the refugee problem.

B. Egypt-Israel

1. Egypt and Israel undertake not to resort to the threat or the use of force to settle disputes. Any disputes shall be settled by peaceful means in accordance with the provisions of Article 33 of the Charter of the United Nations.

2. In order to achieve peace between them, the parties agree to negotiate in good faith with a goal of concluding within three months from the signing of this Framework a peace treaty between them, while inviting the other parties to the conflict to proceed simultaneously to negotiate and conclude similar peace treaties with a view to achieving a comprehensive peace in the area. The Framework for the Conclusion of a Peace Treaty between Egypt and Israel will govern the peace negotiations between them. The parties will agree on the modalities and the timetable for the implementation of their obligations under the treaty.

C. Associated Principles

1. Egypt and Israel state that the principles and provisions described below should apply to peace treaties between Israel and each of its neighbors—Egypt, Jordan, Syria, and Lebanon.

2. Signatories shall establish among themselves relationships normal to states at peace with one another. To this end, they should undertake to abide by all the provisions of the Charter of the United Nations. Steps to be taken in this respect include:

(a) full recognition;

(b) abolishing economic boycotts;

(c) guaranteeing that under their jurisdiction the citizens of the other parties shall enjoy the protection of the due process of the law.

3. Signatories should explore possibilities for economic development in the context of final peace treaties, with the objective of contributing to the atmosphere of peace, cooperation, and friendship which is their common goal.

4. Claims Commissions may be established for the mutual settlement of all financial claims.

5. The United States shall be invited to participate in the talks on matters related to the modalities of the implementation of the agreements and working out the timetable for the carrying out of the obligations of the parties.

6. The United Nations Security Council shall be requested to

endorse the peace treaties and ensure that their provisions shall not be violated. The permanent members of the Security Council shall be requested to underwrite the peace treaties and ensure respect for their provisions. They shall also be requested to conform their policies and actions with the undertakings contained in this Framework.

. . . The following matters are agreed between the parties:

(a) the full exercise of Egyptian sovereignty up to the internationally recognized border between Egypt and mandated Palestine;

(b) the withdrawal of Israeli armed forces from the Sinai;

(c) the use of airfields left by the Israelis near El Arish, Rafah, Ras en Naqb, and Sharm el Sheikh for civilian purposes only, including possible commercial use by all nations;

(d) the right of free passage by ships of Israel through the Gulf of Suez and the Suez Canal on the basis of the Constantinople Convention of 1888 applying to all nations; the Strait of Tiran and the Gulf of Aqaba are international waterways to be open to all nations for unimpeded and nonsuspendable freedom of navigation and overflight;

(e) the construction of a highway between the Sinai and Jordan near Elat with guaranteed free and peaceful passage by Egypt and Jordan; and

(f) the stationing of military forces listed below.

Stationing of Forces

A. No more than one division (mechanized or infantry) of Egyptian armed forces will be stationed within an area lying approximately 50 kilometers (km) east of the Gulf of Suez and the Suez Canal.

B. Only United Nations forces and civil police equipped with light weapons to perform normal police functions will be stationed within an area lying west of the international border and the Gulf of Aqaba, varying in width from 20 km to 40 km.

C. In the area within 3 km east of the international border there will be Israeli limited military forces not to exceed four infantry battalions and United Nations observers.

D. Border patrol units, not to exceed three battalions, will supplement the civil police in maintaining order in the area not included above.

The exact demarcation of the above areas will be decided during the peace negotiations.

Early warning stations may exist to ensure compliance with the terms of the agreement.

United Nations forces will be stations: (a) in part of the area in the Sinai lying within about 20 km of the Mediterranean Sea and adjacent to the international border, and (b) in the Sharm el Sheikh area to ensure freedom of passage through the Strait of Tiran; and these forces will not be removed unless such removal is approved by the Security Council of the United Nations with a unanimous vote of the five permanent members.

After a peace treaty is signed, and after the interim withdrawal is complete, normal relations will be established between Egypt and Israel, including: full recognition, including diplomatic, economic, and cultural relations; termination of economic boycotts and barriers to the free movement of goods and people; and mutual protection of citizens by the due process of law.

Egyptian-Israeli Peace Treaty, March 26, 1979

The Government of the Arab Republic of Egypt and the Government of the State of Israel:

Preamble

Convinced of the urgent necessity of the establishment of a just, comprehensive and lasting peace in the Middle East in accordance with Security Council Resolutions 242 and 338;

Reaffirming their adherence to the "Framework for Peace in the Middle East Agreed at Camp David," dated September 17, 1978;

Noting that the aforementioned Framework as appropriate is intended to constitute a basis for peace not only between Egypt and Israel but also between Israel and each of its other Arab neighbors which is prepared to negotiate peace with it on this basis;

Desiring to bring to an end the state of war between them and to establish a peace in which every state in the area can live in security;

Convinced that the conclusion of a Treaty of Peace between Egypt and Israel is an important step in the search for comprehensive peace in the area and for the attainment of the settlement of the Arab-Israeli conflict in all its aspects;

Inviting the other Arab parties to this dispute to join the peace process with Israel guided by and based on the principles of the aforementioned Framework;

Desiring as well to develop friendly relations and cooperation between themselves in accordance with the United Nations Charter and the principles of international law governing international relations in times of peace;

Agree to the following provisions in the free exercise of their sovereignty, in order to implement the "Framework for the Conclusion of a Peace Treaty Between Egypt and Israel:"

Article I

1. The state of war between the Parties will be terminated and peace will be established between them upon the exchange of instruments of ratification of this Treaty.

2. Israel will withdraw all its armed forces and civilians from the Sinai behind the international boundary between Egypt and mandated Palestine, as provided in the annexed protocol (Annex I), and Egypt will resume the exercise of its full sovereignty over the Sinai.

3. Upon completion of the interim withdrawal provided for in Annex I, the Parties will establish normal and friendly relations, in accordance with Article III(3).

Article II

The permanent boundary between Egypt and Israel is the recognized international boundary between Egypt and the former mandated territory of Palestine, as shown on the map at Annex II, without prejudice to the issue of the status of the Gaza Strip. The Parties recognize this boundary as inviolable. Each will respect the territorial integrity of the other, including their territorial waters and airspace.

Article III

1. The Parties will apply between them the provisions of the Charter of the United Nations and the principles of international law governing relations among states in times of peace. In particular:

a. They recognize and will respect each other's sovereignty, territorial integrity and political independence;

b. They recognize and will respect each other's right to live in peace within their secure and recognized boundaries;

c. They will refrain from the threat or use of force, directly or indirectly, against each other and will settle all disputes between them by peaceful means.

2. Each Party undertakes to ensure that acts or threats of belligerency, hostility, or violence do not originate from and are not committed from within its territory, or by any forces subject to its control or by any other forces stationed on its territory, against the population, citizens or property of the other Party. Each Party also undertakes to refrain from organizing, instigating, inciting, assisting or participating in acts or threats of belligerency, hostility, subversion or violence against the other Party, anywhere, and undertakes to ensure that perpetrators of such acts are brought to justice.

3. The Parties agree that the normal relationship established between them will include full recognition, diplomatic, economic and cultural relations, termination of economic boycotts and discriminatory barriers to the free movement of people and goods, and will guarantee the mutual enjoyment by citizens of the due process of law. The process by which they undertake to achieve such a relationship parallel to the implementation of other provisions of this Treaty is set out in the annexed protocol (Annex III).

Article IV

1. In order to provide maximum security for both Parties on the basis of reciprocity, agreed security arrangements will be established including limited force zones in Egyptian and Israeli territory, and United Nations forces and observers, described in detail as to nature and timing in Annex I, and other security arrangements the Parties may agree upon.

2. The Parties agree to the stationing of United Nations personnel in areas described in Annex I. The Parties agree not to request withdrawal of the United Nations personnel and that these personnel will not be removed unless such removal is approved by the Security Council of the United Nations, with the affirmative vote of the five Permanent Members, unless the Parties otherwise agree.

3. A Joint Commission will be established to facilitate the implementation of the Treaty, as provided for in Annex I.

4. The security arrangements provided for in paragraphs 1 and 2 of this Article may at the request of either party be reviewed and amended by mutual agreement of the Parties.

Article V

1. Ships of Israel, and cargoes destined for or coming from Israel, shall enjoy the right of free passage through the Suez Canal and its approaches through the Gulf of Suez and the Mediterranean Sea on the basis of the Constantinople Convention of 1888, applying to all nations. Israeli nationals, vessels and cargoes, as well as persons, vessels and cargoes destined for or coming from Israel, shall be accorded nondiscriminatory treatment in all matters connected with usage of the canal.

Appendix D

Jordanian-Palestinian Accords Between King Hussein and Chairman Arafat, February 11, 1985

Project for Joint Action

Proceeding from the spirit of the Fez Summit resolutions, approved by Arab states, and from United Nations resolutions relating to the Palestine question,

In accordance with international legitimacy, and

Deriving from a common understanding on the establishment of a special relationship between the Jordanian and Palestinian peoples,

The Government of the Hashemite Kingdom of Jordan and the Palestine Liberation Organization have agreed to move together toward the achievement of a peaceful and just settlement of the Middle East crisis and the termination of Israeli occupation of the occupied Arab territories, including Jerusalem, on the basis of the following principles:

1. The land in exchange for peace (Al-Ard Muqabil Al-Salam) as cited in the UN resolutions, including the Security Council resolutions.

2. The Palestinian people's right to self-determination. The Palestinians will exercise their inalienable right to self-determination when the Jordanians and Palestinians manage to achieve this within the framework of an Arab confederation that is proposed to be established between the two states of Jordan and Palestine.

3. Solving the Palestinian refugees problem in accordance with the UN resolutions.

4. Solving of the Palestine question from all its aspects.

5. Based on this, peace negotiations should be held within the

framework of an international conference to be attended by the five UN Security Council permanent member-states and all parties to the conflict, including the PLO, which is the Palestinian people's sole legitimate representative, within a joint delegation (a joint Jordanian-Palestinian delegation).

Appendix E

The Palestinian Declaration of Independence

In the name of God, the Compassionate, the Merciful.

Palestine, the Land of the three monotheistic faiths, is where the Palestinian Arab people was born, on which it grew, developed and excelled. The Palestinian people was never separated from or diminished in its integral bonds with Palestine. Thus the Palestinian Arab people ensured for itself an everlasting union between itself, its land and its history.

Resolute throughout that history, the Palestinian Arab people forged its national identity, rising even to unimagined levels in its defense, as invasion, the design of others, and the appeal special to Palestine's ancient and luminous place on that eminence where powers and civilizations are joined. . . . All this intervened thereby to deprive the people of its political independence. Yet the undying connection between Palestine and its people secured for the land its character, and for the people its national genius.

Nourished by an unfolding series of civilizations and cultures, inspired by a heritage rich in variety and kind, the Palestinian Arab people added to its stature by consolidating a union between itself and its patrimonial land. The call went out from Temple, Church, and Mosque that to praise the Creator, to celebrate compassion and peace was indeed the message of Palestine. And in generation after generation, the Palestinian Arab people gave of itself unsparingly in the valiant battle for liberation and homeland. For what has been the unbroken chain of our people's rebellions but the heroic embodiment of our will for national independence? And so the people was sustained in the struggle to stay and to prevail.

When in the course of modern times a new order of values was declared with norms and values for all, it was the Palestinian Arab

244APPENDIX E

people that had been excluded from the destiny of all other peoples by a hostile array of local and foreign powers. Yet again had unaided justice been revealed as insufficient to drive the world's history along its preferred course.

And it was the Palestinian people, already wounded in its body, that was submitted to yet another type of occupation over which floated the falsehood that "Palestine was a land without people." This notion was foisted upon some in the world, whereas in Article 22 of the Covenant of the League of Nations (1919) and in the Treaty of Lausanne (1923), the community of nations had recognized that all the Arab territories, including Palestine, of the formerly Ottoman provinces were to have granted to them their freedom as provisionally independent nations.

Despite the historical injustice inflicted on the Palestinian Arab people resulting in their dispersion and depriving them of their right to self-determination, following upon UN General Assembly Resolution 181 (1947), which partitioned Palestine into two states, one Arab, one Jewish, yet it is this Resolution that still provides those conditions of international legitimacy that ensure the right of the Palestinian Arab people to sovereignty and national independence.

By stages, the occupation of Palestine and parts of other Arab territories by Israeli forces, the willed dispossession and expulsion from their ancestral homes of the majority of Palestine's civilian inhabitants was achieved by organized terror; those Palestinians who remained, as a vestige subjugated in its homeland, were persecuted and forced to endure the destruction of their national life.

Thus were principles of international legitimacy violated. Thus were the Charter of the United Nations and its Resolutions disfigured, for they had recognized the Palestinian Arab people's national rights, including the right of the Return, the right to Independence, the right to sovereignty over territory and homeland.

In Palestine and on its perimeters, in exile distant and near, the Palestinian Arab people never faltered and never abandoned its conviction in its rights of Return and Independence. Occupation, massacres and dispersion achieved no gain in the unabated Palestinian consciousness of self and political identity, as Palestinians went forward with their destiny, undeterred and unbowed. And from out of the long years of trial in evermounting struggle, the Palestinian political identity emerged further consolidated and confirmed. And the collective Palestinian national will forged for itself a political embodiment, the Palestine Liberation Organization, its sole legitimate representative, recognized by the world community as a whole, as well as by related regional and international institutions. Standing on the very rock of conviction in the Palestinian people's inalienable right, and on the ground of Arab national consensus, and of international legitimacy, the PLO led the campaigns of its great people, molded into unity and powerful resolve, one and indivisible in its triumphs, even as it suffered massacres and confinement within and without its home. And so Palestinian resistance was clarified and raised into the forefront of Arab and world awareness, as the struggle of the Palestinian Arab people achieved unique prominence among the world's liberation movements in the modern era.

The massive national uprising, the "Intifada," now intensifying in cumulative scope and power on occupied Palestinian territories, as well as the unflinching resistance of the refugee camps outside the homeland, have elevated consciousness of the Palestinian truth and right into still higher realms of comprehension and actuality. Now at last the curtain has been dropped around a whole epoch of prevarication and negation. The Intifada has set siege to the mind of official Israel, which has for too long relied exclusively upon myth and terror to deny Palestinian existence altogether. Because of the Intifada and its revolutionary irreversible impulse, the history of Palestine has therefore arrived at a decisive juncture. Whereas the Palestinian people reaffirms most definitively its inalienable rights in the land of its patrimony:

> Now, by virtue of natural, and the exercise of those
> rights historical and legal right and the sacrifices of
> successive generations who gave of themselves in
> defense of the freedom and independence of their
> homeland; in pursuance of Resolutions adopted by Arab
> Summit Conferences and relying on the authority
> bestowed by international legitimacy as embodied in the
> Resolutions of the United Nations Organization since
> 1947; and in exercise by the Palestinian Arab people of
> its rights to self-determination, political independence,
> and sovereignty over its territory.
>
> The Palestine National Council, in the name of God,
> and in the name of the Palestinian Arab people, hereby
> proclaims the establishment of the State of Palestine on

our Palestinian territory with its capital Jerusalem
(Al-Quds Ash Sharif).

The State of Palestine is the state of Palestinians wherever they
may be. The state is for them to enjoy in it their collective national
and cultural identity, theirs to pursue in it a complete equality of
rights. In it will be safeguarded their political and religious convic-
tions and their human dignity by means of a parliamentary democratic system of governance, itself based on freedom of expression
and the freedom to form parties. The rights of minorities will duly
be respected by the majority, as minorities must abide by decisions
of the majority. Governance will be based on principles of social
justice, equality and non-discrimination in public rights, men or
women, on grounds of race, religion, color or sex under the aegis
of a constitution which ensures the rule of law and an independent
judiciary. Thus shall these principles allow no departure from
Palestine's age-old spiritual and civilizational heritage of tolerance
and religious coexistence.

The State of Palestine is an Arab state, an integral and indivisible
part of the Arab nation, at one with that nation in heritage and
civilization, with it also in its aspiration for liberation, progress,
democracy and unity. The State of Palestine affirms its obligation
to abide by the Charter of the League of Arab States, whereby the
coordination of the Arab states with each other shall be strengthened. It calls upon Arab compatriots to consolidate and enhance
the emergence in reality of our state, to mobilize potential, and to
intensify efforts whose goal is to end Israeli occupation.

The State of Palestine proclaims its commitment to the principles and purposes of the United Nations, and to the Universal
Declaration of Human Rights. It proclaims its commitment as well
to the principles and policies of the Non-Aligned Movement.

It further announces itself to be a peace-loving state, in adherence to the principles of peaceful coexistence. It will join with all
states and peoples in order to assure a permanent peace based
upon justice and the respect of rights so that humanity's potential
for well-being may be assured, an earnest competition for excellence be maintained, and in which confidence in the future will
eliminate fear for those who are just and for whom justice is the
only recourse.

In the context of its struggle for peace in the land of love and
peace, the State of Palestine calls upon the United Nations to bear

special responsibility for the Palestinian Arab people and its homeland. It calls upon all peace- and freedom-loving peoples and states to assist it in the attainment of its objectives, to provide it with security, to alleviate the tragedy of its people, and to help it terminate Israel's occupation of the Palestinian territories.

The State of Palestine herewith declares that it believes in the settlement of regional and international disputes by peaceful means, in accordance with the UN Charter and resolutions. Without prejudice to its natural right to defend its territorial integrity and independence, it therefore rejects the threat or use of force, violence, and terrorism against its territorial integrity, or political independence, as it also rejects their use against the territorial integrity of other states.

Therefore, on this day unlike all others, November 15, 1988, as we stand at the threshold of a new dawn, in all honor and modesty we humbly bow to the sacred spirits of our fallen ones, Palestinian and Arab, by the purity of whose sacrifice for the homeland our sky has been illuminated and our land given life. Our hearts are lifted up and irradiated by the light emanating from the much blessed Intifada, from those who have endured and have fought the fight of the camps, of dispersion, of exile, from those who have borne the standard of freedom, our children, our aged, our youth, our prisoners, detainees and wounded, all those whose ties to our sacred soil are confirmed in camp, village and town. We render special tribute to that brave Palestinian woman, guardian of sustenance and life, keeper of our people's perennial flame. To the souls of our sainted martyrs, to the whole of our Palestinian Arab people, to all free and honorable people everywhere, we pledge that our struggle shall be continued until the occupation ends, and the foundation of our sovereignty and independence shall be fortified accordingly.

Therefore, we call upon our great people to rally to the banner of Palestine, to cherish and defend it, so that it may forever be the symbol of our freedom and dignity in that homeland, which is a homeland for the free, now and always.

In the name of God, the Compassionate, the Merciful.

"Say: 'O God, Master of the Kingdom,
Thou givest the Kingdom to whom Thou wilt,
and seizest the Kingdom from whom Thou wilt,
Thou exaltest whom Thou wilt, and Thou

abasest whom Thou wilt; in Thy hand
is the good; Thou art powerful
over everything."
Sadaga Allahu Al-Azim

The declaration was read by Yasser Arafat to the Palestine National Council in Algiers on November 15, 1988.

References

Sources are listed in the order
that they appear in the text.

Preface

Harkabi, Yehoshafat. *The Bar Kokhba Syndrome.* New York: Rossell Books, 1983.

———. *Palestinians and Israel.* Jerusalem: Keter Publishing House, 1974.

———. *Winds of Change in the Arab Israeli Conflict* (in Hebrew). Tel Aviv: Dvir Publishing Company, 1978. See page 129.

Chapter 1: The Arab-Israeli Conflict: The Arab Positions

Wolfers, Arnold. *Discord and Collaboration.* Baltimore: The Johns Hopkins Press, 1962. See page 71.

Sayegh, Fayez. *A Handful of Mist, the Meaning of Bourguibaism and its Slogans* (in Arabic). Beirut: PLO Research Center, May 1965, July 1966.

Al-Bitar, Nadim. *The Economic Theory and the Road to Arab Unity* (in Arabic). Beirut: Ma'had al-Inma'a al-A'rabi, 1978.

Jiryis, Sabri. "Twenty Years of Armed Struggle: Towards a New Palestinian Alignment," in *Shu'un Filastiniyya* (in Arabic). January–February 1985. See pages 142–143.

Al-Hassan, Khalid. *Jordanian Palestinian Agreement for Joint Action* (in Arabic). Jerusalem: Abu-'Arfa, 1985.

Khalidi, Walid. *Palestine and the Logic of Political Sovereignties* (in Arabic). Beirut: Dar al-Fajr al-Jadid, 1963. See page 7.

Harkabi, Yehoshafat. *Fedayeen Action and Arab Strategy.* London: Institute of Strategic Studies, Adelphi Paper 53, 1968. See page 33.

Chapter 2: The Arab-Israeli Conflict: The Israeli Position

Demographic forecasts:

Friedlander, D. and G. Goldscheier. "Israel's Population: The Challenge of Populism." *Population Reference Bureau,* April 1984.

Sopher, Arnon. "Geography and Demography in Palestine in the Year 2000," in *Approaching the Year 2000: Towards Peace or Another War.* Alouph Hareven, editor. Jerusalem: Van Leer Institute, 1988.

Chapter 3: The Two Streams of Zionism

Bella, Moshe. *The World of Jabotinsky: A Selection* (in Hebrew). Tel Aviv: Defusin Publishing House, 1972. See page 165.

Chapter 4: The Likud in Power

Ne'eman, Yuval. *The Policy of Sobriety* (in Hebrew). Tel Aviv: Revivim, 1984. See page 79.

Shavit, Yaacov. "Between Ideology and Power," in *The Lebanon War* (in Hebrew). Tel Aviv: Hakibbutz Hameuchad, 1983. See page 153.

Von Clausewitz, Karl. *On War.* Edited and translated by M. Howard and P. Paret, Book VIII, chapter 2. Princeton: Princeton University Press, 1976. See page 579.

Naor, Arye. *Cabinet at War: The Functioning of the Israeli Cabinet during the Lebanon War* (in Hebrew). Tel Aviv: Lahav Publishing House, 1986.

Aron, Raymond. *Histoire et Politique.* Paris: Julliard, 1985. See pages 514–515.

Shalev, Arye. *Line of Defense in Judea and Samaria* (in Hebrew). Tel Aviv: University Center for Strategic Studies and Hakibbutz Hameuchad, 1982.

Jabotinsky, Ze've. "The Iron Wall," in Yoseph Nedava, *Ze've Jabotinsky, the Man and His Teachings* (in Hebrew). Tel Aviv: Ministry of Defence Publishing House, 1980. See page 233.

Preuss, Teddy. *Begin—His Regime* (in Hebrew). Jerusalem: Keter Publishing House, 1984. See pages 162 and 170.

Ben Yeruham, *The Book of Betar History and Sources,* Vol. 2, Part 2. Betar convention: 1976. See pages 61–63. Cited in Yaacov Shavit. *Milat 2* (in Hebrew) 1984. See page 395.

Ben-Gurion, David. "The Wordsmith versus the Pioneers of Action" (in Hebrew), 1984.

Eldar, Ysrael. *Meditations on Israel* (in Hebrew). Tel Aviv: Yair, 1980. See pages 246–247.

Chapter 5: Nationalistic Judaism

The Oaths are based on *Ketuvot* 111a and *Song Raba* 2:7; for commentary see Harkabi, Yehoshafat. *The Bar Kokhba Syndrome,* chapter 3.

Blidstein, Gerald J. *Political Concepts in Maimonides Halakha* (in Hebrew). Bar Ilam University Press, 1983.

Ben-Ami, A., ed. *Hakol (All), The Peace Frontier of Israel* (in Hebrew). Tel Aviv: Madaf Publication, 1967. See page 70 for Rabbi Z. I. Kook's conclusions from Nachmanides.

Rabbi Pichnick. *Year by Year, 1968* (in Hebrew). Jerusalem: Heikhal Shlomo. See page 109 for Rabbi Z. I. Kook.

Rabbi Aviner, Shlomo. "The Inheritance of the Country and the Ethical Problem" (in Hebrew) in *Artzi* (My Land). Jerusalem: The Center for Intensification of Eretz Yisrael Consciousness, 1982.

Harkabi, Yehoshafat. *Israel's Position in the Arab Israeli Conflict* (in Hebrew). Tel Aviv: Dvir Publishing Company, 1967. See page 44.

Rabbi Ariel, Yisrael. "Things as They Are," in *Zeffiyya* (in Hebrew). Center for My Brethren, 1984.

Rabbi Kahane, Meir. *Thorns in Your Eyes* (in Hebrew). New York and Jerusalem.

Rabbi Wolpe, Shalom Dov. *The Opinion of the Torah* (in Hebrew). Third edition. Kiryat-Gat, 1983. See note 4, page 146.

Rubinstein, Amnon. *From Herzl to Gush Emunim and Back: The Zionist Dream Revisited.* New York and Tel Aviv: Schocken Books, 1984.

Rabbi Herzog I. H. "The Rights of Minorities in the Jewish State and the Halakha," reprinted in *Year by Year 1986.* Jerusalem: Heikhal Shlomo, 1986.

Nisan, Mordechai. "A New Approach to Israeli Arab Peace and to the Minorities' Rights in the Middle East." *Kivvunim,* No. 24, August 1924. English version was published in *Plural Societies,* Vol. 15, No. 1, the Hague, Netherlands, 1984.

Katz, Yaacov, "Religious Tolerance of Rabbi Menahem HaMeiri," in his *Halakha and Kabala* (in Hebrew). Jerusalem: Magnes Press of the Hebrew University, 1984.

Sivan, Emanuel. *Radical Islam, Medieval Theology and Modern Politics.* New Haven: Yale University Press, 1985.

Smith, W. C. *Islam in Modern History.* Princeton: Princeton University Press, 1957.

Nisan, Mordechai. *The Jewish State and the Arab Problem* (in Hebrew). Tel Aviv: Hadar Publishing House, 1986.

Chapter 6: What Is There to Do?

Ben-Gurion, David. "The Wordsmith versus the Pioneers of Action" (in Hebrew), 1984.

Dotan, S. *The Struggle of Eretz Israel.* Ministry of Defense Publishing House. See page 385 for misunderstanding of the secessionist underground organization of the historical challenge.

Eilam, Yigaal. "The Development of the Defense and Underground Organization," in *History of Eretz Yisrael* (in Hebrew), Vol. 9, Keter and Yad Ben Zvi, 1982. See pages 241 and 246 for numbers of weaponry in 1947.

Heller, Yoseph. *The Struggle for a State* (in Hebrew). Jerusalem, 1985. See pages 309–310 for Lehi contacts with Nazi Germany. See also Dan Margalit in *Kivvunim* (in Hebrew), No. 15, page 89.

Heller, Yoseph. "Between Messianism and Political Realism," in *Contemporary Judaism,* Vol. 2. Jerusalem: The Hebrew University, 1985. For Lehi and the Arab problem.

Index

Abu Jihad, 39
Abu Musa, 6, 39
Abu Nidal, 39, 100
Agudat Yisrael party, 80, 142, 151, 185
"A Handful of Mist" (Sayegh), 4
Ahmed, Sid, 29
Akzin, Professor Benjamin, 16
al-Bitar, Professor Nadim, 9
Algeria, 12, 36, 51, 108
Al-Hadaf, 41
al-Hassan, Khaled, 29–30, 65
Amalek, 149–150, 160, 189–190
Americans. *See* United States
Amirav, Moshe, 135
Annexation/withdrawal debate, 8, 20, 25,
    30, 45–55, 69, 82, 84, 160, 197–199;
    and Egyptian agreement, 87–90; and
    religious extremism, 172, 191; and
    religious justification, 144; and security,
    119–120; U.S. opposition to, 128. *See
    also* Occupied territories
Anti-Israelism, 216, 218–220
Anti-Semitism, 54–55, 91, 130, 179–180,
    203; Anti-Semitism: compared with
    anti-Zionism/anti-Israelism, 216–220
Anti-Zionism, 216–218
Arab extremists, *xxviii,* 7–10, 30, 32, 41,
    55–56, 60, 66, 122–123, 206, 223; and
    religion, 184; and terrorism, 37, 39
Arab-Israeli conflict: recent events, *xii–xiv,
    xvi–xxiii*
Arab Israelis, 50
Arab League, 21
Arab League Summit, Algiers (June
    1988), *xv,* 23–24, 41
Arab League Summit, Algiers (November,
    1973), 14
Arab League Summit, Amman (November
    1987), *xiii*
Arab League Summit, Fez (1982), *xii, xiii,*
    33–34; text of declaration, 229–230
Arab League Summit, Rabat (October,
    1974), 14
Arab Liberation Front, 20
Arab majority, in Israel. *See* Demographic
    problem
Arab moderates, 31–32, 43, 55–57, 223;

and Arab need for peace, 12; effect of
    Israeli policies on, 10–11; and
    terrorism, 37, 39–40
Arab positions, 32–34, 45, 55–57; basic
    changes in, *xii,* in "Declaration of
    Independence", *xviii–xx;*
    destruction-of-Israel goal, *xxviii,* 2–6,
    10, 12, 32, 60, 87, 199, 218; existential
    trend, 58–61; grand design *vs.* policy,
    1–5, 32, 42, 60, 81, 199; Israeli
    absolutism and, 43; Israeli
    understanding of, 203–204;
    modification of, *xii,* 206; and need for
    peace, 12–13; and Palestinian state,
    16–17; and recognition of Israel, 6;
    theory of stages, 4; two-state
    settlement, *xix–xxii See also* Arab
    extremists; Arab moderates; Arab states
Arab Rebellion (1936–39), 20
Arabs: anti-Semitism and anti-Zionism,
    217–218; Begin's dehumanization of,
    109; determination of, 98. *See also*
    Palestinians; and establishment of
    Israel, 59; expulsion from occupied
    lands, 25–26, 57, 147–150, 160, 166,
    198; within Israel, 145–150; Israeli
    withdrawal from West Bank, 46; as
    resident aliens, 151–159
Arab states, 24, 57–58, 61, 81, 128,
    155–156, 224; and Arabs in occupied
    territories, 121; backwardness and
    decentralization, 64–65; exodus of
    British from Palestine, 212; and God's
    favor, 168; and Gulf War, 63; invasion
    of Israel, 78–79; and Israeli settlement,
    63–68, 225; and religious
    fundamentalism, 171–172; results of
    Lebanon War, 102–103. *See also* other
    Arab headings
Arafat, Yasser, *xii, xviii–xx, xxiv,* 6, 18, 21,
    22, 41, 60, 66, 116; accord with
    Hussein (1985), *xiii,* 241–242
"Arafat's Aide on Israel", 41
Arens, Moshe, 89, 116
Argov, Ambassador Shlomo, 100
Ariel, Rabbi Yisrael, 146, 147–148, 150
Arms control negotiations, *xxv*

Armistice Agreement (1949), 116
Aron, Raymond, 108, 215
Ashkenazic Jews, 84
Assad, King, 9–10, 33
Autonomy concept, *xv, xxi, xxii,* 89–90, 117–118, 154
Aviner, Rabbi Shlomo, 145–146, 162
Avineri, Professor Shlomo, 127

Baker, James, *xxv*
Balfour Declaration, 70–71
Bar Kochba Rebellion (132–135 C.E.), 74, 138–139, 210
The Bar Kochba Syndrome (Harkabi), *xiv*
Begin, His Regime (Preuss), 126–127
Begin, Menachem, *xi, xxix,* 17, 42, 49, 69, 73–74, 79, 104, 116–118, 164–165, 199, 217; Camp David Accords and Egyptian peace agreement, *xv,* 87–92; evaluation of, 125–132, 135–137; and Israelis, 81–83, 129–131; and Israel's decline, 107–111; and Lebanon War, 95, 97–99, 101–102, 103; on withdrawal, 53. *See also* Jabotinsky-Begin ethos; Likud coalition government
Beirut, 103, 110
Bella, Moshe, 82–83
Ben-Gurion, David, *xix,* 70, 77, 80, 95, 97, 108, 134, 160, 210–211, 213; assessment of Begin and Jabotinsky, 126–127, 132; and foreign opinion, 205
Ben-Meir, Dr. Yehudah, 155
Bible, 140, 142, 160, 161, 189; and expulsion of non-Jews, 147; and Land of Israel, 145
Bismarck, Otto von, 104, 108
Book of Commandments (Maimonides), 144
Brezhnev, Leonid, *xxiv*
British, 48, 75, 78; and revisionist Zionists, 75, 210–215. *See also* Great Britain
British Mandate, 11, 74, 79, 184

Camp David Accords, *xii, xxv,* 17, 27, 69, 87–92, 101, 113, 118, 129, 136; Egyptian-Israeli Peace Treaty text, 237–240; Framework agreements, *xii, xv,* 87–88, 231–237
Casualties, 122; Arab/Israeli absorption of, 8–9, 43–44; Israeli attack in Beirut, 110
Catholic Church, 180, 189
Catholics, 160
China, 35, 64
Chosen People concept, 83, 145, 153; two historical currents of, 163–165
Christianity, 157–159, 167, 180, 201–202; church/state separation, 171, 174, 176
Christians, 149, 151, 155, 157–159, 204; expulsion from Jerusalem, 180, 220; and religious extremists, 180–183, 188–189
Christians (Lebanese), 103, 113
Citizenship rights, 49, 114–115, 151, 155

Civil rights, 151–152
Civil war, threat of, 112
Clausewitz, Karl von, 94–95, 102
Cold War, *xxiv*
"The Commandment of Genocide in the Torah" (Hess), 149–150, 182
Condominium solution, *xiv, xv, xvi*
Confederation (Palestinians and Jordan), 25–28
Conservative Judaism, 141, 161, 172, 173
Crusades, 157
Cuba, 36
Czechoslovakia, 118

David, 201
Declaration of Independence (Israel), *xix,* 151, 181, 187
Declaration of Independence (Palestinian), *xviii–xix,* 243–48
The Defense Line in Judaea and Samaria (Shalev), 119
DeGaulle, General Charles, 108
Demagoguery, 77, 84, 100, 105, 108–109, 111, 127, 131, 195
Democratic Front (PDFLP), *xiii, xxiv*
Demographic problem, *xiv,* 46–48, 57, 110, 113–114, 119, 121, 222; and public education, 197–198
Dhimmis (minorities), 155–156
Diaspora Jewry, *xii, xxv, xxvi,* 134, 139, 140, 156, 172, 177, 225; mentality of, 77; relationship with Israel and identity, 216–222
Dinstein, Professor Yoram, 91
Discrimination. *See* Non-Jews
Druse, 204

East Bank, 25, 124–125; Palestinians of, 17
Eastern European Jews, 71–73, 79, 113–114; evacuation of, 131–132
East Jerusalem, 24
Economy: of Arab states, 10; under Likud coalition government, *xi,* 84, 104–107, 165, 173–174, 199; in West Bank, 51; and Zionists, 79
Egypt, 10, 34, 206, 231–237; Arab boycott of, *xiii,* Camp David peace treaty, *xii,* 3–4, 13, 84, 87–92, 126–127, 136–137, 237–240; and Sunni fundamentalism, 171
Egyptian-Israeli Peace Treaty (March 1979), 237–240. *See also* Sadat, Anwar
Eitan, Rafael, 93
Eldad, Dr. Yisrael, 74, 134, 136, 213–215
Elections, in occupied territories, *xxi*
Eretz Yisrael, *xviii,* 7, 71, 73, 75, 78, 210; Jews migration to, 138–139; religious commandment to settle, 147–148
Eshkol, Levi, 80, 134
Ethnocentricity, 204–205
Europe, 54, 206, 224
European Common Market, 54
Evron, Boaz, 132–133

Expansionism, 183–184
Expressivist approach, 74–75, 103
Expulsion policy: of Arabs, 25–26, 57,
    147–150, 160, 166, 198; Kahane on,
    162–163; on non-Jews, 190–191; and
    resident aliens, 155
Extremism. *See* Arab extremists; Israeli
    extremists; Nationalistic religious
    extremists

Fahd, Prince of Saudi Arabia, 33
Fantasy *vs.* vision, *xxviii*, 208
Fatah, 20, 22, 41; and terrorism, 40
Fedayeen organizations, 20
Fez resolutions, *xii*, 33–34
"Final Statement of the 19th PNC, The",
    xviii–xx, xxiv
Fishman, Rabbi Yehudah Leib, 151
Foreign governments, 121, 124–125,
    162–163; and Begin, 128; and Diaspora
    Jews, 140; and world opinion, 205, 219.
    See also International relations
France, 204, 217
Fundamentalists, Muslim, *xvi*

"Gardeners", 76, 78, 208
Gaza Strip, *xxi*, 5, 8, 10–12, 17, 21, 48,
    152; Resolution 242 and, 89–91; riots,
    xiii–xiv, 1. *See also* Occupied territories
Genocide, 190
Gentiles, 139–140, 148, 149, 156–157,
    160, 188, 191, 201. *See also* Non-Jews
Germany, 2–4, 108, 194. *See also* Nazi
    Germany
Glass, David, 155
God, 142, 143, 144, 145, 148, 156; and
    holy war, 150; intervention of in
    politics, 177–178; and Jews, 161–165;
    and non-Jews, 152, 157; and religious
    extremists, 167–168, 171; in Torah, 205
Golan Heights, 10
Gold, Rabbi Ze'ev, 151
Gorbachev, Mikhail, *xxiv*, 225
Grand design *vs.* policy: Arabs and, 1–5,
    32, 42, 199; Israel and, 42–43
Great Britain, 61, 116, 201
Great Revolt (66–70 c.e.), 74, 98
Guerrilla warfare, 35–37. *See also*
    Terrorism
Gush Emunim, 69, 90, 143, 144, 162,
    166, 172

Ha'aretz, 16, 136, 156, 159, 213, 215
Habad, 185
Habash, Dr. George, *xiii, xxiv,* 60
Haganah, 108, 211
Halakha, 140–142, 144, 166; and
    distortion of texts, 185–193; and
    government policy, 175–176, 181;
    impact on Arab-Israeli conflict,
    183–193; and non-Jews, 149–150,
    180–181
HaMeiri, Rabbi Menachem, 158, 188
Hananniah b. Teradyon, Rabbi, 178

Hart, Liddell, 206
Hasanein Heikal, Mohammed, 36
Hashemite monarchy. *See* Hussein, King
Hasmoneans, 201
Hassan, Prince, *xvii*
Hawatmeh, Naef, *xiii, xxiv*
Herut party, *xxix–xxx,* 70, 73, 74, 76,
    78–80, 82–83, 89–90, 106, 143, 160;
    and Begin, 125–126; Irgun/Lehi
    undergrounds, 210–216; and Israel's
    decline, 108, 110–112; and occupied
    territories, *xiv,* 118–125; rejection of,
    130–137; younger leaders of, 135–136
Herzl, Theodor, 23, 86, 98
Herzog, Rabbi Yitzhak ha-Levi, 151, 153,
    188–189, 193
Hess, Rabbi Yisrael, 149–150, 161, 182
Hillel, Rabbi, 205
Historical relativism argument, 188–189
History and Policy (Aron), 108
Hitler, Adolf, 214
Holocaust, 110, 114, 139; evacuation of
    survivors, 132
Holy wars *(Jihad),* 40, 150, 168, 194
Hostages, 39
The Human Wolf (Jabotinsky), 203
Hussein, King, 18, 22–23, 59, 60; accord
    with PLO, *xii–xiii,* 241–242; and
    Palestinian/Israeli conflict, 24–28, 30,
    33, 116, 118, 119, 121; and terrorism,
    38; West Bank connections severed by,
    xvi–xvii, xix

Idolatry, 156–159, 160, 180, 188–189
Immigration, to Israel, 8, 50, 79,
    113–114, 138–139; and Diaspora Jewry,
    218, 220–221; of Holocaust survivors,
    212; and religious extremism, 177
India, 48, 75, 211
Indonesia, 168
Instrumentalist approach, 74–75
Intelligentsia (Israeli), 195–198
International peace conference, *xiii,* 30–31
International relations, *xxix,* 201–207, 223.
    See also Foreign governments
Intifada, *xxv, xiv, xviii*
Iran, 63, 128
Iraq, 13, 63, 128
Irgun (Revisionist militia), 74, 78, 79, 93,
    126, 136, 162, 210–212
"Iron Wall" argument, 120–121, 124, 224
"The Iron Wall" Jabotinsky, 121
Isaiah, 167
Islam, 60, 155–156, 173–175, 176, 201;
    and religious fundamentalism, 63,
    171–172
Israel: Arab extremist/moderate debate,
    11–12, 43; and Arab sense of injury, 59;
    army, 78–79, 99, 222; decline of,
    107–113; deterrent capability, 102–103;
    economic conditions, 51, 79, 84,
    104–107; and existential trend to
    conflict, 58–61; extremists in, *xxi–xxii;*
    foreign relations, 144, 201–207; greater,

Israel *(cont'd)*
xxv; militarism xvii–xviii, 43–44, 75, 81,
86; and morality, 86, 90–91, 110–111;
need for peace, 43–45; options for end
of conflict, xi, xxix, 62–68; and
Palestinian people, 14–17, 103;
Partition Resolution and, xix; and
perception of Arab weakness, 64; PLO
and Hussein, xvii, 24–28; political and
military successes, 160–165; political/
military successes, 160–165; security
needs, xvi, xxv See also other Israeli
headings; Judaism; State of Israel
Israeli citizenship, right to, 49, 114–115,
151, 155
Israeli Defense Force (IDF), 120, 158, 161
Israeli extremists, 19, 55–56, 66, 79, 223
Israeli moderates, 55–56, 58–59
Israeli positions, xi–xviii, xx–xxx, 55–57,
60–61; military success and policy
change, 42–44
Italy, 76, 194, 214

Jabotinsky, Eri, 82–83
Jabotinsky, Ze'ev, xi, 70, 72–79, 82–83,
107–108, 118, 121, 127, 203, 210, 214;
evaluation of, 131–135
Jabotinsky-Begin ethos, 73–74, 79, 81–85,
97, 98, 124–127, 143, 203, 208, 217,
223; and Herut, 210; political power
and policies, 160–163, 165; and
realpolitik, 202–203; rejection of,
131–136
Jamayel, President Bashir, 94–95
Japan, 97–98, 194; and kamikaze pilots,
170
Jerusalem, xix, 33, 46, 49, 143, 157;
division of, 51–52; expulsion of
non-Jews, 149, 180; and Great Revolt
(70 C.E.), 98, 194–195
Jewish Agency, xxii, 95, 132, 211–212
Jewish National Fund, 146–147
Jewish religion. *See* Judaism
Jewish state. *See* State of Israel
The Jewish State and the Arab Problem
(Nisan), 183–184
Jewish Underground, 168
Jews: American, xxvii, 129–130, 216,
219–222; and Great Revolt, 98; idea of
superiority, 163–165, 180; identity,
219–221; immigration to Israel, 8, 50,
79, 113–114; intermarriage and,
221–221; and international affairs,
201–207; Mainstream and Revisionist
Zionism, 71–73; morality and
self-righteousness, 110–111, 164–165,
198, 209, 217; in Palestinian state, 51;
See also Diaspora Jewry; Eastern
European Jews
Jihad (holy war), 40, 150, 168
Jiryes, Sabri, 28
Jordan, xix–xx, 6, 59, 65, 89–90; Arab
emigration to, 47; Hussein vs. Hassan
view of, xvii; and occupied territories,

xiv–xv, 115–118, 121, 123; and PLO,
xii–xiii, 14, 17–18, 22–23; and
PLO-Israeli negotiations, 24–28, 197;
terrorism from, 38; and West Bank, 14,
25–26
Jordanian option, xvi
Jordanian-Palestinian Accords (February
1985): text, Appendix D, xii–xiii, 30,
241–242
Jubilee Year, 151–152
Judaism, xii, xix, 42; and Arabs, 155; and
employment, 174; and extremism,
183–193, 199; moderate leaders and,
191–193; and nationalism, 83, 143–147,
165, 172–179; and non-Jews, 164–165;
and politics, 159–165, 171–179; and
statehood, 139–141; and world opinion,
179–183; and Zionism, 138–139. *See also*
Nationalistic religious extremists
Judea, xiv, xxix, 143, 152, 155, 193

Kach movement, 114, 162
Kahane, Rabbi Kalman, 151
Kahane, Rabbi Meir, 136, 212;
discrediting of, 185–187, 191; policies
of, 114, 147–149, 151–152, 155,
162–164, 168–169, 172, 178, 181–182
Katyusha missiles, 103, 110
Kennan, George, 76
Kennedy, John F., 202
Khalidi, Professor Walid, 35
Khomeini, Ayatollah, 171–172, 182
Kibbutzim, 112, 120
"King of Israel", 81, 130
Kiryat Shmona, Galilee, 93
Kissinger, Henry, 34
Kivvunim, 57, 153
Knesset, 147, 149, 151, 173, 177, 182,
186, 205
Kook, Rabbi A. I., 146, 168, 170
Kook, Rabbi Zvi Yehudah, 141, 144–146,
161, 168, 170; on occupied territories,
178

Labor Alignment, xxvii, 85
Labor government, 79–82, 86, 106, 134;
and Sephardic Jews, 112
Labor movement. *See* Mapai
"Land for peace" principle, xii, xv
Land of Israel concept, 138, 144–147,
153–154, 156, 159, 183, 190. *See also*
State of Israel
Laws and legal system, 115–116. *See also*
Halakha; Talmud
Lebanon, 42, 58, 63. *See also* Lebanon
War
Lebanonization, 111–112
Lebanon War, xi, 9, 21, 25, 28, 44, 87,
106, 107, 111–112, 127, 162, 165, 168,
178, 198, 222, 225; errors and
deceptions, 96–102; expanding
consequences of, 102–104, 204; and
false information, 111; judging of, 201;
media coverage of, 219; and Peace

Now, 196–197; strategic failure of, 92–102
Lehi, 74, 79, 136, 210–212; and Nazis, 213–215
Levin, Rabbi Yitzhak Meir, 151
Lewis, Ambassador Samuel, 129
Liberal party, 73
Libya, 12, 33
Likud coalition government, xi, xiv–xv, xxvii, xxix, 24–25, 34, 42, 53, 69, 73, 74, 80–83, 131, 161, 195, 210; and decline of Israel, 107–113; and economy, 104–107; failures of, 84–137; granting of citizenship to Arabs, 49; and Lebanon War, 92–104; and occupied territories, xiv, 113–125; peace with Egypt, 87–92; and religious Jews, 165
Lubavitcher Rebbe, 148, 168

Ma'ariv, xxix, 159
Machiavellianism, 108
Magnes, Dr., 81
Mahfuz, Nagib, 83
Maimonides, 140, 144, 150, 160–161, 180, 191; on non-Jews, 152, 154–159; and Rabbi Herzog, 188–189; and realism, 208
Mainstream Zionism, 70–71, 75–80, 81–82, 85–86, 108; and religious Zionism, 142–143
Mapai (Labor party), xxix–xxx, 76, 79–81, 95, 132, 134, 160, 213
Marshall, George, 203
Marx, Karl, 73, 197
Marxism, 73, 82
Mauritania, 168
"Mechanics", 76, 78, 127, 208
Media, 40, 195
Meditations on Israel (Eldad), 134
Messiah, 139, 140–141, 142, 148, 156, 175, 193. See also Messianiam
Messianism, 165–171, 173, 190; dangers of, 199
Middle East, 9, 24, 34, 75, 81, 86, 93, 155, 161; and Israeli ethnocentricity, 199–200; peace in, 222, 224–225; and religions, 54, 167; and Soviet policy revision, xxiv
Militarism, 75, 161–165, 198, 199
Military strength, 43–44, 81
Mizrachi party, 151, 160, 184
Morality, 86, 90–91, 110–111, 198; and international affairs, 203; tribal, 153–154
Morocco, 168
Moshavim, 120
Muslims, xvi, 151, 155–159, 168, 180, 188. See also Arabs; Islam

Nachmanides, 144
Naor, Aryeh, 135
Napoleon, 97
Nasser, Gamal Abdel, 35
Nationalism: Arab, 9, 13, 63, 212; Israeli,

112–113. See also Nationalistic religious extremists
Nationalistic religious extremists, xi, 66, 143–147, 188–189; coping with, 185–193; and expansionism, 183–184; impact on Arab-Israeli conflict, 183–185; impact on Israel and the Jews, 171–179; Israel's political/military strength, 159–165; and non-Jews, 151–160, 172; public education and, 199; and world opinion, 179–183
National Religious party, 80, 155
National Unity Government, xxvii, 85–86, 87; symposium on, 127–128
Natorei Karta, 170, 172, 184
Nazi Germany, 97–98, 213–214, 217
Ne'eman, Professor Yuval, 90, 114–115
Netanyahu, Benjamin, 53
Netivot Shalom, 184
"A New Approach to Israeli-Arab Peace" (Nisan), 153–155
New Testament, 159, 181, 182
New York Times, 41
New Zionist Organization (NZO), 76
Nirim kibbutz, 120
Nisan, Mordechai, 153–155, 180, 183–184
Noachide commandments, 149, 152, 154–155, 157, 160, 181
Non-Jews, 159–161, 163, 187–188; expulsion of, 148–150, 180–181, 190–191; as idolators, 156–159, 180; killing of, 150, 181; as resident aliens, 151–156, 159, 181
North Vietnam, 43, 52

Occupied territories, xi, xv, 12, 14, 24–28, 42, 81, 87–88, 135, 166, 191; annexation vs. withdrawal, 20, 25, 30, 45–55, 112, 184, 223; Arab majority problem, xiv, 46–48, 57, 110, 113–114, 119–121, 148, 166, 194, 222; arguments for continued occupation, 115–125; autonomy of, xxii; and Begin/Shamir policy, 129, 136–137; coming crisis in, 113–125; current debate, xi, xxix; elections in, xxi; and religious extremists, 143–147, 172; Resolution 242 and, 87–90; U.S. position on, 69, 91. See also Gaza Strip; Uprising; West Bank
One-state settlement, xx–xxii
On War (Clausewitz), 94
Orthodox Judaism, 141, 143–144, 172, 193, 220–221. See also Nationalistic religious extremists
Oz Le-Shalmon, 158
Oz le-Shalom, 184, 190–191

Pakistan, 116, 168
Palestine, 79; British withdrawal from, 75; establishment of Israel and, 42; Land of vs. State of, xxiii
Palestine Liberation Front, 21
Palestine National Council, xiii, 18, 20

Palestinian Communist Party, *xxiv*
Palestinian Covenant, *xxv, xix, xxiii* 15, 18, 29
Palestinian Declaration of Independence, *xviii–xix,* 243–48
The Palestinian-Jordanian Agreement for Joint Action (al-Hassan), 29–30
Palestinian National Council (PNC), *xviii–xx, xxiv*
Palestinians, 10–11, 13, 109, 184, 191, 204, 225; annexation/withdrawal debate, 45–55; Baker's views on, *xxv;* and Camp David Accords, *xv,* 90–92; Diaspora, *xxvi;* education and identity, 15–16, 32; and expulsion from occupied territories, 57; extremists, *xxi–xxii;* moderates, *xviii–xx, xxii;* negotiations and PLO, 200–201; in occupied territories, *xvii, xviii, xxii,* 57, 113–125; and peace negotiations, 197; and PLO, *xiii,* 13–14; and riots, *xiv,* 40, 45; and terrorism, 35–40
Palestinians and Arabs (Harkabi), *xxviii*
Palestinians and Israel (Harkabi), *xxix*
Palestinian state, 50, 67, 123, 201; Arab states endorsement of, 33; Camp David agreement and, 91; in Palestinian Declaration of Independence, *xviii–xx;* and Israeli Arabs, 50; and PLO, 11, 4–5, 13–24
Pan-Arabism, 63
Partition Resolution (Resolution 181) (1947), *xviii–xx,* 30, 42, 61, 120
Peace, 222–225; Israel's need for, 43–44; negotiated vs. dictated, *xxi;* and public education, 197–198; *See also* Camp David Accords; Egyptian-Israeli Peace Treaty
"Peace for peace" slogan, 117
Peace Now, 96, 196–197
Peel partition plan, 61
Peloponnesian War, 205
Pilsudski, Marshal, 135
PLO (Palestine Liberation Organization), *xvii–xxiv,* 6, 9, 48, 60, 109, 116; contradictory messages of, *xxiii;* demands to make upon, *xxiii;* Israel and U.S. recognition, *xii, xx,* 14–15, 34; and Lebanon War, 28, 39, 93–94, 99–100, 103; moderates vs. radicals in, *xviii;* negotiations with, *xii–xviii, xx, xxi, xxiv,* 12–35, 67–68, 197, 200–201; and Palestinian state, 4–5, 11–24; quarrels within, 20–22, 41, 64, 66, 128; recognition of Israel, *xii,* 19; and riots, *xiii, xiv,* 23; as sole Palestinian representative, *xiii, xvi,* 14, 34; and terrorism, *xx,* 35–40, 99–100
"PLO View, Prospect of a Palestinian-Israeli Settlement" (Sharif), 41
The Policy of Sobriety (Ne'eman), 115
Political rights, *xxv,* 151–154
Political settlement, *xii, xxviii–xxix,* 30,

54–55, 61–68, 121–124, 136; *See also* Jordan; PLO (Palestine Liberation Organization); Resolution 242
Politicians, *xxvii,* 195–197
Politics, 159–165, 172–179, 190, 206; and public opinion, 195
Pollard affair, 216
Popular Front (PFLP), *xiii, xxiv,* 41
Population. *See* Demographic problem
Populism, 105–107, 108, 127, 195, 225; in Judaism, 178
PPLO (Part of Palestine Liberation Organization), 31
Preuss, Teddy, 126–127
Public opinion, *xv, xxi,* and Begin leadership, 128–131; and foreign affairs, 202; and intellectuals' role in, 195–201. *See also* World opinion

Rabbis: and nationalistic religious extremism, 185–193
Rabin, I., 99, 120
Rabin government, 34
Racism, 186–187
Radical Islam (Sivan), 171
Ramadan, 176
Rashi, 147–148
Reagan, Ronald, *xx, xxv,* 128, 225
Reagan Plan (September 1982), 51
Realism, 207–209; and Israeli history, 209–216
Realpolitik, 202–203
Redemption, Judaic idea of, 140, 142, 143, 148, 161, 172, 173, 190; religious extremists and, 165–171
Reform Judaism, 141
Rejection Front, 56
Religionists, 84, 111, 177. *See also* Nationalistic religious extremists
Religions, 60; fundamentalism and, 170–172; *See also* Islam; Judaism
Resident aliens, 151–156, 159, 160, 181–182
Resolution 181 (Partition Resolution) (1947), *xviii–xx,* 30, 42, 61, 120
Resolution 242, *xii, xviii, xx,* 19, 27–28, 31, 52, 69, 87–89, 116–117, 128; text, 227–228
Resolution, 338, *xviii, xx,* 31, 88; text, 228
Revisionist Zionism, *xi,* 124, 131–132, 134–136, 160, 162, 164; beginnings, 70–79; and British, 75, 79, 211–215; establishment of state, 79–80, 210–215; and Jabotinsky-Begin ethos, 73–76, 131; settlements and, 119. *See also* Likud coalition government
Revolutionary Judaism, 172
Riots. *See* Uprising, 1987–88
Rishon Lezion, 180–181
River Jordan, 64, 124
Rubinstein, Amnon, 149–150, 182

Sabbath, 141, 176, 178
Sadat, Anwar, *xxix,* 10, 24, 34, 36, 117;

peace agreement with Israel, 2–6, 89–92
"Salami tactics", 10
Salvation Front, 21
Samaria, *xiv, xxi,* 143, 145, 152, 155, 193
Sartre, Jean Paul, 216
Satmar Hasidim, 139, 170
Saudi Arabia, 33, 128
Sayegh, Fayez, 4
Schmidt, Helmut, 128
Schnayerson, Menachem Mendele, 148
Schultz, George, 136
Secularists, 84, 111, 177
Security Council, 24, 30–31, 33, 89; call for Israeli withdrawal, 116–117; *See also* Resolution 242; Resolution 338; United Nations
Self-criticism (Israeli), 110–111, 193, 199–201
Self-determination principle, *xxiii, xxiv,* 6–7, 19–20, 31, 116
Self-righteousness, 110, 164–165, 209, 217
Semantics, 7, 16–17, 19
Sephardic Jews, 80, 84, 112
Settlements, 46–49, 82, 161–162; and Arab negotiations, 52; arguments for, 118–120; and condominium plan, *xiv–xv,* damage wrought by, 59–60; as irreversible, 51; Israeli withdrawal and, 124–125; and Lebanonization, 111–112; U.S. position on, 68–69
Shalev, Aryeh, 119–120
Shamir, Yitzhak, *xvi, xxi, xxii,* 89, 109, 115, 126, 136–137; interpretation of "autonomy", *xiv–xv*
Sharett, Moshe, 80, 126
Sharif, Bassan Abu, 41
Sharon, Ariel, 93, 96, 99, 101–102, 107, 116
Shavit, Yaakov, 93
Shi'ite Islam, 22, 103, 162, 167, 171–172
Shukeiry, Ahmed, 21
Shultz, George, *xx*
Sinai, 10, 42, 51, 117, 128, 136–137, 168; withdrawal from, 89, 91–92
Situational thinking, 209
Sivan, Emanuel, 171
Six Day War, 36, 80–81, 87, 121, 143
Smith, Cantwell, 173
Sokolov, Nahun, 72
Solomon, 201
Soviet Union, 1, 3, 30, 33–34, 52, 97, 102, 203, 215, 225; changing Mideast policy, *xxiv,* and Israeli-PLO negotiations, *xiii, xxiv*
State of Israel, 138, 140–147, 172–173, 177, 179, 182–184, 197, 218; establishment of, 79–80, 188–189, 210–211; and international relations, 201–207; and Messianism, 167–171; and non-Jews, 143–159; and Zionism, 71–80
Stern, Avraham, 214–216

Stern Gang, 74
"Stone Revolution", 38, 40, 161–162
Strategic thinking, 35–41. *See also* Terrorism
"A Strategy for Israel in the 1980s" (Yinon), 57–58
Sunni Islam, 167, 171–172
Super Powers, *xxiv–xxv,* 42, 163
Switzerland, 64
Syria, *xii,* 27, 29, 33, 63, 113, 162; and Arab extremism, 9–11; and Druse, 204; and Lebanon War, 93–97, 99, 102–103; and PLO, 21–22; and "strategic parity", *xiii,* 10; Sunni fundamentalism, 171

Talmud, 138–140, 148, 184, 189
Teachers, 200
Tehiya, 69, 89–90, 136
Temple Mount mosques, 168–169
Terrorism, 9, 27–28
Terrorism, 9, 27–28, 31–32, 35–41, 64, 66, 99–101, 103, 125, 165; Arafat's renunciation of, *xx;* "freelance", 37–38; Israeli fears of, 109–110; and Israel's military, 120; Lebanon War and, 99–101; and West Bank, 46; and Zionist underground, 75, 211–212
Thorns in Your Eyes (Kahane), 155
Thucydides, 205
Torah, 145, 148, 155, 163, 172, 182, 191, 192, 205
Trans-Jordan, 42, 163
Tribal morality, 153–154
Two-state settlement, *xix–xxii*

Ultra-Orthodox Judaism, 170
Underground organizations (Zionist), 210–214
United Nations, *xiii,* 19, 30–31, 61, 163, 202, 218. *See also* Resolution 242; Security Council
United States, 1, 3, 30–31, 34–35, 43, 52, 53, 64, 68–69, 92, 102, 116, 205, 212; agreement with Soviets, 225; attachment to Israel, 10, 203; and Begin, *xv,* 128–129; and Jewish extremism, 177; and Jordanian-PLO peace initiative, *xii;* recognition of PLO, 34; *See also* Jews, American
Universal Bill of Human Rights, 181
Uprising, 1987–88, *xiv,* 8–9, 12, 23, 26, 37, 40–41, 45, 66, 112, 115, 130, 162, 199
Urbach, E. E., 157
Utilitarian argument, 188–189

Vatican, 180
Vietnam War, 102
von Hantig, 214

Waldenberg, Rabbi Eliezer, 149
War of Independence, 79, 108, 120, 123, 210

Wars (Middle East), 2–3, 8, 10, 43–45, 79, 81–82, 122, 161–162, 224. *See also* Lebanon War; Six Day War; Yom Kippur War
Weizmann, Chaim, 70, 77, 134, 160, 210
West Bank, *xxi,* 5, 6, 10–12, 17, 160, 219; demographic problem, 46–48, 57, 110; Hussein's severing of connections with, *xvi–xvii, xix;* and Jordan, 22–23, 25–28; land profiteering in, 105; Palestinian state in, 5, 18, 21; and Peace Now, 196–197; Resolution 242 and, 89–91; riots, *xiii–xiv,* 1; and Shamir policy, 136–137. *See also* Occupied territories
Westernization, of Arab states, 171
When the Cannons Fall Silent (Sid Ahmed), 29
Winds of Change (Harkabi), *xxviii–xxix*
Withdrawal question. *See* Annexation/ withdrawal debate
Wolfers, Arnold, 1
Wolpe, Rabbi S. D., 148–149, 162–163, 168
The Wordsmith versus the Pioneers of Action (Ben-Gurion), 132
World opinion, 30, 42, 48, 64, 66, 179–183, 205, 219
World War I, 69, 104, 204
World War II, 97–98, 214
World Zionist Organization, 57–58, 153

Xenophobia, 191

Yamit settlement, 51, 91, 168
Yedioth Ahronoth (Evron), 132–133
Yellin-Mor, Nathan, 214
Yemen, 12
Yinon, Oded, 57–58
Yishuv (Jewish community in Palestine), *xx, xxii,* 210–211, 212–213
Yitzhak, Rabbi Amnon, 178
Yom Kippur War, 81, 93, 143
Yosef, Chief Rabbi Ovadiah, 158–159, 181
Yosi b. Kisma, Rabbi, 178
Youth: Israeli and extremism, 196; Palestinian and "freelance" terrorism, 37–38

Zealots, 194–195
Zionism, *xx, xxii,* 6, 13, 42, 48, 50, 61, 70–80, 98, 190, 200–201, 225; failure of, 112–113, 172; historic right to Israel, 144–147; and Judaism, 138–139; PLO and, 67; political *vs.* practical, 86; and realism, 207–208; and Redemption, 165–169; and religion's place in, 142–143; and secularism, 142, 197; true historical account of, 210–216. *See also* Mainstream Zionism; Revisionist Zionism
"Zionism is racism" resolution, 19, 31, 218
Zionist Organization, 75, 77
Zionist World Organization, *xxii*